CHRISTIAN HERITAGE CLASSICS

The Twentieth Century

Sherwood Eliot Wirt, Editor

BOARD OF EDITORIAL ADVISERS

Geoffrey W. Bromiley
Helga Bender Henry
Calvin D. Linton
D. Bruce Lockerbie

Spiritual Witness

Classic Christian Writings
of the 20th Century

Sherwood Eliot Wirt, Editor

CROSSWAY BOOKS • WHEATON, ILLINOIS
A DIVISION OF GOOD NEWS PUBLISHERS

Spiritual Witness.

Copyright © 1991 by Sherwood Eliot Wirt.

Published by Crossway Books, a division of
Good News Publishers, 1300 Crescent Street, Wheaton, Illinois 60187.

Cover design: Russ Peterson

First printing, 1991

Printed in the United States of America

Library of Congress Cataloging in Publication Data
Spiritual witness : classic Christian writings of the 20th century
Sherwood Eliot Wirt, editor
    p.   cm.—(Christian heritage classics. The twentieth century)
    1. Theology.   2. Christian life.   I. Wirt, Sherwood Eliot.
II. Series.   III. Series: Christian heritage classics. Twentieth century.
BR53.S68   1991   230—dc20   91-12434
ISBN 0-89107-629-8

99		98		97		96		95		94		93		92		91
15	14	13	12	11	10	9	8	7	6	5	4	3	2	1

To my brother,
Lincoln Brown Wirt

CONTENTS

ACKNOWLEDGMENTS

With this volume Jan Dennis, editor of Crossway Books, and I have completed the task we set ourselves in 1977—to collect and publish a series of classic Christian writings of the past four centuries. The task has brought an avalanche of blessings and accompanying joy as we have immersed ourselves in some of the finest Christian thought to be recorded since A.D. 1600.

My heartfelt thanks go out to all those who contributed to this fourth volume:

To our distinguished board of editorial advisers— Professor Geoffrey W. Bromiley of Fuller Theological Seminary, now retired; Helen Bender Henry, author, literary critic, and wife of Dr. Carl F. H. Henry; Dr. Calvin D. Linton of George Washington University, Washington, DC, retired; and D. Bruce Lockerbie, author and former Staley scholar-in-residence at The Stony Brook School, Long Island, New York.

To the living authors and their publishers who kindly gave permission to reproduce excerpts from their works.

To the heirs and trustees of deceased authors who also provided permission.

To editor Jan Dennis, for his vision and encouragement, and his associate editor, Lila Bishop, for her indispensable help.

To my beloved wife and most perceptive critic, Ruth Evelyn Love Wirt.

In God's time another, abler hand may undertake to extend the Christian Heritage Classics to include all the centuries going back to the first one. First-century writings, of course, have been in print since the first Gutenberg Bible came off the press.

INTRODUCTION

Readers who may wonder at the thirteen selections in this volume (the last in the Christian Heritage Classics series) need some advance warning. This is no beauty contest, although great beauty may be found in these pages. These works were not chosen because of elegance of literary expression any more than were the choices in our seventeenth-, eighteenth-, and nineteenth-century collections.

Like the others, this volume is intended to be an expression of dynamic evangelical thought. The literature represented is a literature not of knowledge but of power. Its aim is not cognitive but causal; it proposes to change the reader, to make him or her a different kind of person. Its target is not just the mind, but also the heart and conscience. Its goal is nothing less than the reconstruction of individuals into the image and likeness of their Creator through the grace of our Lord Jesus Christ.

The twentieth century is unlike any of its predecessors. We who survive in it live perpetually under the dangling sword of Damocles. Our writing is accordingly different. As the decades have rolled by, journalese has gradually been established as the authentic model of written communication. Even evangelicals have shucked off the literary finesse of the past and have turned to sharper phrases and newer versions of the Bible.

Many of the authors chosen for this volume are still alive. Those whose writings appeared in the earlier volumes of the Christian Heritage Classics, by contrast, have stood the test of time. History has a way of casting its own vote. The works of Pascal, Baxter, Madame Guyon, Wesley, Moody, and Spurgeon have been reissued many times, so that choosing excerpts from their writings has been largely a matter of personal taste.

In our twentieth century, the cream is still rising to the top. Eminently worthy authors abound, and your editor and advisers sincerely believe that on the whole they have chosen from among the best. We are prepared nonetheless to receive objections: "Why these? Why not others?" Some readers may have theological reservations; others may contend that some of the chapters hardly qualify as literature or even as proper prose. We have chosen not to defend our choices, believing that the reader who looks for the gold, rather than the dross, will soon find it.

Many libraries were combed and many fine writers considered for inclusion before the final selection was made. We found no dearth of talent. Had a delicately-balanced selection of evangelical writers of different ethnic and geographical backgrounds been our aim, the result might have been quite different. What we sought was rather a volume that would convey Christian truth in its clarity, its purity, its variety, its compassion, its renewing and sustaining power, and above all, in its glory.

We leave it to you, the reader, to decide whether the Holy Spirit has informed the work.

Spiritual Witness

Amy Carmichael, 1867-1951

Honored in our own day as the founder of a great movement, as a poet, a humanitarian, and a spiritual pioneer, Amy Carmichael ranks among the most remarkable women of modern times. Her devotion to her Lord in the midst of personal suffering, so eloquently expressed in her writings, has inspired and ministered to men and women everywhere.

Not many have loved an adopted land as Amy Carmichael loved India. She never married. Born in County Down, Northern Ireland, in 1867, Amy spent most of her life as a missionary of the gospel. The work she began in India in 1896 filled her whole life uninterruptedly for fifty-five years. She never took a furlough. The Dohnavur Fellowship she founded continues to the present day—a great center of healing and training, staffed by qualified workers from all over the world.

God came early into Amy's life. She told about a childish prayer to God to change her brown eyes to blue. Everyone else in her family had blue eyes. The prayer was answered simply, "No." When the people of India later accepted her partly because of her brown eyes and made her "one of them," she understood God's design.

By the time she was seventeen, Amy was leading a Sunday morning class for "shawlies" in a Presbyterian church hall in Belfast. The "shawlies" were poor mill girls who wore shawls instead of respectable hats. In time the class grew to over five hundred girls.

At the age of twenty-four, Amy sensed a call to the mission field. She sailed to Japan where her soul-winning messages and engaging zeal won many to Jesus Christ. But after fifteen months, illness forced her return to England where she slowly recovered. In 1895 she responded to a suggestion that she offer herself to a Church of England mission society for service in India. She was accepted, for Amy's spiritual gifts were already well recognized. Her farewell message at the Keswick convention was a memorable occasion.

Amy was twenty-nine when she finally arrived in the Tinnevelly region of India, which was to be her permanent home. In 1900 the small group of mission workers with whom she worked moved to Dohnavur. It is at this point we pick up the story of Amy's opposition to the temple traffic in children, as she relates it in the following pages.

During the years that followed, the battle for the children was won, not by Amy nor by the British rulers, but by the people of India themselves. The laws were changed, and the practice stopped. For her part, Amy wrote book after book detailing the incredible story of her life and work. In the process she broke fresh journalistic ground in the use of illustrative photography.

In 1931 Amy suffered a tragic fall that left her bedfast for the last twenty years of her life. Out of the pain of those years poems and books were written that still bring solace to sufferers worldwide.

The following text is taken from her own autobiographical writings, principally from Gold Cord, *copyright 1932 by Dohnavur Fellowship (Ft. Washington, PA: Christian Literature Crusade; North Harrow, Middlesex: Dohnavur Fellowship) and from* Lotus Buds *(Dohnavur Fellowship). Used by permission.*

ONE

THE TRAFFIC OF THE TEMPLE
by Amy Carmichael

When on March 7, 1901, we first heard from the lips of a little child the story of her life in a temple house, we were startled and distressed. Our hearts were penetrated with the conviction that such a story ought to be impossible in a land ruled by a Christian power.

The subject was new to us. We knew nothing of the magnitude of what may be called "the secret traffic of India"—a traffic in little children, mere infants oftentimes, for wrong purposes; and we did not appreciate, as we do now, the delicacy and difficulty of the position from a Government point of view, facing the quiet might of the forces on the other side. And though with added knowledge comes an added sense of responsibility, and a fear of all careless appeal to those whose burden is already so heavy, yet with every fresh discovery the conviction deepens that something should be done—and done, if possible, soon—to save at least this generation of children, or some of them, from destruction.

By temple children we mean children dedicated to gods or in danger of being so dedicated. Dedication to gods implies a form of marriage which makes ordinary marriage impossible. The child is regarded as belonging to the gods. In southern India, where religious feeling runs strong and the great temples are the centers of Hindu influence, the traffic is worked upon religious lines. In trying to save the children we have to contend with the perverted religious sense. Something of the same kind exists in other parts of India, and the traffic under another name is common in provinces where temple service as we have it in the south is unknown.

Again, in some areas, owing to the action of the native Government, temple service as such is not recognized. Children in danger of wrong cannot, strictly speaking, be called temple children. Yet there is need for legislation which shall touch all houses where little children are being brought up for the same purpose. The subject is immense and involved, and the thought of it suggests a net thrown over millions of square miles of territory, so finely woven as to be almost invisible, but so strong in its mesh that in no place yet has it ever given way. And the net is alive; it can feel and it can hold.

We ourselves became only gradually aware of what was happening about us. As fact after fact came to light, we were forced to certain conclusions which we could not doubt were correct. At first we were almost alone in these conclusions, because it was impossible to take others with us in our tedious underground hunt after facts. So the question was often asked, "But do the children really exist?"

A copy of a Government document lies before me. It is bravely and clearly worded, and its intention is evident. The high-minded Hindu—and there are such, let it not be forgotten—revolts from the degradation and pollution of this travesty of religion and will abolish it where he can. But let it be remembered that good as this law is, it does not and it cannot touch the great secret traffic itself. That will go on behind the law, and behind the next that is made, and the next, unless measures are devised to ensure its being thoroughly enforced.

A temple woman's son, now living apart from his clan, explains the very early marriage [of temple children] thus: "If not married, they will not be considered worthy of honor. Before the children reach the age of ten they must be married. They become the property of the temple priests and worshipers who go to the temple to chant the sacred songs."

A temple woman told a friend of ours: "The child is dressed like a bride and taken with another girl of the same community, dressed like a boy in the garb of a bridegroom. The child dressed as a bride goes as if to worship the idol in the temple. There the marriage symbol is hidden in a garland, and the garland is put over the idol, after which it is taken to the child's home and put around her neck. After this she is considered married to the god."

A Hindu woman known to us left home with her little daughter and wandered about as an ascetic. She went to a famous temple where it is the custom for such as desire to become ascetics to enter the life by conforming to certain ceremonies ordained by the priests. She shaved her head, took off her jewels, wore a Saivite necklace of berries, and was known as a devotee.

She had little knowledge of the life before she entered it, and only gradually became aware of the character borne by most of her fellow-devotees. When she knew, she fled from them and returned to her own village and the secular life, finding it better than the religious. In telling us about it she said, "I expected whiteness, I found blackness."

She told of the children: "Many babies are brought by their parents and given to temple women for the sake of merit. If the child is old enough to miss her mother, she is carefully watched until she has forgotten her. Sometimes she is shut up in the back part of the house and punished if she runs out into the street. The punishment is severe enough to frighten the child. Sometimes it is branded with a hot iron upon a place which does not show, as under the arm. Sometimes the punishment is nipping with the nail till the skin breaks; sometimes a whipping. As soon as she can understand, she is taught all evil and trained to think it is good."

Thus the child is taught to read poetry. The poetry is almost entirely of a debased character, and so the child's mind is familiarized with sin. Before she knows how to refuse the evil and choose the good, the instinct which would have been her guide is tampered with and perverted till the poor little mind, thus bewildered and deceived, is incapable of choice.

* * *

The road that skirts Red Lake leads through two ancient Hindu towns, from both of which we have children saved, in each case as by a miracle. In the first of these old towns there is a temple surrounded by a mighty wall. There are two large gates and one small side door in the wall; and passing through the small side door, one sees another wall almost as strong as the first, and realizes something of the power that built it.

The temple is in the center of the large enclosure. It is a single tower opening off the inner court. In the outer court a pillared hall is used as stable for the temple elephant, and two camels lounge in the roughly kept garden in front.

This temple, with its double walls, its splendidly carved doors, and expensive animal life is something of a surprise to the visitor, who hardly expects to see so much in a little old country town on the borders of the wilds. But Hinduism has not lost hold of this old remote India yet. There are some who think that the country town is the place to see it in strength.

It was early in August three years ago that we heard of a baby girl in that town, devoted from birth to the god. We set wheels in motion and waited. A month passed and nothing was done. We could not go ourselves and attempt to persuade the mother to change the vow she had made; any movement on our part would only have riveted the links that fettered the child to the god. We had to be quiet and wait.

At last one evening in September, a Hindu arrived in the town with whom our friends who were on the watch had intimate connection. He, too, knew about the child, and he knew a way unknown to our friends by which the mother might be influenced. He consented to try. His arrival just at that juncture appeared to us, who were waiting in daily expectation of an answer of deliverance, as the evident beginning of that answer. Thus our faith was quickened.

Two days later, after dark, there was a rush from the nursery to the bungalow. "The baby has come!" Another moment and we were in the nursery. A woman, one of our friends, was standing with what looked like a parcel wrapped in a cloth hidden under her arm. Even then, though all was safe, she was trembling; and outside two men who were her relations stood on guard. She opened the white cloth, and inside was the baby.

The men assured us that all was right. The mother had been convinced of the wrongness of dedicating the little babe and would give us no trouble. But a day or two later she came and demanded it back. She could not stand the derision of her friends, who told her she had sinned far more in giving her child to those who would break its caste than she ever could have done had she given it to the temple. We pacified her with difficulty and were thankful when the little thing was safe in the Neyoor nursery. In those days, before we knew how best to protect our children, we were glad to have some place even more out of reach than Dohnavur.

The second of these old towns is famous for its rock and its temple built into the rock. Looking down from above, one can see inside the courtyard as into an open well. Connected with this temple, some years ago, was a beautiful young temple woman who had been given as a child—as all temple women must be—to the service of the gods. She had no choice as regarded herself (probably the idea of choice never entered her mind), but for her babe she determined to choose; and yet she knew of no way of deliverance.

But there was a way of deliverance, and if it had been only for this one child's sake and for the relief it must have been to that fear-haunted mother, we are glad with a gladness too deep for words that the nursery was here. For the mother heard of it. There were lions in the path. She quietly avoided them, and through others who were willing to help, she sent her child to us. She herself would not come. She waited a mile or so from the bungalow till the matter was concluded, then returned.

A week later she appeared suddenly at the bungalow. It was only to make sure the little one was safe and well and to sign a paper saying she was wholly given to us. This done, she disappeared again, refusing speech with anyone, and for months we heard nothing of her. Then cholera swept our countryside, and we heard she had taken it and died. We leave her to God her Creator, who alone knows all the story of her life.

*   *   *

Another little girl who came from that same Temple of the Rock has a story very different and far more typical. It was a blazing day in June when the very air leaned heavily upon us, and we felt unequal to the contest, that a cough outside my open door announced a visitor. "Come in!" Another cough, and I looked out and saw a shuffling form disappear round the corner of the house.

I called again and the figure turned. It was a man who had helped us before, but about whose good faith we had doubts; so we asked without much hopefulness what he had to tell us. He said he had reason to believe a certain temple woman known to him had a child she meant to dedicate to the god of a temple a day's journey distant. Then he paused.

"Do you know where she is now?"

"She is on her way to the temple."

"It would be well if she came here instead."

"If that is the Ammal's desire it may be possible to bring her."

"Has she gone far? Could you overtake her?"

"She is waiting outside your gate."

At such a moment it is wise to show no surprise and no anxiety. All the burning eagerness must be covered up with coolness. But in the hour that intervened before the woman "at the gate" could be persuaded to come further, we quieted ourselves in the Lord our God and held on for the little child.

At last the shuffling step and the sound of voices told us they had come: two women, the man, and a child. The child was a baby of something under two, a sad-looking little thing, with great, dark, pathetic eyes looking out from under limp brown curls. She was very pale and fragile; and when the woman who carried her set her down upon the floor and propped her against the wall, she leaned against it listlessly, with her little chin in her tiny hand in a sorrowful, grown-up fashion.

I longed to take her and nestle her comfortably, but of course took no notice of her. Any sign of pity or sympathy would have been misunderstood by the women. All through the interminable talk upon which her fate depended, that child sat wearily patient, making no demands upon anyone; only the little head drooped, and the mouth grew pitiful in its complete despondency.

The ways of the East are devious. The fact that the child had been brought to us did not indicate a decision to give her to us instead of to the temple. The woman and the man who had persuaded her to come had much to say to one another, and there was much we had to explain.

A child given to temple service is not in all cases entirely cut off from her people. If the temple woman's hold on her is sure, her relatives are sometimes allowed to visit her; so far as friendly intercourse goes she is not lost to them. But with us things are different. For the child's own sake we have to refuse all intercourse whatever. Once given to us, she is lost to them as if they never had her. We adopt the little one altogether or not at all.

It is a delicate thing to explain all this so clearly that there can be no misunderstanding about it, without so infuriating the relatives that they will have nothing more to do with us. Naturally their viewpoint is entirely different from ours, and they cannot appreciate our reasons. At such times we lean upon the Invisible and count upon that supernatural help which alone is sufficient for us; we count also upon the prayers of those who know what it is to pray through all opposing forces, till the battle is won by faith which is the victory.

It was strange to watch the women as the talk went on. The "woman" within them had died; there was nothing of it left to which we could appeal. Everything about them was perverted, unnatural. I looked at the insensitive faces and then at the sensitive face of the child, and I entered deeper than ever into the mercifulness of God's denunciation of sin.

Once toward the close of what had been a time of some tension, the leader of the two women suddenly sprang up, snatched at the tired baby, and flung out of the room with her. She had been gradually hardening, and I had felt rather than seen the shutting down of the prison house gates upon that little soul. I then appealed to the sense [in her], not wholly atrophied, the sense that recognizes the supernatural.

God is, I told them briefly; God takes cognizance of what we are and do; God will repay; some time, somewhere, God will punish sin. The arrow struck through to the mark. Startled, indignant, overwhelmed by the sweep of an awful conviction, with a passionate cry she rushed away. We lived through one breathless moment, but the next saw the child dropped into our arms, safe at last.

Facts about any matter of importance are usually other than first stated, but we have reason to believe that in this instance our shuffling friend spoke the truth. The women were really on their way to the temple when he waylaid them. The wonder was that they allowed themselves to be persuaded by him to come to us. But if nothing happened except what we might naturally expect would happen in this work, we might as well give it up at once. If we did not expect our Jericho walls to fall down flat, it would be foolish to continue marching round them.

It was a relief when the women left the compound after signing a paper committing the child to us. There is defilement in the mere thought of evil, but such closer contact with it is a thing by itself. The sense of contamination lasted for days; and yet would that we could go through it every day if the result might be the same! For the child woke up to a new life and became what a child should be.

At first it was very pitiful. She would sit hour after hour as she had sat through that first hour, with her chin in hand, her eyes cast down, and the little mouth pathetic. We found that in accordance with a custom prevailing in the coterie of temple women belonging to the Temple of the Rock, she had been lent by her mother to another woman when she was an infant, the other lending her baby in exchange.

This exchange had worked sadly, for the little one had asked for something which had not been given her, and her two years had left her starved of love and experienced in loneliness. But when she came to us everything changed, for love and happiness took her hands and led her back to baby ways and taught her how to laugh and play. Now there is nothing left to remind us of those first two years but a certain droop of the little mouth when she feels for the moment desolate or wants some extra petting.

*   *   *

The thing we fight is not India or Indian, in essence or development. It is something alien to the old life of the people. It is not allowed in the Vedas.[1] It is like a parasite which has settled upon the bough of some noble forest tree—on it, but not of it. The parasite has gripped the bough with strong and interlacing roots, but it is not the bough.

We think of the real India as we see it in the thinker—the seeker after the unknown God, with his wistful eyes. "The Lord beholding him loved him," and we cannot help loving as we look. And there is the Indian woman hidden away from the noise of crowds, patient in her motherhood, loyal to the light she has. We see the spirit of the old land there; and it wins us and holds us, and makes it a joy to be here to live for India.

The true India is sensitive and very gentle. There is a wisdom in its ways, none the less wise because it is not the wisdom of the West. This spirit which traffics in children is callous and fierce as a ravening beast; and its wisdom descendeth not from above, but is earthly, sensual, devilish. And this spirit, alien to the land, has settled upon it and made itself at home in it, and so become a part of it that nothing but the touch of God will ever get it out. We want that touch of God: "Touch the mountains, and they shall smoke."[2] That is why we write.

For we write for those who believe in prayer—not in the emasculated modern sense, but in the old Hebrew sense, deep as the other is shallow. We believe there is some connection between knowing and caring and praying, and what happens afterward. Otherwise we should leave the darkness to cover the things that belong to the dark. We should be forever dumb about them, if it were not that we know an evil covered up is not an evil conquered. So we do the thing from which we shrink with strong recoil; we stand on the edge of the pit, and look down and tell what we have seen, urged by the longing within us that the Christians of England should pray.

"Only pray?" does someone ask? Prayer of the sort we mean never stops with praying. "Whatsoever he saith unto you, do it"[3] is the prayer's solemn afterword; but the prayer we ask is no trifle. "Arise, cry out in the night; in the beginning of the night watches pour out thine heart like water before the Lord; lift up thine hands toward Him for the life of thy young children."

The story of the children is the story of answered prayer. If any of us were tempted to doubt whether, after all, prayer is a genuine transaction and answers to prayer no figment of the imagination—but something as real as the tangible things about us—we have only to look at some of our children. It would require more faith to believe that what we call the Answer came by chance or by the action of some unintelligible combination of controlling influences, than to accept the statement in its simplicity—God heard: God answered.

*　*　*

In October, 1908, we were told of two children whose mother had recently died. They were with their father in a town some distance from Dohnavur. The source from which our information came was so unreliable that we hardly knew whether to believe it. We prayed a rather tentative prayer: "If the children exist, save them."

For three months we heard nothing; then a rumor drifted across to us that the elder of the two had died in a temple house. The younger, six months old, was still with her father. On Christmas eve our informant arrived in the compound with his usual unexpectedness. The father was near, but would not come nearer because the following day being Friday (a day of ill-omen), he did not wish to discuss matters concerning the child; he would come on Saturday.

On Saturday he came, carrying a dear little babe with brilliant eyes. She almost sprang from him into our arms, and we saw she was mad with thirst. She was fed and put to sleep, and hardly daring yet to rejoice (for the matter was not settled with the father), we took him aside and discussed the case with him.

There were difficulties. A temple woman had offered a large sum for the child and had also promised to bequeath her property to her. He had heard, however, that we had little children who had all but been given to temples and had come to reconnoiter rather than to decide.

The position was explained to him, but the temple meant to him everything that was worshipful. How could anything that was wrong be sanctioned by the gods? The child's mother had been a devout Hindu; and so we went deeper and deeper into things with him. It was evident he became more and more reluctant to leave the little one with us. "Her mother would have felt it shame and eternal dishonor."

We were in the little prayer room, a flowery summerhouse in the garden, when this talk took place. On either side are the nurseries, and playing on the wide verandahs were happy, healthy babes. Their merry shouts filled the spaces in the conversation. Sometimes a little toddling thing would find her way across to the prayer room and break in upon the talk with affectionate caresses. To our eyes everything looked so happy, so incomparably better than anything the temple house could offer.

It was difficult to adjust one's mental vision so as to understand that of the Hindu beside us, to whose thought all the happiness was as nothing because these babes would be brought up without caste. In the temple house caste is kept most carefully. If a temple woman breaks the rules of her community, she is outcasted, excommunicated. "You do not keep caste! You do not keep caste!" the father repeated over and over in utter dismay. It was nothing to him that the babes were well and strong and as happy as the day was long, nothing to him that cleanliness reigned, as far as constant supervision could ensure it, through every corner of the compound.

We did not profess to keep caste; we welcomed every little child in danger of being given to temples, irrespective altogether of her caste. All castes were welcome to us, for all were dear to our Lord. This was beyond him, and he declared he would never have brought his child to us had he understood it before. "Let her die rather. There is no disgrace in death." As he talked and expounded his views, he argued himself further and further away from us in spirit, until he became disgusted with himself for ever having considered giving the baby to us.

All this time the baby lay asleep, and as we looked at the little face and noted the "mother-want," the appealing expression of pitiful weariness even in sleep, it was all we could do to turn away and face the almost inevitable result of the conversation. Once the father, a splendid-looking man, tall and dignified, rose and stood erect in sudden indignation. "Where is the babe? I will take her away and do as I will with her. She is my child!"

We persuaded him to wait awhile as she was asleep, and we went away to pray. Together we [of the fellowship] waited upon God, whose touch turns hard rocks into standing water and flint stone into a springing well, beseeching him to deal with that father's heart and make it melt and yield. And as we waited, it seemed as if an answer of peace was distinctly given to us, and we rose from our knees at rest. But just at that moment the father went to where his baby slept in her cradle, and he took her up and walked away in a white heat of wrath.

The little one was in an exhausted condition, for she had not had suitable food for at least three days. It was the time of our land-winds, which are raw and cold to south India people. It seemed that the answer of peace must mean peace after death of cold and starvation. It would soon be over, we knew—twenty-four hours, more or less, and those great wistful eyes would close, and the last cry would be cried. But even twenty-four hours seemed long to think of a child in distress, and her being so little did not make it easier to think of her dying like that.

So on Sunday morning I shut myself up in my room, asking for quick relief for her, or—but this seemed almost asking too much—that she might be given back to us. And as I prayed, a knock came at the door, and a voice called joyously, "Oh, Amma, Amma, come! The father stands outside the church; he has brought the baby back!"

But the child was almost in collapse. Without a word he dropped the cold, limp little body into our arms and prostrated himself till his forehead touched the dust. We had no time to think of him; we hardly noted his extraordinary submission, for all our thought was for the babe. There was no pulse to be felt; only those far-too-brilliant eyes looked alive. We worked with restoratives for hours, and at last the little limbs warmed and the pulse came back. But it was a bounding, unnatural pulse, and the restlessness which supervened confirmed the tale of the brilliant eyes—the little babe had been drugged.

From that day on till our prayer day, January 6, it was one long, unremitting fight with death. We wrote to our medical comrade in Neyoor and described the symptoms, which were all bad. He could give us little hope. Gradually the brilliance passed from the eyes, and they became what the Tamils call "dead." The film formed after which none of us had ever seen recovery. Then we gathered round the little cot in the room we call Tranquillity, and we gave the babe her Christian name, Vinala, the Spotless One; for we thought that very soon she would be without spot and blameless, another little innocent in that happy band of innocents who see His face.

On the evening of January 5, friends of our own mission who were with us seemed to lay hold for the life of the child with such fresh earnestness and faith that we ourselves were strengthened. Next morning we believed we saw a change in the little, deathlike face, and that evening we were sure the child's life was coming back to her.

It was not till then we thought of the father, who after signing a paper made out for him by our pastor, had returned to his own town. When we heard all that had occurred, we saw how our God had worked for us. It was not fear of his baby's death that had moved the man to return her to us. "What is the death of a babe? Let her die across my shoulders!" After all persuasions had failed, we had tried threats: the thing he proposed to do was illegal. The Collector (chief magistrate) would do justice. The father was not afraid of the law. "What care I for your Collector? How can he find me if I choose to lose myself? How can you prove anything against me?"

In that he spoke the truth. There are ways by which the intention of the law concerning children can be easily and successfully circumvented. Our pleadings had not touched him. "Is she not my child? Was her mother not my wife? Who has the right to come between this child of mine and me, her father?" And so saying, he had departed without the slightest intention of coming back again.

But a Power with which he did not reckon had him in sight; and a Hand was laid upon him, and it bent him like a reed. We hope some ray of a purer light than he had ever experienced found its way into his darkened soul and revealed to him the sin of his intention. But we only know that he left his child and went back to his own town. God had heard: God had answered.

*   *   *

We would never willingly disguise one fraction of the truth in our desire to win sympathy and true cooperation. And yet there is a joy that is worth it all a thousand times. Who that has known it will doubt it? Many a bitter storm has come. There have been the shock and the darkness of new knowledge of evil and grief beside which all other pain pales, the grief of helplessness in the face of unspeakable wrong.

But still, above and within and around, like an atmosphere, like a fountain, there has been something bright, even that sweet original joy which nothing can darken or quench.

If Thy first glance so powerful be
A mirth but opened and sealed up again,
What wonders shall we feel when we shall see
Thy full-orbed love!
When Thou shalt look us out of pain,
And one aspect of Thine spend in delight,
More than a thousand worlds' disburse in light
In heaven above!

And not alone, oh, not alone, shall we see Him as He is.
There will be the little children too.

Think through me, thoughts of God,
My Father, quiet me,
Till in Thy holy presence, hushed,
I think Thy thoughts with Thee.

Think through me, thoughts of God,
That always, everywhere,
The stream that through my being flows
May homeward pass in prayer.

Think through me, thoughts of God,
And let my own thoughts be
Lost like the sand—pools on the shore
Of the eternal sea.

*   *   *

I have no word,
But neither hath the bird,
And it is heard;
My heart is singing, singing all day long,
In quiet joy to Thee who art my Song.

For as Thy majesty
So is Thy mercy,
So is Thy mercy,
My Lord and my God.

How intimate Thy ways with those who wait
About Thy gate;
But who could show the fashion of such ways
In human words, and hymn them to Thy praise?

Too high for me,
Far shining mystery,
Too high to see;
But not too high to know, though out of reach
Of words to sing its gladness into speech.

*   *   *

Broken pitchers—and the light shone out.
Broken box—and the ointment was poured
   forth.
Broken bread—and the hungry were fed.
A broken Body—and the world was redeemed.

As Thou wast broken, O my Lord, for me,
Let me be broken, Lord, for love of Thee.

*   *   *

Father, hear us, we are praying,
Hear the words our hearts are saying,
We are praying for our children.

Keep them from the powers of evil,
From the secret, hidden peril,
Father, hear us for our children.

From the whirlpool that would suck them,
From the treacherous quicksand, pluck them,
Father, hear us for our children.

From the worldling's hollow gladness,
From the sting of faithless sadness,
Father, Father, keep our children

Through life's troubled waters steer them,
Through life's bitter battle cheer them,
Father, Father, be Thou near them.

Read the language of our longing,
Read the wordless pleadings thronging,
Holy Father, for our children.

And wherever they may bide,
Lead them Home at eventide.

NOTES

1. The body of ancient Hindu sacred scriptures.
2. Psalm 144:5
3. John 2:5

Peter Taylor Forsyth, 1848-1921

For evangelicals brought to commitment to Jesus Christ on a hearty diet of Scripture, or perhaps suddenly transplanted from a life of sin into the Kingdom of God, it may be difficult to understand how a convinced "liberal," a person who claims to be "emancipated" from Biblical faith, can ever find the way back to it. Yet such was the experience of Peter Taylor Forsyth.

A brilliant student of the literary classics and a master of scientific criticism, he graduated with first-class honors from the University of Aberdeen, Scotland. Leaving his native city at age twenty-two, he studied for a term at the University of Göttingen, Germany, where his interest turned toward religion. At first he approached the Bible as he had the classics, primarily from the viewpoint of a critic; but when in 1876 he entered the Congregational church ministry and began to apply the New Testament to his pastoral responsibilities, he underwent a transformation. He said, "It pleased God by the revelation of his holiness and grace . . . in the Bible, to bring home to me my sin. . . . Whereas I first thought that what the churches needed was enlightened instruction and liberal theology, I came to be sure that what they needed was evangelization."[1]

This radical change in his theology, which became apparent in subsequent pastorates in London and Manchester, has been described as a conversion. Forsyth himself expressed the change convincingly and vividly by saying, "I was turned from a Christian to a believer, from a lover of love to an object of grace."[2]

By the turn of the century, Forsyth had become an ardent champion of "the positive Gospel," which he expounded in some twenty-five books with such titles as The Cruciality of the

Cross, The Work of Christ, The Person and Place of Jesus Christ, and The Justification of God. *In 1907 he delivered the Lyman Beecher lectures on preaching at Yale University.*

Meanwhile the liberalizing trend in British mainline theology burst into full bloom twenty years before it arrived in the United States. "Our being," declared R. J. Campbell, minister of London's City Temple, "is the same as God's. . . . Every man is a potential Christ."[3] In the ensuing debate, authentic evangelicalism became virtually voiceless. Peter Forsyth found himself, not unlike Athanasius many centuries before him, contending against the whole theological world.

What makes Forsyth's turnaround especially remarkable is the ambience in which it took place. He was a man steeped in the tradition of European classicism. One of his early books carried the title, Religion in Recent Art. *His literary style was that of a poet writing prose. In his personal life he suffered from frail health; after the death of his wife, he suffered a breakdown. Yet his keen mind and gracious, warm, outgoing natural qualities brought him to the leadership of his denomination and to the deanship of the faculty of theology at the University of London. Today he ranks among the significant Christian voices of the twentieth century. The following pages, taken from* The Soul of Prayer *by P. T. Forsyth, published by Independent Press (London) 1916 and reprinted in 1954, are reproduced by permission of The United Reformed Church in the United Kingdom, 86 Tavistock Place, London, WC1H 9RT.*

THE SOUL OF PRAYER
by Peter Taylor Forsyth

It is a difficult and even formidable thing to write on prayer, and one fears to touch the Ark. But perhaps the effort to look into its principle may be graciously regarded by him "who ever liveth to make intercession" as itself a prayer to know better how to pray. All true prayer promotes its own progress and increases our power to pray.

The worst sin is prayerlessness. Overt sin, or crime, or the glaring inconsistencies which often surprise us in Christian people are the effect of this, or its punishment. We are left by God for lack of seeking him. The history of the saints shows often that their lapses were the fruit and nemesis of slackness or neglect in prayer. Their life, at seasons, also tended to become inhuman by their spiritual solitude.

Only living prayer keeps loneliness humane. It is the great producer of sympathy. Trusting the God of Christ, and transacting with Him, we come into tune with men. Our egoism retires before the coming of God, and into the clearance there comes with our Father our brother. We realize man as he is in God and for God, his Lover. When God fills our heart, he makes more room for man than the humanist heart can find.

Prayer is an act, indeed the act, of fellowship. We cannot truly pray even for ourselves without passing beyond ourselves and our individual experience. If we should begin with these, the nature of prayer carries us beyond them. Even private prayer is common prayer.

Not to want to pray, then, is the sin behind sin. And it

ends in not being able to pray. That is its punishment—spiritual dumbness, or at least aphasia, and starvation. We do not take our spiritual food, and so we falter, dwindle, and die. "In the sweat of your brow you shall eat your bread."[4] That has been said to be true both of physical and spiritual labor. It is true both of the life of bread and of the bread of life.

Prayer brings with it, as food does, a new sense of power and health. We are driven to it by hunger, and, having eaten, we are refreshed and strengthened for the battle which even our physical life involves. For heart and flesh cry out for the living God.[5] God's gift is free; it is, therefore, a gift to our freedom. Without this gift always renewed, our very freedom can enslave us. The life of every organism is but the constant victory of a higher energy, constantly fed, over lower and more elementary forces. Prayer is the assimilation of a holy God's moral strength.

We must work for this living. To feed the soul we must toil at prayer. And what a labor it is! "He prayed in an agony."[6] We must pray even to tears if need be. Our cooperation with God is our receptivity; but it is an active, a laborious receptivity, an importunity that drains our strength away if it do not tap the sources of the Strength Eternal. We work, we slave, at receiving. To him that hath this laborious expectancy, it shall be given.[7] Prayer is the powerful appropriation of power, of divine power. It is therefore creative.

Prayer is not mere wishing. It is asking—with a will. Our will goes into it. It is energy. *"Orare est laborare."*[8] We turn to an active Giver; therefore we go into action. For we could not pray without knowing and meeting Him in kind. If God has a controversy with Israel, Israel must wrestle with God. Moreover, He is the Giver, not only of the answer, but first of the prayer itself. His gift provokes ours. He beseeches us, which makes us beseech Him. And what we ask for chiefly is the power to ask more and to ask better. We pray for more prayer. The true "gift of prayer" is God's grace before it is our facility.

*   *   *

Thus prayer is, for us, paradoxically, both a gift and a conquest, both a grace and a duty. When we look up from under it, it is a load, but those who look down to it from God's side see it as a blessing. It is like great wings—they increase the weight but also the flight. To be denied duty is to be denied God. No cross, no Christ.

We are so egoistically engrossed about God's giving of the answer that we forget His gift of the prayer itself. But it is not a question simply of being willing to pray, but of accepting and using as God's will the gift and power to pray. In every act of prayer, we have already begun to do God's will, for which above all things we pray. The prayer within all prayer is, "Thy will be done."

Prayer has its great end when it lifts us to be more conscious and more sure of the gift than the need, of the grace than the sin. As petition rises out of need or sin, in our first prayer it comes first; but it may fall into a subordinate place when, at the end and height of our worship, we are filled with the fullness of God. "In that day you will ask me nothing."[9]

Inward sorrow is fulfilled in the prayer of petition; inward joy in the prayer of thanksgiving. And this thought helps to deal with the question as to the hearing of prayer, and especially its answer. Or rather as to the place and kind of answer. We shall come one day to a heaven where we shall gratefully know that God's great refusals were sometimes the true answers to our truest prayer. Our soul is fulfilled if our petition is not.

* * *

When we begin to pray, we may catch and surprise ourselves in a position like this. We feel to be facing God from a position of independence. If He starts from His end, we do from ours. We are His vis-a-vis; He is ours.

But this is not the Christian idea; it is only a crude stage of it. [In the New Testament] we are taught that only those things are perfected in God which He begins; that we seek only because He found; we beseech Him because He first besought us. If our prayer reaches or moves Him, it is because He first reached and moved us to pray.

The prayer that reached heaven began there, when Christ went forth. It began when God turned to beseech us in Christ—in the appealing Lamb slain before the foundation of the world.[10] The Spirit went out with the power and function to return with our soul. Our prayer is the answer to God's. Herein is prayer, not that we prayed Him, but that He first prayed us, in giving His Son to be a propitiation for us. So we pray because we were made for prayer, and God draws us out by breathing Himself in.

We feel this especially as prayer passes upwards into praise. When the mercy we sought comes home to us, its movement is reversed, and it returns as thanksgiving. "Great blessings which are won with prayer are worn with thankfulness." Prayer may spring from self-love, and be so far natural; for nature is all of the craving and taking kind. But praise is supernatural. It is of pure grace. And it is a sign that the prayer was more than natural at heart.

Spare some leisure, therefore, from petition for thanksgiving. If the Spirit moves conspicuously to praise, it shows that He also moved latently the prayer. "Prayer and thanks are like the double motion of the lungs; the air that is drawn in by prayer is breathed forth again by thanks."

In prayer we do not think out God; we draw Him out. Prayer is where our thought of God passes into action and becomes more certain than thought. In all thought which is not mere dreaming or brooding, there is an element of will. We do not simply spread our thought before God, but we offer it to Him, press it on Him.

We can offer God nothing so great and effective as our obedient acceptance of the mind and purpose and work of Christ. It is not easy. It is harder than any idealism. But then it is very mighty. At first it groans, at last it glides. As there are thoughts that seem to think themselves in us, so there are prayers that pray themselves in us. And, as those are the best thoughts, these are the best prayers.

Prayer is often represented as the great means of the

Christian life. But it is no mere means, it is the great end of that life. It is truer to say that we live the Christian life in order to pray, than that we pray in order to live the Christian life. Our prayer prepares for our work and sacrifice, but all our work and sacrifice still more prepare for prayer.

We cannot move fast to such a fine product. It is a growth in grace. And the whole history of the world shows that nothing grows so slowly as grace, [and] nothing costs as much as free grace.

*   *   *

A chief object of all prayer is to bring us to God. But we may attain His presence and come closer to Him by the way we ask Him for other things, concrete things or things of the Kingdom, than by direct prayer for union with Him. The prayer for deliverance from personal trouble or national calamity may bring us nearer Him than mere devout aspiration to be lost in Him. The poor woman's prayer to find her lost sovereign may mean more than the prayer of many a cloister.

Prayer is never rejected so long as we do not cease to pray. The chief failure of prayer is its cessation. Our importunity is a part of God's answer, both of His answer to us and ours to Him. He is sublimating our idea of prayer and realizing the final purpose in all trouble, which is to drive us farther in on Himself.

The joiner, when he glues together two boards, keeps them tightly clamped till the cement sets and the outward pressure is no more needed; then he unscrews. So with the calamities, depressions, and disappointments that crush us into close contact with God. Instant relief would not establish the habit of prayer. If we got all we asked for, we should soon come to treat God as a convenience or the request as magic. The reason of much bewilderment about prayer is that we are less occupied about faith in God than about faith in prayer.

In God's eyes the great object of prayer is the opening

or restoring of free communion with Himself. In this sense every true prayer brings its answer with it, in our obtaining a deeper and closer place in God and His purpose. If prayer is God's great gift, it is inseparable from the Giver, who is, after all, His own great gift. We find that the complete answer to prayer is the Answerer, and the hungry soul comes to itself in the fullness of Christ.

*   *   *

Prayer is the highest use to which speech can be put. It is the highest meaning that can be put into words. It breaks through language and escapes into action. Words fail us in prayer oftener than anywhere else; and the Spirit must come in aid of our infirmity, set out our case to God, and give to us an unspoken freedom in prayer. We are taken up from human speech to the region of the divine Word, where Word is deed. Prayer contains the very heart and height of truth, but especially in the Christian sense of truth: reality and action. In prayer the inmost truth of our personal being locks with the inmost reality of things.

True prayer does not allow us to deceive ourselves. It relaxes the tension of our self-inflation. It produces a clearness of spiritual vision. There are fervent prayers which, by making people feel good, may do no more than foster the delusion that natural vigor or robust religion, when flushed enough, can do the work of the Kingdom of God. So by prayer we acquire our true selves. If my prayer is not answered, I am. If my petition is not fulfilled, my person, my soul, is.

Not to pray is not to discern—not to discern the things that really matter. The mind may see acutely and clearly, but the personality perceives nothing subtle and mighty, because the natural powers are unschooled, unchastened, and unempowered by the energy of prayer. It is not always hard to tell among Christian men those whose thought is matured in prayer, whose theology [has become] a hymn, whose energy is disciplined, whose work becomes love poured out, as by many a Salvationist lass, and whose temper is subdued to that illuminated humility in which a man truly finds his soul. The deeper we go into things, the more do we enter a world where the mastery and the career is not to talent but to prayer.

In prayer we do not ask God to do things contrary to nature. So far from crossing nature, we give it tongue. We lift it to its divinest purpose, function, and glory. Nature excels itself in our prayer. If there be a divine teleology in nature at all, prayer is the *telos*.

True prayer is the supreme function of the personality which is the world's supreme product. It is personality with this function that God seeks above all to rear. The praying personality has an eternal value for God as an end in itself. This is the divine fullness of life's time and course, the one achievement that survives with more power in death than in life. The intercession of Christ in heaven is the continuity and consummation of His supreme work on earth. To share it is the meaning of praying in the Spirit.

The soul's growth is often visible only to the Savior whom we keep near by prayer, whose search we invoke, and for whose action we make room in prayer. Our certainty of Him is girt round with much uncertainty, but in prayer we become more and more sure that He is sure, and knows all things, and hesitates or falters never, and commands all things to His end. All along Christ is being darkly formed within us as we pray.

This is the mark of real life: we possess our souls in the prayer which is real communion with God. We enter by faith upon that which to sight and history is but a far future reversion. When [God] comes to our prayer, He brings with Him all that He purposes to make us. We are already the "brave creature" He means us to be. We can pierce to what we are at our true center and true destiny, i.e., what we are to God's grace. Laws and injunctions, such as "love your neighbor," even "love your enemy," then become life principles, and they are law pressures no more. The yoke is easy. When all is forgiven to seventy times seven, there is no friction and no grief any more.[11] We taste love and joy. All the pressure of life then goes to form the crystals of faith. It is God making up His jewels.

*   *   *

When we are in God's presence by prayer, we are right, our will is morally right, we are doing His will. However unsure we may be about other acts and efforts to serve Him, we know we are right in this. If we ask truly but ask amiss, it is not a sin, and He will in due course set us right in that respect.

We are sure that prayer is according to His will and that we are just where we ought to be. And that is a great matter for the rightness of our thought and of the aims and desires proposed by our thoughts. It means much both as to their form and their passion. If we realize that prayer is the acme of our right relation to God, if we are sure that we never are so right with Him in anything we do as in prayer, then prayer must have the greatest effect and value for our life.

The effect of our awful war [World War I] will be very different on the prayerful and the prayerless. It will be a sifting judgment. It will turn to prayer those who did not pray and increase the prayer of those who did. But some, whose belief in God grew up only in fair weather and not at the cross, it will make more skeptical and prayerless than ever. It will present them with a world more confused and more destitute of a God than before, which can only lead to renewed outbreaks of the same kind as soon as the nations regain strength.

Every true prayer carries with it a vow. If it does not, it is not in earnest, not of a piece with life. Can we pray in earnest if we do not in the act commit ourselves to do our best to bring about the answer? What is the value of praying for the poor if all the rest of our time and interest is given only to becoming rich? Where is the honesty of praying for our country if in our most active hours we are chiefly occupied in making something out of it? If we pray for our child that he may have God's blessing, we are really promising that nothing shall be lacking on our part to be a divine blessing to him.

To begin our prayer with a petition for the hallowing of God's name and to have no real place for holiness in our life is not sincere. To begin the day with prayer is but a formality unless it go on in prayer, unless for the rest of it we pray in deed what we began in word. One has said that while prayer is the day's best beginning, it must not be like the handsome title page of a worthless book.

Prayer is for the religious life what original research is for science—by it we get direct contact with reality. We touch the last reality directly in prayer. It is the climate in which God's manifestation bursts open into inspiration. We are left with God in Christ as His own Mediator and His own Revealer. He is directly with us and in us. We transcend these two thousand years as if they were but one day.

So many of us pray because we are driven by need rather than kindled by grace. Our prayer is a cry rather than a hymn. It is a quest rather than a tryst. It trembles more than it triumphs. It asks for strength rather than exerts it. How different was the prayer of Christ! All the divine power of the Eternal Son went to it. It was the supreme form taken by His Sonship in its experience and action.

Nothing is more striking in Christ's life than His combination of selflessness and power. His consciousness of power was equal to anything, and egoism never entered Him. His prayer was accordingly. It was the exercise of His unique power rather than of His unique need. It came from His uplifting and not His despair. It was less His duty than His joy. It was more full of God's gift of grace than of man's poverty of faith, of a holy love than of a seeking heart.

In His prayer He poured out neither His wish nor His longing merely, but His will. He knew He was heard. He knew it with such power and certainty that He could bless with His overflow and promise His disciples they would be heard in His name. It was by His prayer that He countered and foiled the godless power in the world, the kingdom of the devil. "Satan has desired to have you, but I have prayed for you."[12]

His prayer means so much for the weak because it arose

out of this strength and its exercise. It was chiefly in His prayer that He was the Messiah, the Revealer and Wielder of the power and Kingship of God. His power with God was so great that it made His disciples feel it could only be the power of God. And it was so great because it was spent on God alone.

So true is it that the Kingdom of God comes not with observation,[13] that the greatest things Christ did for it were done in the night and not in the day; His prayers meant more than His miracles. And His great triumph was when there were none to see, as they all forsook Him and fled. He was mightiest in His action for men, not when He was acting on men, but on God. He did most for His public in entire solitude. There He put forth all His powers.

The power of prayer answers to the omnipotence of grace. Those who feel they owe everything to God's grace need have no difficulty about the range of prayer. They may pray for everything.

* * *

It is an art—this great and creative prayer—this intimate conversation with God. *Magna ars est conversari cum Deo* (to converse with God is a great art), says Thomas à Kempis. It has to be learned. In social life we learn that conversation is not mere talk. There is an art in it, if we are not to have a table of gabblers. How much more is it so in the conversation of heaven! We must learn that art by practice and by keeping the best society in that kind. Associate much with the great masters in this kind, especially with the Bible, and chiefly with Christ. Cultivate His Holy Spirit. He is the grand master of God's art and mystery in communing with man. And there is no other teacher, at least, of man's art of communion with God.

The will of God is that men should pray everywhere.[14] He wills to be entreated. Prayer is that will of God's making itself good. When we entreat we give effect to His dearest will. And in His will is our eternal liberty. In this will of His,

ours finds itself and is at home. It ranges the liberties of the
Father's house. But here prayer must draw from the cross,
which is the frontal act of our emancipation as well as the central revelation of God's own freedom in grace. The action of
the Atonement and of its release of us is in the nature of
prayer.

When we are told to pray without ceasing, it seems to
many tastes today to be somewhat extravagant language. And
no doubt that is true. Why should we be concerned to deny
it? Measured language and the elegant mean is not the note of
the New Testament. The peace of God is not the calm of culture, it is not the charm of breeding.

Every great forward movement in Christianity is associated with much that seems academically extravagant. Erasmus
is always shocked with Luther.[15] There is nothing so abnormal,
so unworldly, so supernatural in human life as prayer—nothing that is more of an instinct, it is true, but also nothing that
is less rational among all the things that keep above the level
of the silly. The whole Christian life as it is lived from the cross
and by the cross is rationally an extravagance. This "pray
without ceasing"[16] [is] far from being absurd, [just] because it
is extravagant. Every man's life is in some sense a continual
state of prayer. Every life is a draft on the unseen. If you are
not praying toward God, you are toward something else. You
pray as your face is set—toward Jerusalem or Babylon. The
man whose passion is habitually set upon pleasure, knowledge, wealth, honor, or power is in a state of prayer to these
things or for them. These are his real gods, on whom he waits
day and night. He may from time to time go on his knees in
church and use words of Christian address and petition. He
may even feel a momentary unction in so doing, but it is a
flicker; the other devotion is his steady flame.

*   *   *

To cultivate the ceaseless spirit of prayer, use more frequent
acts of prayer. To learn to pray with freedom, force yourself
to pray. The great liberty begins in necessity.

Do not say, "I cannot pray. I am not in the Spirit." Pray till you are in the Spirit. It is often hard enough to take up the task which in half an hour you enjoy. It is often against the grain to turn out of an evening to meet the friends you promised. But once you are in their midst, you are in your element. So if you are averse to prayer, pray the more. Do not call it lip-service. That is not the lip-service God disowns. What is unwelcome to God is lip-service that is untroubled at not being more. As appetite comes with eating, so prayer with praying. Our hearts learn the language of the lips.

Go into your chamber, shut the door, and cultivate the habit of praying audibly. Write prayers. Formulate your soul. Pay no attention to literary form, only to spiritual reality. Read a passage of Scripture, and then sit down and turn it into a prayer, written or spoken. Learn to be particular, specific, and detailed in your prayer so long as you are not trivial.

General prayers, literary prayers, and stately phrases are, for private prayer, traps to the soul. To formulate your soul is one valuable means to escape formalizing it. Speaking with God discovers us safely to ourselves. Face your special weaknesses and sins before God. Force yourself to say to God exactly where you are wrong. When anything goes wrong, don't ask to have it set right without asking in prayer what it was in you that made it go wrong.

It is somewhat fruitless to ask for a general grace to help specific flaws, sins, trials, and griefs. Let prayer be concrete, actual, a direct product of life's real experiences. Pray as your actual self, not as some fancied saint. Let it be closely relevant to your real situation. Pray without ceasing in this sense. Pray without a break between your prayer and your life. Pray so that there is a real continuity between your prayer and your whole actual life.

Do not allow your practice in prayer to be arrested by scientific or philosophic considerations as to how answer is possible. That is a valuable subject for discussion, but it is not entitled to control our practice. Criticism of prayer dissolves in the experience of it. In this region we are not to be regulated by science, but by God's self-revelation.

Keep close to the New Testament Christ, and then ask for anything you desire in that contact. Ask for everything you can ask in Christ's name. If prayer is not a play of the religious fantasy or a routine task, it must be the application of faith to a concrete actual and urgent situation. Only remember that prayer does not work by magic and that stormy desire is not fervent, effectual prayer.

If you may not come to God with the occasions of your private life and affairs, then there is some unreality in the relation between you and Him. If some private crisis absorbs you, some business or family anxiety of little moment to others but of much to you, and if you may not bring that to God in prayer, then one of two things [has happened]. Either it is not you, in your actual reality, that came to God, but it is you in a pose—you in some role which you are trying with poor success to play before Him. You are praying in court-dress. You are praying as you imagine one should pray to God, as another person than you are.

Either that, or you are not praying to a God who loves, helps, and delivers you in every pinch of life, but only to one who uses you as a pawn for the victory of His great Kingdom. You are not praying to Christ's God, but to [one] who cares only for the great actors in His Kingdom or for the calm people who do not deeply feel life's trials.

God has old prayers of your long maturing by Him. What wine you will drink with Him in his Kingdom!

Before prayer can expect an answer, it must be itself an answer. That is what is meant by prayer in the name of Christ. It is prayer which answers God's gift in Christ, with whom are already given us all things. Natural or instinctive prayer is one thing; supernatural prayer is another. It is the prayer not of instinct but of faith. "The best thing in prayer," says Luther, "is faith."

* * *

We pray and pray, and no answer comes. The boon does not arrive. Why? Perhaps we are not spiritually ready for it. It

would not be a real blessing. But the persistence, the importunity of faith, is having a great effect on our spiritual nature.
I have often found that what I sought most, I did not get at
the right time, not until it was too late, not till I had learned
to do without it, till I had renounced it in principle, though
not in desire.

Perhaps it had lost some of its zest by the time it came,
but it meant more as a gift and a trust. That was God's right
time—when I could have it as though I had it not. If it came,
it came not to gratify me, but to glorify Him and be a means
of serving Him. One recalls that most pregnant saying of
Schopenhauer: "All is illusion—the hope or the thing
hoped."[17] If it is not true for all, it is true for very many. Either
the hope is never fulfilled, or else its fulfillment disappoints.
God gives the hoped-for thing, but sends leanness into the
soul. The mother prays to have a son—and he breaks her
heart, and were better dead. Hope may lie to us, or the thing
hoped may dash us.

But though he slay me, I will trust.[18] God does not fail.
Amid the wreck of my little world, He is firm, and I in Him.
I justify God amid the ruins; in His good time I shall arrive.
More even than my hopes may go wrong. I may go wrong.
But my Redeemer lives; and, great though God is as my
Fulfiller, He is greater as my Redeemer. He is great as my
hope, but He is greater as my power. What is the failure of my
hope from Him compared with the failure of His hope in me?
If He continues to believe in me, I may well believe in Him.

God's object with us is not to give just so many things
and withhold so many; it is to place us in the tissue of His
Kingdom. He would lift us to confident business with Him,
to commerce of loving wills. The painter wrestles with the sit-
ter till he gives him back himself, and there is a speaking likeness. So man with God.

He gives or refuses things, therefore, with a view to that
communion alone. It is that spiritual personal end, and not an
iron necessity, that rules God's course.

Is there not a constant spiritual interaction between God
and man as free spiritual beings? How that can be is one of

the great philosophic problems. But the fact that it is, is of the essence of faith. It is the unity of the universe. Many systems try to explain how human freedom and human action are consistent with God's omnipotence and omniscience. None succeed. How secondary causes like man are compatible with God as the Universal and Ultimate Cause is not rationally plain. But there is no practical doubt that they are compatible.

And so it is with the action of man on God in prayer. We may perhaps, for the present, put it thus, that we cannot change the will of God, which is grace, and which even Christ never changed but only revealed or effected. But we can change the intention of God, which is a matter of treatment, in the interest of grace, according to the situation of the hour.

If we are guided by the Bible, we have much ground for this view of prayer. Does not Christ set more value on importunity than on submission? "Knock, and it shall be opened." I would refer also to the parable of the unjust judge, [and] to the incident of the Syrophoenician woman, where her wit, faith, and importunity together did actually change our Lord's intention and break his custom. Then there is Paul beseeching the Lord thrice for a boon, and urging us to be instant, insistent, continual in prayer.[19]

We have Jacob wrestling. We have Abraham pleading, yea, haggling, with God for Sodom. We have Moses interceding for Israel and asking God to blot his name out of the book of life, if that were needful to save Israel. We have Job facing God, withstanding Him, almost bearding Him, and extracting revelation. And we have Christ's own struggle with the Father in Gethsemane.[20]

It is a wrestle on the greatest scale—all mankind taxed as in some great war or some great negotiation of state. And the effect is often exhaustion. The result of true prayer is not always peace.

So when God yields to prayer in the name of Christ, to the prayer of faith and love, He yields to Himself who inspired it. Christian prayer is the Spirit praying in us. It is prayer in the solidarity of the Kingdom. It is God dealing with God. And when God yields, it is not to an outside influence, but to Himself.

When we resist the will of God, we may be resisting what God wills to be temporary and to be resisted, what He wills to be intermediary and transcended. We resist because God wills we should. We are not limiting God's will, any more than our moral freedom limits it. That freedom is the image of His, and, in a sense, part of His. We would be defrauding Him and His freedom if we did not exercise ours. So the prayer which resists his dealing may be part of His will and its fulfillment.

By God's will (let us say) you are born in a home where your father's earnings are a few shillings a week, like many an English laborer's. Is it God's will that you acquiesce in that and never strive out of it? It is God's will that you are there. Is it God's will that you should not resist being there? Or may it be that it is His will that you should wisely resist it? Do we ourselves not appoint problems and make difficulties for those we reach, for the very purpose of their overcoming them? We set questions to children of which we know the answer quite well. The real answer to our will and purpose is not the solution but the grappling, the wrestling. And we may properly give a reward not for the correct answer, but for the hard and honest effort. That work is the prayer, and it has its reward apart from the solution.

Let us beware of a pietist fatalism which thins the spiritual life, saps the vigor of character, makes humility mere acquiescence, by banishing the will from prayer as much as thought has been banished from it. In time all effort will seem less pious than submission. And so we fall into the ecclesiastical type of religion, drawn from an age whose first virtue was submission to outward superiors. We shall come to canonize decorum and subduedness in life and worship. We shall think more of order than of effort, more of law than of life, more of fashion than of faith, of good form than of great power.

But was subduedness the mark of the New Testament men? Our [Christianity] may gain some beauty in this way, but it loses vigor. It may gain style, but it loses power. It may consecrate manners, but it impoverishes the mind. It may regulate prayer by the precepts of intelligence instead of by the needs and faith of the soul.

A young man began his prayer, in my own hearing, with the words, "O God, we have come to have a chat with Thee." It was gruesome. No prayers, certainly no public prayers, should be "chats with God." Lose the importunity of prayer, reduce it to soliloquy or even to colloquy with God, make it mere walking with God in friendly talk, and precious as that is, you tend to lose the reality of prayer at last. You may have beautiful prayers, but as ineffectual as beauty so often is, and as fleeting. Redemption turns down into mere revelation, faith to assent, and devotion to a phase of culture.

But close with God, cling to him with your strength, not your weakness only, with your active and not your passive faith, and He will give you strength. He may lift you from your feet. But it will be to lift you from earth and set you in the heavenly places which are theirs who fight the good fight and lay hold of God as their eternal life.

NOTES

1. R. M. Brown, *P. T. Forsyth: Prophet for Today* (Philadelphia: Westminster, 1952), p. 20.
2. *Ibid.*, p. 22.
3. *Ibid.*, p. 27.
4. Cf. Genesis 3:19.
5. Cf. Psalm 84:2.
6. Cf. Luke 22:44.
7. Cf. Mark 4:25.
8. "To pray is to work." (Attributed to Augustine, but its origin is unknown.)
9. John 16:23.
10. Cf. Revelation 13:8.
11. Cf. Matthew 18:22.
12. Luke 22:31.
13. Cf. Luke 17:20.
14. 1 Timothy 2:8.
15. Desiderius Erasmus (1466?-1536) was a Dutch Renaissance scholar, a Roman Catholic who at first favored the Reformation led by Luther, but later opposed it as being too extreme.
16. 1 Thessalonians 5:17.
17. Arthur Schopenhauer (1788-1860), possibly in *Counsels and Maxims*.
18. Cf. Job 13:15.
19. Matthew 7:7-8; Luke 18:2-6; Mark 7:25-30; 2 Corinthians 12:7-9; Romans 12:12.
20. Genesis 32:24 ff.; Genesis 18:23-32; Exodus 32:32; Job 7:19-21; Mark 14:36.

G. K. Chesterton, 1874-1936

In his own words, Chesterton was "intolerably showy and assertive." He was sometimes pugnacious toward his many opponents. He was grossly overweight. He drank too much. He withstood women's suffrage. He disliked foreigners and Jews. He ended life as a rather combative Roman Catholic.

And yet, in the words of George Bernard Shaw (no Christian), this man was a "colossal genius" who exercised an amazing influence over his generation. He was a painter, puppeteer, poet, dramatist, essayist, epigrammatist, philosopher, author of detective fiction, biographer, and supremely a journalist and critic. He kept the English-speaking world shaking its head at his versatility while chuckling at his humor. Asked which one book he would like to take if he knew he would be wrecked on a desert island, Chesterton replied, "I think I would like to take Thomas's Guide to Practical Shipbuilding."

At the time he wrote his famous book Orthodoxy, *from which our extracts are taken, Chesterton was a loyal communicant member of the Church of England. At age thirty-four, after having left University College, London, without seeking a degree, he and his pen took on the whole gamut of Christianity's opponents: the evolutionists, rationalists, Fabian socialists, spiritualists, and free sex advocates, all of whom flourished in the post-Victorian years.* Orthodoxy *was published in 1908 by John Lane, London, six years before the outbreak of World War I, at a time when the very existence of sin was being questioned or denied by English liberals.*

Chesterton's skill in attacking the fallacies in rival systems of thought made him a strong voice in intellectual circles. He challenged the biological implications of Darwinism with an

*affirmation of joy in creation. He sensed as did few of his con-
temporaries that the Christian gospel is glad tidings of great joy
to all people. "Praise," he wrote, "should be the permanent pulsation of the soul. Man is more man when joy is the fundamental thing in him."*

*Gilbert Keith Chesterton was born in Kensington, London,
into a rather well-to-do family. His parents retained the disciplines of Calvinism but repudiated its theology, as they believed
in complete freedom of thought. Young Gilbert proved a rather
unruly pupil at school, but displayed talent in poetry and art. At
age twenty, now six feet, two inches in height, he matriculated
at the university, but remained there only a year.*

*He went to work for a small British publishing house that
specialized in books on spiritualism and the occult. Two years
later he married Frances Blogg, an ardent Anglo-Catholic,
whose influence fostered his growing interest in Christianity.
They had no children.*

*The following pages, taken by permission from the book
Orthodoxy, give no hint of Chesterton's later ecclesiastical
interest in the Roman church. Their theme is the integrity of the
Christian faith as opposed to the inconsistency of its critics. The
respect with which he addressed some of his unbelieving adversaries is particularly refreshing.*

THREE

THE PARADOXES OF CHRISTIANITY
by G. K. Chesterton

I was a pagan at the age of twelve and a complete agnostic by the age of sixteen. All I had hitherto heard of Christian theology had alienated me from it. I did, indeed, retain a cloudy reverence for a cosmic deity and a great historical interest in the Founder of Christianity. But I certainly regarded Him as a man; though perhaps I thought that, even in that point, He had an advantage over some of His modern critics.

I read the scientific and skeptical literature of my time—all of it, at least, that I could find written in English and lying about; and I read nothing else; I mean I read nothing else on any other note of philosophy. The penny dreadfuls which I also read were indeed in a healthy and heroic tradition of Christianity; but I did not know this at the time. I never read a line of Christian apologetics. I read as little as I can of them now.

It was Huxley[1] and Herbert Spencer[2] and Bradlaugh[3] who brought me back to orthodox theology. They sowed in my mind the first wild doubts of doubt. Our grandmothers were quite right when they said that Tom Paine and the free-thinkers unsettled the mind. They do. They unsettled mine horribly. The rationalist made me question whether reason was of any use whatever; and when I had finished Herbert Spencer, I had got as far as doubting (for the first time) whether evolution had occurred at all. As I laid down the last of Colonel Ingersoll's atheistic lectures, the dreadful thought broke across my mind, "Almost thou persuadest me to be a Christian."[4] I was in a desperate way.

This odd effect of the great agnostics in arousing doubts deeper than their own might be illustrated in many ways. I take only one. As I read and reread all the non-Christian or anti-Christian accounts of the faith, from Huxley to Bradlaugh, a slow and awful impression gradually but graphically grew upon my mind—the impression that Christianity must be a most extraordinary thing. It was attacked on all sides and for all contradictory reasons. I will give such instances as I remember at random of this contradiction in the skeptical attack.

Thus I was much moved by the eloquent attack on Christianity as a thing of inhuman gloom, for I thought (and still think) sincere pessimism the unpardonable sin. Insincere pessimism is a social accomplishment, rather agreeable than otherwise; and fortunately nearly all pessimism is insincere. If Christianity was, as these people said, a thing purely pessimistic and opposed to life, then I was quite prepared to blow up St. Paul's Cathedral.[5]

But the extraordinary thing is this: they did prove to me in chapter 1 that Christianity was too pessimistic; and then in chapter 2, they began to prove to me that it was a great deal too optimistic. One accusation against Christianity was that it prevented men, by morbid tears and terrors, from seeking joy and liberty in the bosom of nature. But another accusation was that it comforted men with a fictitious providence and put them in a pink-and-white nursery.

One great agnostic asked why nature was not beautiful enough and why it was hard to be free. Another great agnostic objected that Christian optimism, "the garment of make-believe woven by pious hands," hid from us the fact that nature was ugly and that it was impossible to be free. One rationalist had hardly done calling Christianity a nightmare before another began to call it a fool's paradise. This puzzled me; the charges seemed inconsistent. The state of the Christian could not be at once so comfortable that he was a coward to cling to it, and so uncomfortable that he was a fool to stand it. If it falsified human vision, it must falsify it one way or another; it could not wear both green- and rose-colored spectacles.

I rolled on my tongue with a terrible joy, as did all young men of that time, the taunts which Swinburne[6] hurled at the dreariness of the creed:

> Thou hast conquered, O pale Galilean,
> The world has grown gray with Thy breath.

But when I read the same poet's accounts of paganism (as in [his drama] Atalanta of Calydon), I gathered that the world was, if possible, more gray before the Galilean breathed on it than afterward. The poet maintained, indeed, in the abstract, that life itself was pitch dark. And yet, somehow, Christianity had darkened it. The very man who denounced Christianity for pessimism was himself a pessimist. I thought there must be something wrong. And it did for one wild moment cross my mind that perhaps those might not be the very best judges of the relation of religion to happiness who, by their own account, had neither one nor the other.

It must be understood that I did not conclude hastily that the accusations were false or the accusers fools. I simply deduced that Christianity must be something even weirder and more wicked than they made out. A thing might have these two opposite vices, but it must be a rather queer thing if it did.

Here is another case of the same kind. I felt that a strong case against Christianity lay in the charge that there is something timid . . . and unmanly about all that is called Christian, especially in its attitude toward resistance and fighting. The great skeptics of the nineteenth century were largely virile. In comparison, it did seem that there was something weak and overpatient about Christian counsels.

The gospel paradox about the other cheek . . . a hundred things made plausible that Christianity was an attempt to make a man too like a sheep. I read it and believed it. But . . .

now I found that I was to hate Christianity not for fighting too little, but for fighting too much. Christianity, it seemed, was the mother of wars. Christianity had deluged the world with blood. I had got thoroughly angry with the Christian because he never was angry. And now I was told to be angry with him because his anger had been the most huge and horrible thing in human history.

It was the fault of poor old Christianity (somehow or other) both that Edward the Confessor[7] did not fight and that Richard Coeur de Lion[8] did. The Quakers (we were told) were the only characteristic Christians, and yet the massacres of Cromwell[9] and Alva[10] were characteristic Christian crimes. What could it all mean? What was this Christianity which always forbade war and always produced wars? What could be the nature of the thing which one could abuse first because it would not fight, and second because it was always fighting? In what world of riddles was born this monstrous murder and this monstrous meekness? The shape of Christianity grew a queerer shape every instant.

I take a third case, the strangest of all because it involves the one real objection to the faith. The one real objection . . . is simply that it is one religion. I mean the doctrine that there is one great unconscious church of all humanity founded on the omnipresence of the human conscience. I believed this doctrine of the brotherhood of all men in the possession of a moral sense, and I believe it still—with other things. And I was thoroughly annoyed with Christianity for suggesting (as I supposed) that whole ages and empires of men had utterly escaped this light of justice and reason.

But then I found an astonishing thing. I found that the very people who said that mankind was one church, from Plato to Emerson, were the very people who said that morality had changed altogether and that what was right in one age was wrong in another.

I saw the same thing on every side. Thus, certain skeptics wrote that the great crime of Christianity had been its attack on the family. Certain phrases in the epistles or the marriage service were said by the anti-Christians to show contempt for woman's intellect. But I found that the anti-Christians themselves had a contempt for woman's intellect, for it was their great sneer at the church on the continent that "only women" went to it. Or, again, Christianity was reproached with . . . being too plain and for being too colored . . . restraining sexuality too much [and] too little. . . .

I wished to be quite fair then, and I wish to be quite fair now; and I did not conclude that the attack on Christianity was all wrong. I only concluded that if Christianity was wrong, it was very wrong indeed. If this mass of mad contradictions really existed, quakerish and bloodthirsty, too gorgeous and too threadbare, austere yet pandering preposterously to the lust of the eye, the enemy of women and their foolish refuge, a solemn pessimist and a silly optimist, if this evil existed, then there was in this evil something quite . . . unique. The only explanation which immediately occurred to my mind was that Christianity did not come from heaven, but from hell. Really, if Jesus of Nazareth was not Christ, He must have been Antichrist.

And then in a quiet hour a strange thought struck me. Suppose we heard an unknown man spoken of by many men. Some men said he was too tall and some too short; some objected to his fatness, some lamented his leanness; some thought him too dark and some too fair. One explanation would be that he might be an odd shape. But there is another explanation. He might be the right shape. Perhaps the extraordinary thing is really the ordinary thing, at least the normal thing, the center. Perhaps, after all, it is Christianity that is sane and all its critics that are mad—in various ways.

I went over all the cases and found the key fitted so far. The fact that Swinburne was irritated at the unhappiness of Christians and yet more irritated at their happiness was easily explained. It was no longer a complication of diseases in Christianity, but a complication of diseases in Swinburne. The restraints of Christians saddened him simply because he was more pessimistic than a healthy man should be.

* * *

All sane men can see that sanity is some kind of equilibrium. Paganism declared that virtue [lay] in a balance; Christianity declared it was in a conflict: the collision of two passions apparently opposite. Take the case of courage. Courage is almost a contradiction in terms. It means a strong desire to live taking the form of a readiness to die. "He that will lose his life, the same shall save it," is a piece of everyday advice for sailors or mountaineers. It might be printed in an Alpine guide or a drill book.

This paradox is the whole principle of courage. A man cut off by the sea may save his life if he will risk it on the precipice. He can only get away from death by continually stepping within an inch of it. A soldier surrounded by enemies, if he is to cut his way out, needs to combine a strong desire for living with a strange carelessness about dying. He must seek his life in a spirit of furious indifference to it.

No philosopher, I fancy, has ever expressed this romantic riddle with adequate lucidity, and I certainly have not done so. But Christianity has done more. It has held up . . . the banner of . . . Christian courage, which is a disdain of life.

This is the thrilling romance of orthodoxy. People have fallen into a foolish habit of speaking of orthodoxy as something heavy, humdrum, and safe. There never was anything so perilous or so exacting as orthodoxy. It was sanity, and to be sane is more dramatic than to be mad. It was the equilibrium of a man behind madly rushing horses, seeming to stoop this way and to sway that, yet in every attitude having the grace of statuary and the accuracy of arithmetic. It is always easy to be a modernist, as it is easy to be a snob. It is always simple to fall; there are an infinity of angles at which one falls, only one at which one stands. In my vision the heavenly chariot flies thundering through the ages, the wild truth reeling but erect.

*   *   *

A short time ago Mrs. Besant[11] in an interesting essay announced that there was only one religion in the world, that all faiths were only versions or perversions of it, and that she was quite prepared to say what it was. According to Mrs. Besant this universal church is simply the universal self. It is the doctrine that we are really all one person, that there are no real walls of individuality between man and man. If I may put it so, she does not tell us to love our neighbors; she tells us to be our neighbors.

That is Mrs. Besant's thoughtful and suggestive description of the religion in which all men must find themselves in agreement. And I never heard of any suggestion in my life with which I more violently disagree. I want to love my neighbor, not because he is I, but precisely because he is not I. I want to adore the world, not as one likes a looking glass because it is one's self, but as one loves a woman because she is entirely different.

If souls are separate, love is possible. If souls are united, love is obviously impossible. A man may be said loosely to love himself, but he can hardly fall in love with himself, or if he does, it must be a monotonous courtship. If the world is full of real selves, they can be really unselfish selves. But upon Mrs. Besant's principle the whole cosmos is only one enormously selfish person.

It is just here that Christianity is on the side of humanity and liberty and love. Love desires personality, therefore love desires division. It is the instinct of Christianity to be glad that God has broken the universe into little pieces, because they are living pieces. No other philosophy makes God actually rejoice in the separation of the universe into living souls. But according to orthodox Christianity this separation between God and man is sacred, because this is eternal.

*   *   *

It is commonly the loose and latitudinarian Christians who pay quite indefensible compliments to Christianity. They talk as if there had never been any piety or pity until Christianity came, a point on which any medieval would have been eager to correct them. They represent that the remarkable thing about Christianity was that it was the first to preach simplicity or self-restraint, or inwardness and sincerity.

They will think me very narrow (whatever that means) if I say that the remarkable thing about Christianity was that it was the first to preach Christianity. Its peculiarity was that it was peculiar, and simplicity and sincerity are not peculiar, but [are] obvious ideals for all mankind. Christianity was the answer to a riddle, not the last truism uttered after a long talk.

Only the other day I saw in an excellent weekly paper of Puritan tone this remark—that Christianity when stripped of its armor of dogma (as who should speak of a man stripped of his armor of bones) turned out to be nothing but the Quaker doctrine of the Inner Light. Now, if I were to say that Christianity came into the world specially to destroy the doctrine of the Inner Light, that would be an exaggeration. But it would be very much nearer to the truth.

The last Stoics, like Marcus Aurelius,[12] were exactly the people who did believe in the Inner Light. Their dignity, their weariness, their sad external care for others, their incurable internal care for themselves, were all due to the Inner Light, and existed only by that dismal illumination. Notice that Marcus Aurelius insists, as such introspective moralists always do, upon small things done or undone; it is because he has not hate or love enough to make a moral revolution. He gets up early in the morning, just as our own aristocrats living the Simple Life get up early in the morning, because such altruism is much easier than stopping the games of the amphitheater or giving the English people back their land.

Marcus Aurelius is the most intolerable of human types. He is an unselfish egoist. An unselfish egoist is a man who has pride without the excuse of passion. Of all conceivable forms of enlightenment, the worst is what these people call the Inner Light. Of all horrible religions, the most horrible is the worship of the god within.

Anyone who knows anybody knows how it would work; anyone who knows anyone from the Higher Thought Center knows how it does work. That Jones shall worship the god within him turns out ultimately to mean that Jones shall worship Jones. Let Jones worship the sun or moon, anything rather than the Inner Light. Let Jones worship cats or crocodiles, if he can find any in his street, but not the god within.

Christianity came into the world firstly in order to assert ... that a man had not only to look inwards, but to look outwards, to behold with astonishment and enthusiasm a divine company and a divine captain. The only fun of being a Christian was that a man was not left alone with the Inner Light, but definitely recognized an outer light fair as the sun, clear as the moon, terrible as an army with banners.

* * *

That a man may love God, it is necessary that there should be not only a God to be loved, but a man to love Him. That external vigilance which has always been the mark of Christianity (the command that we should watch and pray) has expressed itself both in typical western orthodoxy and in typical western politics, but both depend on the idea of a divinity transcendent, different from ourselves.

We find that insofar as we value democracy and the self-renewing energies of the West, we are much more likely to find them in the old theology than the new. If we want reform, we must adhere to orthodoxy, especially in this matter of insisting on the immanent or the transcendent deity. By insisting specially on the immanence of God, we get introspection, self-isolation, quietism, social indifference—Tibet. By insisting specially on the transcendence of God, we get wonder, curiosity, moral and political adventure, righteous indignation—Christendom. By insisting that God is inside man, man is always inside himself. By insisting that God transcends man, man has transcended himself.

All Christianity concentrates on the man at the crossroads. The vast and shallow philosophies, the huge syntheses of humbug, all talk about ages and evolution and ultimate developments. The true philosophy is concerned with the instant. Will a man take this road or that? That is the only thing to think about, if you enjoy thinking.

There is a great deal of real similarity between popular fiction and the religion of the western people. Life (according to the faith) is very like a serial story in a magazine: life ends with the promise (or menace) "to be continued in our next." Also, with a noble vulgarity, life imitates the serial and leaves off at the exciting moment. For death is distinctly an exciting moment.

But the point is that a story is exciting because it has in it so strong an element of will, of what theology calls free will. You cannot finish a sum how you like, but you can finish a story how you like. When somebody discovered differential calculus, there was only one differential calculus he could discover. But when Shakespeare killed Romeo, he might have married him to Juliet's old nurse if he had felt inclined. And Christendom has excelled in the narrative romance exactly because it has insisted on the theological free will.

This is the real objection to that torrent of modern talk about treating crime as disease. The fallacy of the whole thing is that evil is a matter of active choice whereas disease is not. If a man is to be saved from influenza, he may be a patient. But if [a forger] is to be saved from forging, he must be not a patient but an impatient. All moral reform must start in the active, not the passive will.

*   *   *

This is the . . . most astounding fact about this faith—that its enemies will use any weapon against it, the swords that cut their own fingers and the firebrands that burn their own homes. Men who begin to fight the church for the sake of freedom and humanity end by flinging away freedom and humanity if only they may fight the church.

This is no exaggeration. I could fill a book with the instances of it. Mr. Blatchford set out, as an ordinary Bible-smasher, to prove that Adam was guiltless of sin against God. In maneuvering to maintain this he admitted, as a mere side issue, that all the tyrants from Nero to King Leopold II[13] were guiltless of any sin against humanity. I know a man who has such a passion for proving that he will have no personal existence after death that he falls back on the position that he has no personal existence now. In order to prove that he cannot go to heaven, he proves that he cannot go to Hartlepool.[14]

I have known people who protested against religious education with arguments against any education, saying that the child's mind must grow freely or that the old must not teach the young. I have known people who showed that there could be no divine judgment by showing that there can be no human judgment, even for practical purposes. They burned their own corn to set fire to the church; they smashed their own tools to smash it.

We do not admire, we hardly excuse, the fanatic who wrecks this world for love of the other. But what are we to say of the fanatic who wrecks this world out of hatred of the other? He sacrifices the very existence of humanity to the nonexistence of God.

And yet the thing hangs in the heavens unhurt. Its opponents only succeed in destroying all that they themselves justly hold dear. They do not destroy orthodoxy. They do not prove that Adam was not responsible to God; how could they prove it? The secularists have not wrecked divine things, but the secularists have wrecked secular things, if that is any comfort to them. The Titans did not scale heaven, but they laid waste the world.

*   *   *

Modern masters of science are much impressed with the need of beginning all inquiry with a fact. The ancient masters of religion were quite equally impressed with that necessity. They began with the fact of sin—a fact as practical as potatoes. Whether or not a man could be washed in miraculous waters, there was no doubt at any rate that he needed washing. But certain religious leaders in London, not mere materialists, have begun in our day not to deny the highly disputable water, but to deny the indisputable dirt. Certain new theologians dispute original sin, which is the only part of Christianity which can really be proved. Some followers of the Reverend R. J. Campbell,[15] in their almost too fastidious spirituality, admit divine sinlessness, which they cannot see even in their dreams. But they essentially deny human sin, which they can see in the street.

*   *   *

I find the history of Christianity, and even of its Hebrew origins, quite practical and clear. It does not trouble me to be told that the Hebrew God was one among many. I know He was, without any research to tell me so. Jehovah and Baal looked equally important, just as the sun and the moon looked the same size.

It is only slowly that we learn that the sun is immeasurably our master, and the moon only our satellite. Believing that there is a world of spirits, I shall walk in it as I walk in the world of men, looking for the things that I like and think good. I shall search the land of void and vision until I find something fresh like water and comforting like fire, until I find some place in eternity where I am literally at home. And there is only one such place to be found.

I have now said enough to show that I have in the ordinary arena of apologetics a ground of belief. But I will not pretend that this curt discussion is my real reason for accepting Christianity, instead of taking the moral good of Christianity as I should take it out of Confucianism.

I have another far more solid and central ground for submitting to it as a faith, instead of merely picking up hints from it as a scheme. And that is this: that the Christian church in its practical relation to my soul is a living teacher, not a dead one. It not only certainly taught me yesterday, it will almost certainly teach me tomorrow.

Plato has taught you a truth; but Plato is dead. Shakespeare has startled you with an image; but Shakespeare will not startle you with any more. But imagine what it would be to live with such men still living—to know that Plato might break out with an original lecture tomorrow, or that at any moment Shakespeare might shatter everything with a single song. The man who lives in contact with what he believes to be a living church is a man always expecting to meet Plato and Shakespeare tomorrow at breakfast. He is always expecting to see some truth that he has never seen before.

* * *

This therefore is my reason for accepting the [Christian] religion and not merely the scattered and secular truths out of the religion. I do it because the thing has not merely told this truth or that truth, but has revealed itself as a truth-telling thing. All other philosophies say the things that plainly seem to be true; only this philosophy has again and again said the thing that does not seem to be true, but is true. It is convincing where it is not attractive, [and] it turns out to be right.

Theosophists[16] for instance will preach an obviously attractive idea like reincarnation; but if we wait for its logical results, they are spiritual superciliousness and the cruelty of caste. Christianity preaches an obviously unattractive idea, such as original sin, but when we wait for its results, they are pathos and brotherhood, and a thunder of laughter and pity, for only with original sin can we at once pity the beggar and distrust the king.

Orthodoxy makes us jump by the sudden brink of hell; it is only afterward that we realize that jumping was an athletic exercise highly beneficial to our health. It is only afterward that we realize that this danger is the root of all drama and romance. The strongest argument for the divine grace is simply its ungraciousness. The unpopular parts of Christianity turn out when examined to be the very props of the people.

But this larger and more adventurous Christian universe has one final mark difficult to express, yet as a conclusion of the whole matter I will attempt to express it. All the real argument about religion turns on the question of whether a man who was born upside down can tell when he comes right way up. The primary paradox of Christianity is that the ordinary condition of man is not his sane or sensible condition; that the normal itself is an abnormality. That is the inmost philosophy of the Fall.

In Sir Oliver Lodge's[17] interesting new catechism, the first two questions were: "What are you?" and "What, then, is the meaning of the Fall of man?" I remember amusing myself by writing my own answers to the questions, but I soon found that they were very broken and agnostic answers. To the question, "What are you?" I could only answer, "God knows." And to the question, "What is meant by the Fall?" I could answer with complete sincerity, "That whatever I am, I am not myself."

That is the prime paradox of our religion; something that we have never in any full sense known, is not only better than ourselves, but even more natural to us than ourselves.

It is said that paganism is a religion of joy and Christianity of sorrow; it would be just as easy to prove that paganism is pure sorrow and Christianity pure joy. Such conflicts mean nothing and lead nowhere. Everything human must have in it both joy and sorrow; the only matter of interest is the manner in which the two things are balanced or divided. And the really interesting thing is this, that the pagan was (in the main) happier and happier as he approached the earth, but sadder and sadder as he approached the heavens.

The gaiety of the best paganism, as in the playfulness of Catullus[18] or Theocritus,[19] is indeed an eternal gaiety never to be forgotten by a grateful humanity. But it is all a gaiety about the facts of life, not about its origin. To the pagan the small things are as sweet as the small brooks breaking out of the mountain, but the broad things are as bitter as the sea.

When the pagan looks at the very core of the cosmos, he is struck cold. Behind the gods, who are merely despotic, sit the fates, who are deadly. Nay, the fates are worse than deadly; they are dead. And when the rationalists say that the ancient world was more enlightened than the Christian, from

their point of view they are right. For when they say "enlightened," they mean darkened with incurable despair.

It is profoundly true that the ancient world was more
modern than the Christian. The common bond is in the fact
that ancients and moderns have both been miserable about
existence, about everything, while medievals were happy
about that at least. I freely grant that the pagans, like the moderns, were only miserable about everything—they were quite
jolly about everything else. I concede that the Christians of
the Middle Ages were only at peace about everything—they
were at war about everything else. But if the question turns
on the primary pivot of the cosmos, then there was more cosmic contention in the narrow and bloody streets of Florence
than in the theater of Athens or the open garden of Epicurus.
Giotto[20] lived in a gloomier town than Euripides,[21] but he
lived in a gayer universe.

The mass of men have been forced to be gay about the
little things, but sad about the big ones. Nevertheless it is not
native to man to be so. Man is more himself, man is more
manlike, when joy is the fundamental thing in him, and grief
is superficial. Melancholy should be an innocent interlude, a
tender and fugitive frame of mind; praise should be the permanent pulsation of the soul. Pessimism is at best an emotional half-holiday; joy is the uproarious labor by which all
things live.

Yet according to the apparent estate of man as seen by
the pagan or the agnostic, this primary need of human nature
can never be fulfilled. Joy ought to be expansive, but for the
agnostic it must be contracted. It must cling to one corner of
the world. Grief ought to be a concentration, but for the
agnostic its desolation is spread through an unthinkable eternity. This is what I call being born upside down. The skeptic
may truly be said to be topsy-turvy, for his feet are dancing
upwards in idle ecstasies, while his brain is in the abyss.

To the modern man the heavens are actually below the
earth. The explanation is simple: he is standing on his head,
which is a very weak pedestal to stand on. But when he has
found his feet again, he knows it. Christianity satisfies sud-

denly and perfectly man's ancestral instinct for being the right way up; satisfies it supremely in this, that by its creed joy becomes something gigantic and sadness something special and small.

The vault above us is not deaf because the universe is an idiot; the silence is not the heartless silence of an endless and aimless world. Rather the silence around us is a small and pitiful stillness like the prompt stillness in a sickroom. We are perhaps permitted tragedy as a sort of merciful comedy, because the frantic energy of divine things would knock us down. We can take our own tears more lightly than we could take the tremendous levities of the angels. So we sit perhaps in a starry chamber of silence, while the laughter of the heavens is too loud for us to hear.

Joy, which was the small publicity of the pagan, is the gigantic secret of the Christian. And as I close this chaotic volume, I open again the strange small book from which all Christianity came; and I am again haunted by a kind of confirmation. The tremendous figure which fills the Gospels towers in this respect, as in every other, above all the thinkers who ever thought themselves tall. His pathos was natural, almost casual.

The Stoics, ancient and modern, were proud of concealing their tears. He never concealed His tears; He showed them plainly on His open face at any daily sight, such as the far sight of His native city. Yet He concealed something. Solemn supermen and imperial diplomats are proud of restraining their anger. He never restrained His anger. He flung furniture down the front steps of the Temple and asked men how they expected to escape the damnation of hell.

Yet He restrained something. I say it with reverence; there was in that shattering personality a thread that must be called shyness. There was something that He hid from all men when He went up a mountain to pray. There was something that He covered constantly by abrupt silence or impetuous isolation. There was some one thing that was too great for God to show us when He walked upon our earth; and I have sometimes fancied that it was His mirth.

NOTES

1. Thomas Huxley (1825-1895), biologist, exponent of Darwinism, father of Julian and Aldous Huxley, coined the term "agnostic" (literally "not knowing") as to God's existence, and applied it to himself.
2. Herbert Spencer (1820-1903), philosophic and scientific writer, adopted the designation agnostic. He considered God unknowable, but held progress to be a supreme law of the universe.
3. Charles Bradlaugh (1833-1891) was a prominent British freethinker and atheist.
4. Robert Ingersoll (1833-1899) was an American orator whose attacks on Christianity won wide publicity. He frequently lectured on "The Mistakes of Moses."
5. St. Paul's Cathedral, a landmark of London, was designed by Sir Christopher Wren in the seventeenth century.
6. Algernon Charles Swinburne (1837-1909) was an English poet.
7. Edward the Confessor (1003-1066) was acclaimed king of England in 1042.
8. Richard Coeur de Lion (the Lion-Hearted, 1157-1199), king of England, led a crusade to the Holy Land.
9. Oliver Cromwell (1599-1658), one-time Lord Protector of England, commanded troops that committed massacres in Catholic Ireland.
10. Fernando Alvarez de Toledo, Spanish Duke of Alva (1508-1583), commanded troops that committed massacres in Protestant Holland.
11. Annie Besant (1847-1933) was an English theosophist and a political leader in India, where she served as president of the Indian National Congress.
12. Marcus Aurelius (121-180), Roman emperor and Stoic philosopher, tarnished his reputation for wisdom by persecuting Christians.
13. Leopold II, king of the Belgians (1835-1909), was widely criticized for his harsh treatment of the natives of the African Congo, which had become a Belgian colony.
14. Hartlepool is an English seaport.
15. R. J. Campbell (1867-1956) was minister of London's City Temple (Congregational). He later abandoned his liberal views and became a priest of the Church of England.
16. Theosophy is a form of mystical religious thought. Cf. Annie Besant, above.
17. Sir Oliver Lodge (1851-1940), English physicist, attempted to reconcile science and religion.
18. Gaius Valerius Catullus (84?-54 B.C.) is regarded as one of ancient Rome's outstanding lyric poets.
19. Theocritus was a Greek pastoral poet of the third century B.C.
20. Giotto de Bondone (1276-1337) was a pre-Renaissance Florentine painter, sculptor, and architect.
21. Euripides (fifth century B.C.), master of Greek tragedy, resided in Athens.

Ole Hallesby, 1879-1961

For Ole Kristian Hallesby the year 1902 marked the beginning of a new life. At the time he was on his way to becoming another liberal theologian in the state Church of Norway (Lutheran). A farmer's son, his early roots were in the deeply pious Haugean tradition, founded by lay leader Hans Nielsen Hauge (1771-1824).[1] Hallesby tells us, "Our family has been a believing and praying family for three generations. During my whole life I have walked in the prayers of my parents and forebears."

As a theological student at the University of Oslo, however, Hallesby soon absorbed the skeptical views of the liberal faculty. One day, after five years of such studies, he made an appointment with one of his lecturers, a Professor Petersen. He explains that this man's "conservative and warm-hearted Christianity appealed very little to me during my whole theological course." Professor Petersen was evidently well aware of the young man's theological stance and spent only half a minute or so in counseling his student. Then, Hallesby tells us, "He looked me straight in the eye and said, 'Will you not become a Christian, Hallesby?'"

The young man later wrote, "That day I received a mortal wound, which within a half year brought me to my knees before my crucified Savior." Leaving both the university and the state church, Hallesby became, like Hauge before him, an itinerant lay preacher and saw spiritual awakening in many places he visited. Later he studied at the University of Berlin and, after receiving his doctorate, returned to Norway. He became chairman of dogmatics at the Free Faculty of Theology in Oslo, a position he held from 1909 to 1952. Carl Wisloff informs us, "In a sense he became the teacher of a whole generation of Norwegian ministers." Also as chairman of the Norwegian Lutheran Home Mission, he led the various mission societies of the nation away from dependence upon liberal connections.

In 1940 Hitler's military and naval forces invaded Norway, sealing its borders and seizing its government. For five years Norway was an occupied country, ruled by a traitor, Vidkun Quisling, who was backed by Nazi troops. A "home front" resistance movement arose, in which many churches took an active role. Ole Hallesby became a leader in the church's resistance effort until his arrest in 1943 by the occupation forces. The next two years he spent in a Nazi concentration camp until liberation in 1945. In 1947 he became the first president of the International Fellowship of Evangelical Students, an organization still active and operating in many countries.

During his long teaching career as Norway's leading independent theologian, Hallesby wrote textbooks on dogmatics and ethics, as well as many devotional books such as Prayer and Why I Am a Christian. These two alone have been translated into many languages and have sold millions of copies. The reason is obvious. Having himself been caught in the crucible of skepticism, Hallesby well understood the symptoms and characteristics of the doubting syndrome and could identify sympathetically and helpfully with the victims.

The following excerpt is reprinted from his Why I Am a Christian, translated by Clarence J. Carlsen, copyright 1958 by Augsburg Publishing House. Used by permission of Augsburg Fortress.

FOUR

WHY I AM A CHRISTIAN
by Ole Hallesby

There are two kinds of doubters.

First, there are those who love to doubt, because their skepticism shields them from the accusations of conscience. They will not give up the selfish life they are living, either in coarse and open sins, in ordinary love of the world, or in the self-sufficiency of outward morality. When their conscience disturbs them, doubt is the best means they have of pacifying it.

That is why we see people defending their skepticism as a precious possession, with which they would not part. They select literature which strengthens their doubt. They seize every opportunity to debate questions pertaining to Christianity. Even if they do not succeed in convincing their opponent in debate, they themselves at least feel more secure every time they have been able to bewilder their believing opponent and drive him to the wall.

If we should ask ordinary, average worldly people what it means to become a Christian, their answers would vary somewhat as to form, but the substance would be the same and would be about as follows.

"Well, this is what happens. A man becomes restless and unhappy and can no longer enjoy life, due either to sickness, sorrow, poverty, or old age. This inner unrest compels him to seek peace with God. And the God to whose will he must conform his life is a severe and exacting Lord. The least He requires is this: You must quit practically everything from which you derive any pleasure, such as dancing, drinking, card playing, the theater, and the society of congenial and interesting people, if these people are worldly. And then you must begin to do things which you do not care to do at all. You must go to church and hear sermons which have a beginning but scarcely an ending. You must read the Bible, which is of course a good book, but exceedingly tiresome, because you have already heard everything that it contains. You must pray to God every day, and several times a day, if the Lord is to be satisfied. You must begin to associate with these believers or 'Bible readers' who, as a rule, are good people but helplessly stupid, narrow, and tiresome. For they must always sing and read and pray when they get together. And you can never get a sensible word out of them about ordinary things."

That is, I believe, about the answer you would get. To them Christianity is an onerous burden, a yoke beneath which they must bend in order to satisfy the Lord. To every doubter of this type who may happen to be reading this, it is not to you that I [write]. The doubters to whom I venture to proffer my help are of a different description.

They are in distress because of their doubt. They are tired of painful uncertainty. They long for the peaceful rest which calm and impregnable assurance affords. But every time they think they have found solid ground upon which to stand, they sink back into the bottomless sea of doubt.

Their inner uncertainty becomes even more distressing to them whenever they come in touch with friends and companions who have found God. To the latter, God is no longer a problem, the unrealized object of their thinking, seeking, and longing. To them God is a living reality. They have experienced God. Theirs is the assurance of experience with its peace, joy, and power.

It is to these sincere, seeking, but distressed doubters that I venture to offer my assistance. I, too, have passed through the various stages of doubt. I have felt its anguish. But I also know a way out of doubt and into faith, a way which is open to all doubters. And this way does not do violence to any of our human faculties, not even to our reasoning powers.

This way was pointed out by Jesus over 1900 years ago. He put it in these words: "If anyone chooses to do God's will, he will find out whether my teaching comes from God or whether I speak on my own."[2] Here he promises to give personal assurance on the basis of experience. He names only one condition—if anyone chooses to do God's will.

Jesus tells us in these words something very important about doubt and the cause of doubt. Many are of the opinion that the cause of their doubt is their great knowledge or the keenness of their intellects. Others are more modest and think that their doubt is due to the fact that they lack knowledge and do not have a sufficiently keen intellect.

It is due to none of these. The cause of your doubt is something entirely different. You lack certain experiences. That is why you find yourself in doubt and uncertainty.

In offering you my help to overcome doubt, I shall not meet your doubts with logical arguments. I shall rather, as well as I can, point out the experiences through which you must pass in order to cope successfully with doubt. At the same time I shall try to indicate the course you must pursue in order to gain these experiences. If you will follow this course and thus gain these experiences, you will find that your experiences themselves will dispel your doubts. Life itself will do it in its own simple way.

My first bit of advice is this: Read the New Testament.

You may reply, "If I could only believe what it says, I would be helped; but it is the very message of the Bible about which I am in doubt. I do not deny the Bible. On the contrary, I desire to be a believer, but I cannot make myself believe. I doubt it instead of believing it."

To this I would say: I know that such is your condition. I am well acquainted with it and shall not take too much for granted. I suppose that you doubt the supernatural origin of Scripture and likewise that you doubt most, perhaps all, of the miraculous accounts in the New Testament. Nevertheless I ask you to read the New Testament.

Jesus never required His listeners to accept and beforehand approve of a greater or lesser number of dogmas about

Himself. He urged them rather to come to Him, hear His voice, and follow Him.

What happened? All who honestly did so, experienced Jesus and soon became personally convinced of the truth of what He said about Himself. When they later gave expression to that which they had experienced ... the result was the New Testament Scriptures.

Now take your New Testament and read it for the purpose of ascertaining the "will of God."

"But," you say, "it is so difficult for me to read the New Testament. All the accounts of miracles and the many other questionable thoughts and expressions distract and even offend me, and make it difficult for me to read with a calm and open mind."

My friend, I remember this well from the time when I was a doubter. My advice to you is that for the time being, you omit reading everything too offensive to your intellect. Read the remainder. It is fully sufficient to help you out of doubt and into personal assurance with respect to the Christ and the whole Scriptural testimony concerning Him.

Even if you omit the things I have mentioned, you will find on practically every page of the New Testament something which you must without doubt recognize as the "will of God." By that I mean eternal truths, independent of time, place and persons; as true today as in the time of Christ, as true at the North Pole as at the Equator, as true and eternally applicable with reference to kings as to beggars.

If you have followed this advice and read the New Testament, Jesus will stand before you in a new light. Morally, you have become mature enough to see the uniqueness of the person of Jesus. You knew before that Jesus was the noblest man known to history. Now you have the moral qualifications for evaluating this aspect of Jesus.

Indeed, you now discover that that perfect mind which was in Jesus is the most incomprehensible thing about Him. From the experiences you have had with your own selfish life and your own evil mind, you have become psychologically or, rather, morally qualified to evaluate the absolute uniqueness of His human life. After you yourself have tried [as Jesus taught] to do to others as you would have them do to you, and have not succeeded in doing so for even one whole day, you ask yourself: "After all, who was Jesus, who was able to do this very thing throughout a whole lifetime, without a single misstep or mistake and in such a natural and matter-of-fact way, as though there were no other way of living life?"

You now have the inner qualifications for experiencing the miraculous in the person of Jesus. The real miraculous, the real supernatural aspect of Jesus is His mind of absolute goodness. Here you are face to face with the supernatural, the absolute. You are in possession of an inner, direct, personal assurance concerning the most unique miracle in our universe.

Can you prove that the mind of Jesus was supernatural? Can I prove it to you? No, but remember that I said at the beginning that doubt cannot be overcome by logical arguments, but by experience only. All I promised you was that I would point out the experiences you would have to go through in order to rid yourself of doubt and receive personal assurance.

And that is what I have done. When you, with your own moral experience, stand before Jesus as He is presented to us in the New Testament, you will (as millions before you have done) experience the mind of Christ as a miracle, a supernatural mind.

Note now that you can become assured of this miracle, this fundamental miracle with respect to Jesus, even though you still doubt the miracles which it is said Jesus performed. If you have experienced that miraculous aspect of Jesus which is fundamental, namely, that His inner being is different from that of all the rest of us, that He, according to His ethical nature, is essentially different from all other people, you have also reached a new position with regard to the other miraculous aspects of His life and Person.

When a person has experienced something of the miraculous, the brunt of his difficulties in connection with miracles is broken. This follows according to the laws of psychology.

Many things seem self-contradictory and absurd as long as we only think and speculate about them. But as soon as we experience them, the inconsistency vanishes. As soon as our minds have experienced actual facts, our whole intellectual basis is changed, and inconsistencies and absurdities vanish. A great deal which formerly seemed absurd to you will now become self-evident and natural. And that in spite of the fact that you can by no means explain everything.

If you have experienced that Jesus according to His inner, ethical nature is essentially different from all other persons, it is no longer an inconsistency to your mind. On the contrary, when the New Testament states that He has a different origin from all the rest of us, it appears something very reasonable. Neither is it an inconsistency to our minds when He Himself says that He existed before His life on earth as the eternal Son of God.

If such is the case, neither is it an inconsistency that His birth took place in a manner different from ours. When the New Testament says that He became incarnate by a creative act of God's own Spirit, our minds say, that is only natural. That is the way it had to be. And if there is a fundamental difference between His inner ethical person and ours, it cannot be an inconsistency when the New Testament says that He is endowed with power different from any that we have. If He is in possession of a power different from any we possess, and by means of which He governs His own Person, why should He not be able to deal with the natural world in a way different from that in which we are able to deal with it?

Moreover, if He is in possession of a unique inner life, it cannot be an inconsistency when the New Testament says that in death, too, He was different from us, insofar as He broke the usual bonds of death and arose bodily from the grave on the third day.

In a similar way I could go through all the miracles we are told Jesus performed. Let me point out that it is only my personal experience of the miraculous element in the person of Jesus that has given me a new attitude with regard to the various other miraculous accounts. It is only in connection with the Person of Jesus that these miracles become plausible—I might almost say self-evident.

My next bit of advice is this: Begin to pray to God. Begin at the same time as you begin to read the New Testament.

"But I doubt the value of prayer," you say.

Yes, I know that. But begin nevertheless.

"Then I will be praying without being perfectly sincere about it, and that will never do."

There is where you make a mistake. To pray does not mean that you are to begin to offer such prayers as you hear others pray—your father or mother or pastor, for instance. To do so would certainly be insincerity on your part, and that will never do. Insincerity in one's relationship to God is more dangerous than any other kind of insincerity.

To pray is to speak candidly and confidentially with God. Why cannot you do that even though you are a doubter? You speak with human beings; why should you not speak with God, the Highest Being? He is invisible, it is true; but is not the real person in men also invisible? That which is visible to your eye is only flesh and blood. You must believe that they have an inner being and by faith establish contact with that being and thus become certain of their being!

"Very well," you say, "but what shall I say when I pray?"

Begin by telling God the truth, that you are in doubt about Him and that you do not believe in prayer. Ask Him to draw near to you and speak with you in order that your doubts may be removed and you may become certain of Him and certain that He hears your prayer.

I am prepared to hear someone say, "I have tried to pray, but not with the result of which you speak. I have received no answer, and I have prayed very earnestly. I cried to God the time my mother was struggling with death, the time my own child lay writhing in pain. In my distress I cried to God to intervene and help them out of pain and me out of doubt, that I might be certain that God is and that He hears and answers when we human beings pray. But there was no answer. And that was the greatest disappointment of my life."

With this, too, I am well acquainted. When I was a doubter I had a similar experience. Permit me to tell a little about it; perhaps it will be of some help to you.

For a long time I was an irreligious doubter. I thought that if there were a personal God, He did not concern Himself about each and every individual. However, the more I studied the religious history of the human race, the clearer it became to me that religion is a phase of human soul-life that resides inherently in persons in the same way as poetry and music, and which will not permit itself to be removed from life.

I observed that there were, indeed, irreligious individuals, but not irreligious peoples. I observed, further, that the irreligious individual is an artificial product, found only among sophisticated and hyper-cultured people in divers periods, especially periods of decadence. I also saw that this artificial product was the result of the suppression of innate religious tendencies, either on the part of the parents of young children, or on the part of individuals themselves at a more mature age.

In the latter instance the suppression was accomplished, as a rule, by great effort, the individual quelling his religious feelings and longings by means of a so-called intellectual or scientific view of life.

I observed, furthermore, that even in irreligious individuals the inherent religious desires are so strong that sophistication must give way to nature. The religious longings of these people often protrude through their "intellectual" unbelief. Moreover, I saw that religion does not by any means degrade an individual. On the contrary I was forced to admit that religion is the most exalting element in all human history, even though in exceptional instances it has been corrupted.

I observed that nations were sound and strong as long as their religions were vital, and that they became unfitted for life when religion became an empty form to most of their people. And I saw, further, that the religious individuals were the noblest our race had produced, and that in religion they possessed a means of elevating others which I could not find elsewhere.

These and similar reflections opened the way for the innate religious tendencies which I, too, possessed, but had suppressed for a long time. The desire to be in touch with the eternal began to assert itself. This soon led me to think of prayer.

The "intellectually" and "scientifically" established view of life which I had adopted had left a peculiar feeling of emptiness within me. This feeling soon began to pass over into restlessness. Now and then I felt an inner anxiety which I could not understand and which was, therefore, the more annoying. Gradually it dawned on me that I had, after all, pursued a wrong course in thinking that a man could and should live his life without conscious fellowship with God.

I now said to myself, "My inner emptiness is due to the fact that my soul-life lacks the religious element. There is something about religious meditation and especially prayer that will fill the great void in my soul. My soul-life will become harmonious and balanced again when I become established in fellowship with God."

I began to pray.

Notice the attitude I had when I began to pray. I did not believe in answer to prayer on God's part. I denied the very possibility of God being able or willing to give any freedom to what a capricious individual might happen to ask of Him. I saw in prayer nothing but a purely subjective movement in my soul upward toward the eternal. I had no other effect of prayer in mind than a purely subjective one—that my soul might become concentrated upon God and the eternal. I looked upon that as a sound and profitable diversion from my soul's concentration upon temporal and corruptible things.

In the second place, I did not turn to God to speak candidly and confidentially with Him. It was by no means my intention to cease my worldly and selfish life. On the contrary, my attempt to pray was a semi-conscious or unconscious effort to find peace and rest in order that I might keep up my worldly life, undisturbed by the more or less clear reproaches of my conscience.

That is the reason I was unsuccessful in prayer. I did not get in touch with God. My prayer was a monologue, a soliloquy. It did not rise to heaven; but was like the smoke from Cain's sacrifice, which lay close to the earth.[4] My attempt to pray was, accordingly, very brief. The little sincerity that was left in me revolted against a religiosity of this kind, against such "fellowship" with God.

Permit me now to tell you what happened when I really began to pray in such a way that I received an answer and entered into fellowship with the unseen God. That did not take place until I was in dire need. It was no longer merely a question of a little inner emptiness or restlessness, or some little outward need or sorrow or reversal from which I desired to be freed through my supplications. Now it was my sin that made me restless. And it finally made me so restless that I did not dare to live in it any longer.

First I tried to break with my sinful habits. I dare say that I made a serious attempt, but failed completely. The more I saw of my own life, the clearer it became that my real sinfulness lay in my self-loving and self-centered heart. It was not long before I had to admit that I was helpless in this struggle.

Then it was that I turned to God in earnest prayer.

I had turned to God before for the sake of a little religious diversion and for relief from the feeling of emptiness and restlessness which annoyed me. Now I turned to God in order to speak candidly and confidentially with Him.

The first thing I said to Him was this: "Lord, speak to me. Speak in such a way that I will understand that it is You speaking. Tell me what You have to tell about my life and my heart. I do not come to You with the intention of deceiving You, but to be reconciled to You and to be saved from my sins. Do to me whatever You will. I have no demands to make on You. I only pray You to save me. Use whatever means You may find necessary."

That is the substance of what I said to Him; the wording may have been slightly different.

And I received an answer. Not exactly what I thought beforehand it would be. But from that moment He gripped my soul so powerfully that I could not deny the fact without being untrue to myself.

At first there were many difficulties. Often He did not hear me at all, or the answer was so indistinct that I was not certain of it in my own mind. But from that time nothing could scare me away from Him or cause me to lose courage. Had I not told Him that He could use whatever means He might find necessary? I had to rest satisfied with what He did, even though I did not always understand His ways with me.

When He delayed answering me, I was impelled more than ever to examine myself diligently before Him, asking myself if there was anything wrong with my life or with my heart which He by this means desired to point out to me.

We have now reached the point that will determine whether you are to remain a doubter or be delivered from skepticism. The question is simply this: Are you willing to break with your former manner of life or not? If you are unwilling to break with the sinful life you have been living, then put aside every hope of ever being rid of your doubts.

There is no other way to salvation than by honestly breaking with sin, the narrow but safe way of repentance. Don't think that God has ordained a separate way of salvation for doubters. In this respect there's no difference; we must all pass through the gate of repentance if we desire to have fellowship with God.

You recall, no doubt, that on Good Friday Jesus was sent from Pilate to Herod. King Herod [Antipas][5] was much pleased at this. For a long time he had been desirous of seeing Jesus because he hoped to watch Him perform a miracle before his eyes. The account of their meeting closes with these characteristic words: "He questioned him in many words; but He answered nothing" (Luke 23:9).

The person who turns to Jesus without seeking salvation

from his sins receives no answer to his prayers even if, like King Herod, he uses "many words."

If you are among these, don't go away saying, as so many do, that Christianity is only imagination and vain talk; that they have cried aloud and wept in their distress but received no reply. Don't allow such cheap talk to mislead you. Give heed once again to the plain words of Jesus, "If anyone chooses to do God's will, he will find out whether my teaching comes from God or whether I speak on my own."[6]

The moment you turn to Christ for the purpose of making an honest accounting of all your sins, and of being saved from your former manner of life, you will be answered by your invisible Savior. The answer may come in a way somewhat different from what you had thought, but you will nevertheless receive the answer you need. And it will be one which will both frighten you and beckon you at the same time.

As you begin to pray, you will have additional new experiences which will enable you to learn experimentally what is the very essence of Christianity, and thus obtain true Christian assurance. As you read in the New Testament about Christ and live in fellowship with Him, confiding to Him each day the facts concerning your inner as well as your outward life, you will (like all the rest of us) experience a singular attitude of confidence toward Him arising in your heart.

He who has seen the sunlight has no need of anyone to explain to him that it is light and not darkness. Likewise he who in prayer enters deeper and deeper into fellowship with Christ as He is given to us in the New Testament, has no need of anyone to explain to him that he is in fellowship with God. He apprehends here the life, the words, and the mighty acts of the Absolute One.

Confronted with the Absolute, there is only one thing for a person to do—submit in unconditional obedience and yield in absolute confidence. If we have experienced what Soren Kierkegaard expresses in the words, "Before God we are always in the wrong," then we know Christ as our real, true Lord.

To submit to Him does not make us stunted or spineless beings. On the contrary, we experience an inner emancipation. The more wholeheartedly and unreservedly we submit to Him, the more we succeed both in finding ourselves and in being ourselves.

If you have had these experiences, my doubting friend, you are prepared to receive full assurance concerning Christ and His wonderful salvation. Up to this time you have not been prepared. This is a fact frequently overlooked. Especially in our day it seems as if people have forgotten that there is no other way of becoming personally assured of the Christian faith than this—the way of the sinner, the way that leads through complete despair of self.

Please remember our agreement: I did not take it upon myself to prove to you the truth of Christianity. I promised to point out the experiences through which you would have to pass in order to become personally convinced of the truth of Christianity. I also promised to show you what to do in order to gain these experiences. I have now followed you step by step into the world of experience which opens itself to you through earnest prayer and the reading of the New Testament. We have now reached the point where you in fellowship with your Savior have become a helpless sinner. From the depths of your soul you cry out for full assurance that all sins be forgiven and that you be received into fellowship with God.

You long for an experience such as they who came to Jesus had. He spoke a word to them, a creative word, which lifted them out of their inner distress and restlessness and transformed them into confident and glad disciples.

Permit me to say a few words about the attitude you should take while waiting for this experience. First, it is not for you to force yourself into this assurance. That is the work of the Holy Spirit. As the great apostle [Paul] expressed it, "The Spirit bears witness with our spirit that we are the children of God."[7]

You should continue to speak candidly with God. Search yourself daily before Him. Ask Him each day to direct your attention to everything in your life which directly or indirectly might hinder the Spirit from making you a partaker in the fulness of salvation. Use diligently the Word of God [that is, the Bible], whether it appeals to you or not, and whether you think it helps you or not. Pray humbly that the Spirit of God may make the Word helpful to you, even though you may not always be certain at the time as to how it is helping you.

I advise you to participate in the Lord's Supper.

Let me further advise you to seek the fellowship of people who, you are convinced, live wholeheartedly with Christ. All religions create fellowships. Christianity does so in a special sense. Jesus Christ desires to bind together His disciples into a holy brotherhood of the finest and most intimate kind. Seek out the church of God and participate in its life and work. The Christian's life should be like an ellipse which revolves about two foci or fixed points—the secret chamber and the communion of saints. Seek out one or two Christians to whom you can confidentially open your heart and with whom you can share everything.

In conclusion permit me to mention the last, the decisive experience that leads to Christian assurance in its fulness.

Some fair day, or perhaps some dark night, the miracle will take place in you as it has in millions before you, unexpectedly, and as a rule, suddenly. It may be a brief passage of Scripture which will become "living" to your soul. As through a little window you will look through this passage into the world of invisible things. Everything will be clear to your inner eye. You will see the Savior, the cross, and God's eternal love in an entirely new light.

You will see now what you have in your Savior. Your sins and the wickedness of your heart will be lost in the boundless depths of grace. They will be like sparks from the funnel of a steamer as they fall into the great ocean. You will be certain that your sins are forgiven, that you are loved of God, that you are His child.

It will be as clear as daylight to you. You will not be able to understand how you could have lived so long without being able to grasp the simple truth that Christ stepped into your place, atoned for all your sins, and made you free.

You have now received assurance, an assurance of which you could not have dreamed before. Now all the doubters and blasphemers and infidels in the world could come, if they wanted to, and stand in array before you with all their doubts and misgivings. They would not move you a hair's breadth.

Having had this experience, you will wonder especially at one or two things. First, that it was the cross which gave you the assurance. You could never have dreamed of that before. Up to this time the cross had been the most perplexing thing in Christianity. Like many others before you, you thought that the cross was the very thing in Christianity that made Christianity doubtful and was the reason for your skepticism. And now it is your experience that the cross was what brought to your soul the final solution and opened to you all the glories of the Kingdom of heaven.

No one now needs to tell you that the cross is the great heart of Christianity. Now you see that the cross shines forth from every page of the New Testament. And now you understand why the greatest of all the apostles, wherever he went, even in the world's greatest centers of culture, proclaimed nothing else save the cross.

The other thing which will cause you to wonder after you have had this experience is that your assurance is not based upon a mental solution of the mystery of the cross. Christ's vicarious suffering and death is still an impenetrable mystery to your intellect. The remarkable thing now is that the unintelligible aspect of the cross no longer causes you any intellectual distress. It is no longer a source of doubt.

The miracle consists in this, that our Lord opens to you the invisible, eternal world in a new way. It is the work of the Spirit in the dispensation of salvation to establish contact between the eternal and the temporal world, between visible and invisible reality. You experience Christ and the realm of grace and salvation of which He is the central figure in a direct, intuitive way. You experience Him as a present, blessed reality.

In the moment that you, with your new spiritual senses, apprehend the invisible world of grace in which the cross is the center, in that moment a new life dawns upon your whole inner and outward being. You see your relation to God from the perspective of eternity. You see what the cross of Christ and the death of Christ mean to you—what it means to be "in Christ." You experience with all your new spiritual senses what it means to be a child of God by grace alone. Your soul is filled with unspeakable joy and with that peace which passes all understanding.

At the same time your attitude toward outward things, toward other human beings and the rest of the world about you, has also changed. Looking upon your fellow men and women in this light, you see them no longer as individuals who by mere chance happen to cross your path in various ways, nor as people who are a little more or less pleasing. You look first and last toward that within them which is eternal and immortal.

This gives you, in the first place, a deep respect for them. In the second place, you become earnestly concerned about their souls. In other words, you have begun to look upon life as Jesus did. That means you go with Him into the work of saving them.

The world of things, too, appears different to your eye when you view it in the clear light of eternity. You will find that things which you formerly deemed indispensable no longer mean much to you. You will have similar experiences in connection with your reading, your associations, and your pleasures.

Are all your doubts and difficulties now [permanently] solved? No, likely not. But you have experienced what Jesus promised you. The statements of the Bible concerning Christ have become the Word of God to you. This has given you a faith in the Bible which enables you freely and gladly to live and die by it.

You may still come upon passages in the Bible which give you trouble. Here I have a bit of advice to offer you. Be honest with yourself. Don't try to conceal from yourself the fact that you are still uncertain and in doubt on some points. Acknowledge it openly to yourself. Above all, speak with God about it in prayer.

And be patient! Take time! Let God quietly prepare you for and give you those experiences which will dispel these doubts also. Confess openly that you do not have personal assurance with regard to certain articles of the Christian faith.

But say also that you are in all humility longing and praying that you may share the Christian church's apostolic faith at every point and that you are looking forward to the day when, together with the living church of God, you can freely confess every article of the Christian faith.

NOTES

1. Hauge's testimony appears in *Spiritual Awakening,* vol. 3 of the Christian Heritage Classics (Wheaton, IL: Crossway Books, 1986).
2. John 7:17.
3. Cf. Matthew 7:12.
4. Hallesby is using poetic imagery to illustrate the Biblical scene in which Cain's offering of thanks to God did not receive divine favor (Genesis 4:5).
5. Herod Antipas, tetrarch of Galilee, was the son of Herod the Great.
6. John 7:17.
7. Romans 8:16.

Sundar Singh, 1889-1929?

He was a tall, impressive young man with a heavy beard and sturdy physique. Wearing a turban and the traditional saffron robe of the sadhu, carrying little more than his Urdu New Testament, he walked barefoot mile after mile through the fields and villages of his native India, sharing with anyone he met the unsearchable riches of Christ.

This was Sundar Singh, one of the twentieth century's most remarkable evangelists, whose very appearance in the western world at age thirty seemed to many almost a reincarnation of Jesus of Nazareth. He was licensed to preach by the Diocesan Mission Council of the Church of England, but returned the license to his bishop so that he might be free to preach the gospel in his own way. To win India for Christ he became a sadhu, one of his culture's "holy men," but his evangelistic vision soon extended far beyond his homeland.

He visited Palestine, preached in the Anglican cathedral in Jerusalem, and later addressed Coptic Christians in Egypt. He traveled to Germany and lectured to theological students at the University in Wittenberg, the home of Martin Luther. Ten thousand came to hear him in Neuchatel, Switzerland. Later he was guest of the Anglican bishop of Winchester, England, and of the Lutheran archbishop in Uppsala, Sweden. In Denmark Her Imperial Majesty, the Dowager Empress of Russia, asked him to bless her with the laying on of hands; but he refused, saying that since his hands had once torn up the Scriptures, he was unworthy to bless anyone.

In 1920, at age thirty-one, he toured the United States and attracted tremendous crowds in the major eastern cities. He then traveled by train to the Midwest for meetings in Chicago,

Iowa, Kansas, and on to San Francisco, where he embarked for Australia. Huge throngs came to hear him in Sydney, Melbourne, Adelaide, and Perth, before he returned to India.

Sundar Singh's 1921 reception in the Far East was equally enthusiastic. Translators conveyed his messages to cosmopolitan crowds in Rangoon, Singapore, Peking, Hankow, Kyoto, and Tokyo, among other cities. In Penang, Muslim and Hindu religious leaders arranged his public meeting, and after he had spoken, a fellow Sikh invited him to speak in the Sikh temple.

More remarkable than all his travels, perhaps, is the story of Sundar Singh's conversion, which he shares with us in the following pages. He was born in the town of Rampur in northern India, the youngest son of a distinguished family. His mother, a broad-minded and devout reader of Hindu scriptures, was on friendly terms with the women of the American Presbyterian Mission in Rampur, and sent young Sundar to the mission school. She died soon after enrolling him. His father strenuously objected to his son's embracing Christianity, but in later years committed his own life to Jesus Christ.

The story of Sundar Singh's many missionary visits to Tibet, which he began when nineteen years of age, is fascinating. In those years Tibet was a closed country, and his trips were invariably subject to many dangers. In April, 1929, when almost forty, he set out once again on an evangelistic journey to Tibet. He was never seen again.

The following excerpts are taken from his book, With and Without Christ, *copyright 1929 Harper & Brothers; copyright renewed 1957. Reprinted by permission of HarperCollins Publishers.*

FIVE

WITH AND WITHOUT CHRIST
by Sundar Singh

I was born in a family that was commonly considered Sikh, but in which the teaching of Hinduism was considered most essential, and my dear mother was a living example and faithful exponent of its teaching. She used to rise daily before daylight, and, after bathing, would read the Bhagavad Gita and other Hindu scriptures.

I was influenced more than the rest of the family by her pure life and teaching. She early impressed on me the rule that my first duty on rising in the morning was that I should pray to God for spiritual food and blessing, and only after that should I breakfast. At times I insisted that I must have food first, but my God-fearing mother, sometimes with love and sometimes with punishment, fixed this habit firmly in my mind, that I should first seek God, and after that other things.

Although at that time I was too young to appreciate the value of these things, yet later on I realized it, and now whenever I think of it I thank God for that training. I can never be sufficiently thankful to God for giving me such a mother, who in my earliest years instilled in me the love and fear of God. Her bosom was for me my best theological school, and she prepared me, as much as she was able, to work for the Lord as a sadhu.

For some years my mother instructed me from the holy books of the Hindu scriptures, and then handed me over to a Hindu pundit and to an old Sikh sadhu. They used to come to our house for two or three hours daily to teach me. I recognize that I got some degree of consolation from this teaching, but I was still hungering for real peace. They taught me with great sympathy and freely gave me the benefit of their experiences, but they had not themselves had that real blessing for which my soul was craving, so how could they help me to get it?

I often used to read the Hindu scriptures till midnight, that I might in some way quench the thirst of my soul for peace. My father would object, saying, "It is bad for your health to read so late." Though there was much in my home to make me happy, I was not attracted by it. My father often remonstrated with me, saying, "Boys of your age think of nothing but games and play, but how has this mania possessed you at so early an age? There is plenty of time to think of these things later in life. I suppose you must have got this madness from your mother and the sadhu."

I frequently asked the pundit to explain my spiritual difficulties for me. He said, "Your difficulties seem to be of a new and strange kind. I can only say that when you grow up and get more experience and knowledge about spiritual life, these difficulties will disappear of themselves. Don't worry about these things at present, but do what your father advises you."

I said to him, "Suppose I do not live till I grow up, then what will happen? I feel very hungry now for spiritual food. If you do not know where I can get it, then say so."

The pundit said, "You cannot understand these deep spiritual things now. You cannot get to this grade of spirituality all at once. To get to it, a long time is essential. Why are you in such a hurry? If this hunger is not satisfied in this life, it will be satisfied in your next rebirths, provided that you keep on trying for it."

I spoke to the sadhu several times about my difficulties, but he gave me a somewhat similar answer: "Do not worry about it. When you get knowledge, all these difficulties will disappear."

I replied, "No doubt it is true that when I obtain this

perfect ultimate knowledge, my difficulties will disappear, but even at this stage the little knowledge that I have should remove some of my difficulties. And I do not see how this increase of knowledge will be able to do much, for it looks as if further knowledge will result in my needs and difficulties being still more clearly seen by me, and how will these new needs be met?"

The sadhu replied, "Not with imperfect, finite knowledge, but with perfect and final knowledge will your needs be met; for when you get perfect knowledge, you will realize that this need, or want, is only an illusion, and that you yourself are Brahma (God) or a part of him; and when you realize this, then what more will you need?"

I persisted, "Excuse me, but I cannot believe this, for if I am a part of Brahma, or am myself Brahma, then I should be incapable of having any Maya (illusion). But if Maya is possible in Brahma, then Brahma is no longer Brahma, for he has been subordinated to Maya. Hence Maya is stronger than Brahma himself, and Maya will not then be illusion but will be a reality that has overcome Brahma, and we shall have to think of Brahma himself as Maya, and that is blasphemy. Instead of helping me, you are throwing me into a whirlpool. I shall be most thankful to you if from your experience and knowledge you can help me to know him so that I may satisfy my spiritual hunger and thirst in him. But please remember that I do not want to be absorbed in him, but I do want to obtain salvation in him."

Then he said, "Child, it is useless to waste time on these things now. The time will come when you yourself will understand these things."

Again I was disappointed. I could not find anywhere the spiritual food for which I hungered, and in this state of unrest I remained till I found the Living Christ.

From my earliest years my mother impressed on me that I should abstain from every kind of sin and should be sympathetic and helpful to all in trouble. One day when my father had given me some pocket money, I ran off to the bazaar to spend it. On the way I saw a very old woman famished with cold and hunger. When she asked help from me, I felt such pity that I gave her all my money.

I came back home and told my father that he should give the poor woman a blanket, or she would die of cold. He put me off by saying that he had often helped her before and that it was the turn of the neighbors to do their part.

When I saw that he was not willing to help her, by stealth I extracted five rupees from his pocket, intending to give them to her to buy a blanket with. The thought that I should be able to help her gave me great satisfaction, but the thought that I was a thief pricked my conscience. My distress was further increased in the evening when my father, on discovering that the rupees were missing, asked me if I had taken them, and I denied it. Though I had escaped punishment, my conscience so tormented me the whole night that I could not sleep.

Early in the morning I went to my father and confessed my theft and my lies and gave back the money. In spite of the fear that he would punish me, the burden was at once removed from my heart. But instead of punishing me, he took me in his arms and with tears in his eyes said, "My son, I have always trusted you, and now I have good proof that I was not wrong." He not only forgave me, but spent the five rupees on a blanket for the old woman and gave me another rupee to buy sweets.

After that he never refused when I asked for anything, and on my part I decided that I would never do anything that should be against my conscience or against my parents' will.

Some time after this, my mother died, and a few months later my elder brother also died. This brother's nature and turn of mind were very like my own. The loss of these two dear ones was a great shock to me; especially did the thought that I should never see them again cast me into despondency and despair, because I could never know into what form they had been reborn, nor could I even guess what I was likely to be in my next rebirths. In the Hindu religion the only consolation for a broken heart like mine was that I should submit to my fate and bow down to the inexorable law of karma.

Now another change came into my life. I was sent for my secular education to a small primary school that had been opened by the American Presbyterian Mission in our village at Rampur. At that time I had so many prejudices against Christianity that I refused to read the Bible at the daily Bible lessons. My teachers insisted that I should attend, but I was so opposed to .this that the next year I left that school and went to a Government school at Sanewal three miles away where I studied for some months.

To some extent I felt that the teaching of the gospel on the love of God attracted me, but I still thought it was false and opposed it. So firmly was I set in my opinions, and so great was my unrest, that one day in the presence of my father and others I tore up a Gospel and burned it.

Though according to my ideas at that time, I thought I had done a good deed in burning the Gospel, yet my unrest of heart increased, and for two days after that I was very miserable. On the third day, when I felt I could bear it no longer, I got up at three in the morning, and after bathing I prayed that if there was a God at all, he would reveal Himself to me, show me the way of salvation, and end this unrest of my soul. I firmly made up my mind that if this prayer was not answered, I would before daylight go down to the railway and place my head on the line before the incoming train.

I remained till about half-past four, praying and waiting and expecting to see Krishna, or Buddha, or some other Avatar of the Hindu religion, but they appeared not. However, a light shone in the room. I opened the door to see where it came from, but all was dark outside. I returned inside, and the light increased in intensity and took the form of a globe of light above the ground, and in this light there appeared, not the form I expected, but the Living Christ whom I had counted as dead.

To all eternity I shall never forget His glorious and loving face nor the few words He spoke, "Why do you persecute me? See, I have died on the cross for you and for the whole world."[1] These words were burned into my heart as by lightning, and I fell on the ground before Him. My heart was filled with inexpressible joy and peace, and my whole life was entirely changed. Then the old Sundar Singh died, and a new Sundar Singh, to serve the Living Christ, was born.

After a little while I went to my father, who was still sleeping, and told him of the appearance and that I was now a Christian. He said, "What are you talking about? It is only three days since you burned their book. Go away and sleep, you silly boy," and he himself turned over again.

Later on I told the whole family what I had seen, and that I was now a Christian. Some said I was mad, some that I had dreamed; but when they saw that I was not to be turned, they began to persecute me. But the persecution was nothing compared with that miserable unrest I had had when I was without Christ; and it was not difficult for me to endure the troubles and persecution which now began.

The thought of being a sadhu had long been in my mind, and I now decided that as a sadhu I would serve the Lord Christ. There were two or three other boys at that time who also wanted to become Christians. Two, because of the punishment given them by their parents, went back, but another went to Khanna and was baptized there by the Rev. E. P. Newton. But shortly afterward that boy's father went to him with a story that his mother was dying and enticed him back. Very soon after, he died, apparently of poison.

When it became difficult for me to remain at Rampur, Mr. Newton advised me to go into the Christian Boys' Boarding School at Ludhiana. There the missionaries, Drs. Wherry and Fife, received me very kindly and protected me in every way. But I was shocked when I saw the unchristian life of some of the Christian boys and of some of the local Christians, for I had the idea that those who followed the Living Christ must be like angels; in this I was sadly mistaken.

It is quite possible that had I not had that appearance of the Living Christ and received new life from Him, I should have stumbled and gone astray and have become an enemy of Christianity. Even as it was, I decided to leave the school and these Christians and live apart and, as a sadhu, follow Christ wherever He should lead me in His work. During the summer holidays I went to Subathu and Simla, and instead of returning to school, I was baptized and began to go about as a sadhu and preach the gospel.

Non-Christian seekers after truth, in order to find it, willingly suffer unbelievable hardships; and had all who claim to be Christian been as true or as wholehearted in their efforts to spread the Kingdom of the Living Christ, the whole world would long ago have become Christian. But we have to confess that in this the Christian church has signally failed.

Now, through living with Christ and having had experience of Him, I have learned this secret, that before ever I knew Him or believed on Him as my Savior, He, unknown to me, was working in my soul like medicine working in the eye. For the eye cannot see the medicine that is in it which is clearing the sight, though it feels its presence.

My restless soul searched for Him but though He was near me, He was hidden from my view and was trying to bring me to Himself. I was in the world's garden like a child whose mother had hidden herself behind a bush. The child began to cry, and as soon as the gardener heard him, he came, and to soothe him offered him one kind of fruit after another. But he threw them all down and kept on crying, "I don't want them. I want my mother." At last his mother came out from behind the bush, and taking him in her arms, kissed him and wiped his tears. Safe in her arms, he found what he wanted.

Without Christ I was without hope and full of fear about the future life. Now, by His presence, He has turned fear into love and hopelessness into realization. In fellowship with Him who is the Resurrection and the Life, we are freed from fear of death and, by sharing in that victory over death, enter into eternal life. He is at the same time present in both worlds. He was in the physical world and was at the same time in the spiritual world.

It is characteristic of this new life that it constrains one to bring others to Christ, not by compulsion but from the desire to let others share in the joy of this wonderful experience. However sore one's trials may be, they are forgotten in the joy of that service.

Once I went to preach at a village two miles from my old home at Rampur. I spoke for a long time, and it was dark before I finished, and then all the people left me and went to their houses. Tired and hungry, I sought rest under a tree. I had had no food all day, and it was against my principles to beg. As I lay there weak and hungry, Satan tempted me with the thought that when I was at my home, I always had every comfort, but now that I had left all for Christ's sake, I was poor and hungry.

Then in spite of it all, my heart was filled with a wonderful peace and joy that not only overcame the temptation but compelled me to break out into song, and till midnight I praised the Lord; and after this these words broke from my lips, "When I had ease and comfort at home, I knew nothing of this wonderful peace. But now when all is gone, I have found in Christ this peace which the world can neither give nor take away."

Some of the people had been aroused by my singing, and two of them came to me. They were greatly impressed when I told them a little of my experience, but when they heard that I had not eaten since morning, they were very perturbed that I had not told them. They at once prepared some food and gave it to me, and I thanked God and them, and having eaten it, I lay down and slept.

The next day I preached in a few villages nearby and then went to Rampur. There also the people listened well. In the evening I went to my home. At first my father refused to see me or to let me in, because by becoming a Christian I had dishonored the family. But after a little while, he came out and said, "Very well, you can stay here tonight, but you must get out early in the morning; don't show me your face again."

I remained silent, and that night he made me sit at a distance that I might not pollute them or their vessels, and then he brought me food. He gave me water to drink by pouring it into my hands from a vessel held high above, as one does who gives a drink to an outcaste. When I saw this treatment, I could not restrain the tears from flowing from my eyes that this father, who used to love me so much, now hated me as if I were untouchable.

In spite of all this, my heart was filled with inexpressible peace. I thanked him for this treatment also, and said, "It does not matter if you have forsaken me,[2] because I have taken Christ for the love of Him who gave His life for me, and His love is unchangeable and is far greater than yours. Before I became a Christian, I dishonored Christ, but He did not forsake me; now I do not complain. I thank you for your past love to me and also for this present treatment." I said goodbye respectfully and went away. In the fields I prayed and thanked God, and then slept under a tree. In the morning I continued my way.

When I first began preaching, I went to my own village and to the villages in its neighborhood, but after that I went on extended tours all over India. Little by little, the Lord sent me in the way of His service to different countries of the world, and after many years my unceasing prayer was answered, and my father also turned to the Lord.

My opinion is that the nations which owe their uplift to the blessings of the gospel of Christ have, in our days, often turned away from Him and disobeyed His commands. Instead of their people having individually accepted Him as their Savior, they have too often forsaken Him and dishonored Him by denying His divinity.

Before we can know the divinity of Christ, we must be made new creatures. The old nature, sin-stained and fallen, is incapable of knowing Him. A new life and a new nature must be ours before we can know Him who is the image of the invisible God, and in whose image we have been created; only then shall we know Him.

Though I have had to go through various kinds of suffering, it has all been for me a means of great blessing, and with thankful heart I can truly say from my experience that every word is literally true in the promises of the Lord who said, "No one who has left home or brothers or sisters or mother or father or children or fields for me and the gospel will fail to receive a hundred times as much in this present age (homes, brothers, sisters, mothers, children and fields, and with them, persecutions) and in the age to come, eternal life."[3] I have found not only a hundredfold, but a hundred times a hundredfold, and if there are any to whom this promise is not fulfilled, it does not mean that the Lord's promise is not true; it means that there is something wrong in their lives, or that God has "provided some better thing"[4] concerning them.

Some time ago in Hardwar, I saw a sadhu lying on a bed of spikes. I went to him and asked, "What aim have you in wounding and torturing your body in this way?"

He replied, "Don't you know that much when you are yourself a sadhu? It means austerity and the mortifying of the flesh. I worship God in this way, but I confess that the pricks of these spikes are not so bad as the pain I get from my sins and evil desires. My object is to crush the desires of self that I may gain salvation."

I asked, "How long have you been doing this, and how far have you succeeded in your object?"

He replied, "I began this eighteen months ago, but I have not yet gained my object, nor is it possible to do it in so short a time. Many years, and indeed many births, will be necessary to accomplish it."

Then I told him of my own experience of failure when I tried to gain salvation by my own efforts, and of how, in an instant, the Lord Jesus changed my heart and calmed my restless soul with that true peace, gaining what he was expecting to torture himself for through many rebirths. I added, "If in this present birth, you cannot be successful, then what proof have you that you will gain it in any future birth? Now, not because I am in any way worthy or have any right, but by His grace and mercy, I have been freed from the pricks of my sin and evil desires and temptations and have yielded myself up to Him who can take away not only my sins, but the sins of the whole world. For as the spikes have pierced the hands and feet of that Sinless One on behalf of sinners, so now by His sacrifice we are saved from sin and its consequences."

When he heard this, he made no attempt to agree, but

said, "I can never admit that salvation can be obtained as a free gift, and in one short life."

Then I saw another ascetic who, with a rope tied to his feet, was being swung about from a tree with his head downwards. I went away, and after awhile returned when he had been untied and had rested. I asked him what motive he had and what profit there might be in such trying austerity.

He said, "I do not feel like saying anything just now, but as you are a brother sadhu, I will explain my motive in a few words. Think for a moment why people are so amazed when they see me hanging head down, when the Creator himself has hung all mankind upside down in their mothers' wombs. I want to remind myself and all men that when we entangle ourselves in our sin, we turn ourselves upside down in the sight of God, even though in the eyes of the world we appear to be right side up. I want also to keep on reforming myself until I am satisfied that at last I am right side up before God."

I replied, "You have strange ideas. It is true the world is upside down, but we should not adopt their upside-down ways of doing things. How can we, by our own efforts, free ourselves from the entanglements of sin? It is a task beyond our strength. Hence the Lord of Love became man that He might set us free from our bondage; and to set the world aright, He uses as His servants those whom He has saved and set free."

On this the sadhu gave a sign that he did not wish the conversation to continue, so I rose and came away.

In Jerusalem I met a Jewish rabbi who was liberal in his views. I asked him his opinion of Christ and of the future of the Promised Land. He said, "I myself await the appearing of the Messiah and the restoration of the Promised Land, but I know not if this longing will be fulfilled in this life or in the next. Nor can I say with certainty whether the Jesus who was crucified in this town was the Messiah, or if the Messiah is still to come. Of course, I am obliged to acknowledge that Jesus was a great prophet whom my nation treated with extreme harshness and cruelty."

Those who have had the opportunity of living in contact

with the followers of different religions in other lands and who have made a sympathetic study of their needs, bear witness that without the touch of the Living Christ, their lives have no abiding peace and hope.

Once in Peking the subject of my address was Christ, the Universal Savior. At the close of the meeting, a Chinese doctor came to me and said, "Christ was born only some two thousand years ago, but long before that we had teachers like Confucius in our country. How then is it possible to say that Christ is universal? The teaching and example of Confucius and our other teachers are sufficient for us."

I answered, "You make a mistake when you say that Christ came only two thousand years ago. Long before His Incarnation, He was in the world, but the world knew Him not;[5] but those who knew Him were glad. I am not against Confucius and his teaching, but tell me in what things China as a nation has progressed through his teaching and example and, in particular, what benefit you yourself have received."

He replied, "This teaching is not a morsel that can be swallowed and its effect seen at once. Its influence will slowly make itself apparent."

I said, "The teaching of Christ is not only good doctrine, it is 'Spirit and life' as well, and millions and millions who have accepted Him have obtained new life through Him."

The doctor said, "This new life and change cannot come from without; it depends on our own efforts."

I said, "It is true that the act of receiving depends on us, but we cannot get this new life through our own efforts. A bitter tree cannot of itself become sweet, but it can be grafted into a sweet tree. Similarly sinful man, through faith, can be grafted into Christ, and Christ's life flowing into him changes him into a new creature, and this is salvation."

But the doctor was called away to attend a patient, and our conversation ended.

In Germany a leading psychologist asked me about my spiritual experience and peace of heart, "What proof have you that spiritual peace and satisfaction is the result of the presence of the Holy Spirit or of the Living Christ in your heart, or that they are not subjective, but have an objective reality?"

I replied, "The existence of hunger and thirst in us is the proof that there is, besides them, some objective reality such as food and water that will satisfy them. Can you tell me of any man in the whole world who, by his imagination alone, has been able for any considerable time to satisfy his hunger and thirst? It is an utter impossibility. It is possible that he may by autosuggestion be able to work up a subjective mental state in which for a time he does not feel his hunger. But it is not possible that a man should, by autosuggestion alone, obtain for his whole life full satisfaction of soul and 'the peace that passes all understanding.'[6] That can be obtained only in Him who has created this spiritual hunger and thirst in us. And when we live in conscious union with Him and obtain from Him this satisfaction of heart, our whole being bears witness that we have at last obtained that reality which we so passionately longed for."

A German gentleman who was an interested supporter of missions asked me, "What form of church organization will be adopted if all India becomes Christian?"

I replied, "There is no country in the world that is wholly Christian, and there never will be, and even if India ever becomes Christian, it will be only to the extent that any of the countries of the West are Christian. For as long as the world lasts, good and bad, earnest and indifferent will always be found. Only if all were changed in heart and life could we say that the Kingdom of heaven had come, but then the world would not be the world, it would be heaven. As for the church, people are continually introducing changes in worship and creating new sects, but they are not satisfied with any of them. The real need is not that we should adopt new forms, but that through the Living Christ, rivers of living water should begin to flow through us.

"When the water of a Himalayan mountain stream reaches the plains, men dig canals for it; but away among the great mountains it makes its own way past cliff and rock and valley, and no one digs a channel for it. So the new life at first makes its way through the lives of individual Christians, and they feel no need of organizing channels for it; but when it flows through whole communities, they will organize channels, or churches, for it to meet their needs.

"But the time will come when the man-made sects will disappear, and there will be only one Church of the Living Christ, and there shall be one fold and one Shepherd."[7]

After a meeting which I had in Cambridge [England], a promising Hindu student came to me. He had been a mission schoolboy in India. He said that while he was at that school, his heart had been so drawn toward Christ that he had decided to become a Christian. He had gone to the missionary and had asked for baptism, but as he was under the age for baptism required by Government, the missionary could not do it.

Still he was determined that when he reached the required age, he would be baptized. After this he entered a mission college, and later on had been sent by his parents to England. "When I was preparing to come here," he said, "I was overjoyed because I was to have the good fortune to be sent to a Christian country and receive education and spiritual blessings in the land from which our good missionaries had come.

"But after I had landed and had lived here for some time and had seen the conduct and ways of life of the people, I was greatly disillusioned. During my vacations I visited France, Switzerland, Germany, and other countries on the continent, and found that the people there were worse heathens than are to be found in non-Christian countries. In the latter countries, if people are not Hindus, they are Mohammedans; if not Mohammedans, they follow some other religion; but in these European countries if they are not Christians, they are nothing at all and have no religion except worldliness. And this applies not merely to the common people, but to some of the highly educated leading men as well. Even some of my professors have told me that they do not specially believe in any religion, but look on all as equal."

I replied to him, "To a great extent I agree with you, for

my experience is somewhat similar. I know there are many who call themselves Christians without having had any kind of experience of Christ. I call them Christians-without-Christ. If the members of a church are without Christian life, that is churchianity without Christianity. The religion of those Christians who deny the deity of Christ is truly Christianity-without-Christ. They are shells without kernels and bodies without souls. Mere civilization and moral life, however beautiful it may be, is like a cold and lifeless statue. Do not be upset about this. It is no fault of our Living Lord. It is not He who has failed, but the people who have failed to understand and follow Him, for they have given Him no chance to change their lives and make a paradise of their hearts."

In Boston [Massachusetts] an educated man who was a Christian-without-Christ asked me, "If God is Love, why does He hide Himself from the world? He should show Himself and save men from their error and destruction."

I replied, "Once He revealed himself to the world in Christ, and now He shows Himself to every soul of man who seeks Him with his whole heart. It is true that He is Love, but He is at the same time a consuming fire,[8] for He consumes all things that are unclean and unholy and contrary to His will. The sun by its heat and light helps the growth of a tree, but if there is any sickness or defect in the tree, the same sun and its heat will wither it instead of helping it. This is no fault of the sun, but it is due to a condition in the life of the tree itself. So the God of Love, the Light of Life, gives every man every kind of help for his spiritual growth; but man turns this life-giving light to his destruction. By his disobedience and foolishness he brings injury on himself and becomes his own enemy."

We should ever be watchful and prayerful, for if the light that is in us becomes darkness, then how great will be that darkness! Though our eyes are little, they see many things, great and small, far and near. If the pupil is affected, then not only is darkness created in the eye, but for us the whole world is darkened. So we must pray that the light that is within us be not darkened, and also that our light may shine before men, so that we may glorify our Father which is in heaven.

It is necessary that we should live in the world like a diver who, when diving for pearls in the ocean, either holds his breath that water may not enter his lungs or else continues to breathe through an air tube as long as he is in the water. We must be in the world but not of the world. We must be like these two kinds of divers. We must stop breathing the air of the world and, being dead to it, should be alive unto God, and by means of the tube of prayer that reaches up to the eternal God, should breathe the Holy Spirit. Thus while living in the world, we shall find the precious pearl of salvation.

In closing, let me add this from my own experience. Without Christ I was like a fish out of water or like a bird in the water. With Christ I am in the ocean of Love, and while in the world, am in heaven. For all this, to Him be praise and glory and thanksgiving for ever.

NOTES

1. Cf. Acts 9:4; 1 John 2:2.
2. Cf. Psalm 27:10.
3. Mark 10:29-30.
4. Cf. Hebrews 11:40.
5. Cf. John 1:10.
6. Philippians 4:7.
7. Cf. John 10:16.
8. Cf. Hebrews 12:29.

Dietrich Bonhoeffer, 1906-1945

For American evangelicals wanting to understand Dietrich Bonhoeffer, the barriers of language and culture can be formidable. We may easily appreciate him as the young German theologian who loved Jesus Christ and dared to oppose Hitler. We may admire his brilliant intellect, his courage, his nobility of character, his sympathy for the Jews, and his love for his fellow prisoners. We can deplore his early death as a martyr at age thirty-nine.

One can admit all this and yet remain ignorant of Bonhoeffer the man, the theologian, and churchman, the creative genius, perhaps the one Christian scholar to emerge from war-torn Germany whose message today's evangelicals can embrace and espouse. To Bonhoeffer we owe such memorable expressions as "the Man for others," "cheap grace," and "religionless Christianity."

Born in Breslau, Bonhoeffer moved in 1912 when his distinguished father was offered the chair of psychology and neurology at the University of Berlin. From the beginning it was expected that Dietrich would be a scholar. At seventeen he enrolled at the University of Tübingen as a Lutheran student in theology. Two years later, following travels in Italy and North Africa, he studied in Berlin, where at age twenty-one he took his doctorate. There followed a year in Spain as curate to a German congregation and a year of study at Union Theological Seminary, New York. Two things impressed him about American Christians: He admired their social drive, but was appalled by their weak theology.

Returning to Germany, he found the Nazi movement had swept the nation, and by opposing it he became a marked man.

At this time he first began writing The Cost of Discipleship. *After Hitler came to power in 1933, Bonhoeffer joined a group of conspirators who were determined to rid Germany of the Nazi regime. He aligned himself with them despite his personal conviction that the church should remain politically pacifist in doctrine (he had tried to visit Gandhi in India).*

From 1935 to 1937 Bonhoeffer directed a secret seminary for German ministerial students in the outlawed "confessing church"—a dangerous project that the Nazis finally shut down. By this time friends in America and Britain realized that Bonhoeffer was certain to be arrested, and they arranged for him to get out of Germany. He flew to New York in 1939, but after only a few weeks he became convinced that his place was with his fellow Christians in his native land. "I will have no right to participate in the reconstruction of Christian life in Germany after the war," he wrote, "if I do not share the tribulations of this time with my people."

On his return he was severely restricted and forbidden to lecture, preach, or publish. Finally in 1943 he was arrested and spent eighteen months in a Berlin prison. After the attack on Hitler's life failed in July, 1944, Bonhoeffer's part in the conspiracy was uncovered. He was moved to Buchenwald, then to Schonberg, and finally to Flossenburg, where, on direct orders of Himmler, he was executed on April 8, 1945, only a few days before the arrival of the liberating American army. His last act was to conduct a worship service for the prisoners. His final words were, "This is the end; for me the beginning of life!"

These selections from The Cost of Discipleship, *reproduced by permission of the publishers, Macmillan, New York, and SCM Press, London, provide a glimpse into what Jesus Christ really meant to Dietrich Bonhoeffer.*

SIX

GRACE AND DISCIPLESHIP
by Dietrich Bonhoeffer

Cheap grace is the deadly enemy of our Church. We are fighting today for costly grace.

Cheap grace means grace sold on the market like cheapjack's wares. The sacraments, the forgiveness of sin, and the consolations of religion are thrown away at cut prices. Grace is represented as the Church's inexhaustible treasury, from which she showers blessings with generous hands, without asking questions or fixing limits. Grace without price, grace without cost! The essence of grace, we suppose, is that the account has been paid in advance; and, because it has been paid, everything can be had for nothing. Since the cost was infinite, the possibilities of using and spending it are also infinite. What good would grace be if it were not cheap?

Cheap grace means grace as a doctrine, a principle, a system. It means forgiveness of sins proclaimed as a general truth, the love of God taught as the Christian "conception" of God. An intellectual assent to that idea is held to be sufficient of itself to secure remission of sins.

The church which holds the correct doctrine of grace has, it is supposed, *ipso facto* a part in that grace. In such a church the world finds a cheap covering for its sins; no contrition is required, still less any real desire to be delivered from sin. Cheap grace therefore amounts to a denial of the living Word of God, in fact, a denial of the Incarnation of the Son of God.

Cheap grace means the justification of sin without the justification of the sinner. Grace alone does everything, we are told, so everything can remain as it was before. "All for sin could not atone."[1] The world goes on in the same old way, and we are still sinners "even in the best life," as Luther said.

Well, then, let the Christian live like the rest of the world. Let him model himself on the world's standards in every sphere of life, and not presumptuously live a life under grace that differs from his old life under sin. That was the heresy of the enthusiasts. Let the Christian beware of rebelling against the free and boundless grace of God and desecrating it. Let him not attempt to erect a new religion of the letter by endeavoring to live a life of obedience to the commandments of Jesus Christ!

The world has been justified by grace. The Christian knows that and takes it seriously. He knows he must not strive against this indispensable grace. Therefore—let him live like the rest of the world! Of course we would like to go and do something extraordinary, and it demands a great deal of self-restraint to refrain from the attempt and content ourselves with living as the world lives. Yet it is imperative for the Christian to achieve this renunciation and self-effacement.

He must let grace be grace indeed, lest he destroy the world's faith in the free gift of grace. Let the Christian rest content with his worldliness and with this renunciation of any standard higher than the world's. He is doing it for the sake of the world rather than for the sake of grace. Let him be comforted and rest assured in his possession of this grace— for grace alone does everything.

Instead of following Christ, let the Christian enjoy the consolations of his grace! That is what we mean by cheap grace, the grace which amounts to the justification of sin without the justification of the repentant sinner who departs from sin and from whom sin departs. Cheap grace is not the kind of forgiveness of sin that frees us from the toils of sin. Cheap grace is the grace we bestow upon ourselves.

Cheap grace is the preaching of forgiveness without requiring repentance, baptism without church discipline, communion without confession, absolution without contrition. Cheap grace is grace without discipleship, grace without the cross, grace without Jesus Christ, living and incarnate.

Costly grace is the treasure hidden in the field; for the sake of it a man will gladly go and sell all that he has. It is the pearl of great price, for which to buy the merchant will sell all his goods.[2] It is the kingly rule of Christ, for whose sake a man will pluck out the eye which causes him to stumble; it is the call of Jesus Christ at which the disciple leaves his nets and follows Him.

Costly grace is the gospel which must be sought again and again, the gift which must be asked for, the door at which a man must knock.[3]

Such grace is costly because it calls us to follow, and it is grace because it calls us to follow Jesus Christ. It is costly because it costs a man his life, and it is grace because it gives a man the only true life. It is costly because it condemns sin, and grace because it justifies the sinner. Above all, it is costly because it cost God the life of His Son: "You were bought at a price."[4] And what has cost God much cannot be cheap for us. Above all, it is grace because God did not reckon His Son too dear a price to pay for our life, but delivered Him up for us.[5] Costly grace is the Incarnation of God.

Costly grace is the sanctuary of God. It has to be protected from the world and not thrown to the dogs. It is therefore the living word, the Word of God, which He speaks as it pleases Him. Costly grace confronts us as a gracious call to follow Jesus. It comes as a word of forgiveness to the broken spirit and the contrite heart. Grace is costly because it compels a man to submit to the yoke of Christ and to follow Him. It is grace because Jesus says, "My yoke is easy and my burden is light.[6]

On two separate occasions Peter received the call, "Follow me." It was the first and last word Jesus spoke to His disciple.[7] A whole life lies between these two calls. The first occasion was by the lake of Gennesareth, when Peter left his nets and his craft and followed Jesus at His word. The second occasion is when the Risen Lord finds him back again at his old trade. Once again the call is, "Follow me."

Halfway between the two calls comes Peter's confession, when he acknowledged Jesus as the Christ of God. Three times Peter hears the same proclamation that Christ is his Lord and God. Each time it is the same grace of Christ calling Peter to follow and revealing itself to him in his confession.

This grace was certainly not self-bestowed. It was the grace of Christ Himself, now prevailing upon the disciple to leave all and follow Him, inviting Peter to the supreme fellowship of martyrdom for the Lord he had denied, and thereby forgiving him all his sins. In the life of Peter grace and discipleship are inseparable. He had received the grace that costs.

As Christianity spread and the church became more secularized, this realization of the costliness of grace gradually faded. The world was Christianized, and grace became its common property. It was to be had at low cost. [But] whenever the church was accused of being too secularized, it could always point to monasticism as an opportunity of living a higher life within the fold, and thus justify the other possibility of a lower standard of life for others.

And so we get the paradoxical result that monasticism, whose mission was to preserve in the Church of Rome the primitive Christian realization of the costliness of grace, afforded conclusive justification for the secularization of the church. By and large the fatal error of monasticism lay not so much in its rigor (though even here there was a good deal of misunderstanding of the precise content of the will of Jesus), as in the extent to which it departed from genuine Christianity by setting itself up as the individual achievement of a select few, and so claiming a special merit of its own.

When the Reformation came, the providence of God raised Martin Luther to restore the gospel of pure, costly grace. Monasticism had transformed the humble work of discipleship into the meritorious activity of the saints. The bottom having thus been knocked out of the religious life, Luther laid hold upon grace. Just as the whole world of monasticism was crashing about him in ruins, he saw God in Christ stretching forth His hand to save.

The grace extended to him was a costly grace, and it shattered his whole existence. Once more he must leave his nets and follow. The first time was when he entered the monastery, when he had left everything behind except his pious self. This time even that was taken from him. He obeyed the call, not through any merit of his own, but simply through the grace of God.

Luther did not hear the word, "Of course you have sinned, but now everything is forgiven, so you can stay as you are and enjoy the consolations of forgiveness." No, Luther had to leave the cloister and go back to the world, not because the world in itself was good and holy, but because even the cloister was only a part of the world.

It is a fatal misunderstanding of Luther's action to suppose that his discovery of the gospel of pure grace offered a general dispensation from obedience to the command of Jesus, or that it was the great discovery of the Reformation that God's forgiving grace automatically conferred upon the world both righteousness and holiness. On the contrary, for Luther the Christian's calling in the world is sanctified only insofar as that calling registers the final, radical protest against the world.

Only insofar as the Christian's secular calling is exercised in following Jesus does it receive from the gospel new sanction and justification. It was not the justification of sin, but the justification of the sinner that drove Luther from the cloister back into the world. The grace he had received was costly grace. It was grace, because it was like water on parched ground, comfort in tribulation, freedom from the bondage of a self-chosen way, and forgiveness of all his sins. And it was costly, for far from excusing him from good works, it meant that he must take the call to discipleship more seriously than ever before.

It was grace because it cost so much, and it cost so much because it was grace. That was the secret of the gospel of the Reformation—the justification of the sinner.

Yet the outcome of the Reformation was the victory, not of Luther's perception of grace in all its purity and costliness, but of the vigilant religious instinct of man to find the place where grace is to be obtained at the cheapest price. Luther had said that grace alone can save; his followers took up his doctrine and repeated it word for word. But they left out its invariable corollary, namely, the obligation of discipleship.

Judged by the standard of Luther's doctrine, that of his followers was unassailable, yet their orthodoxy spelled the end and destruction of the Reformation as the revelation on earth of the costly grace of God. The justification of the sinner in the world degenerated into the justification of sin and the world. Costly grace was turned into cheap grace without discipleship.

[Luther] always looked upon [grace] as the answer to a sum, an answer which had been arrived at by God, not by man. But his followers then changed the "answer" into the data for a calculation of their own. That was the root of the trouble. If grace is God's gift of Christian life, then we cannot for a moment dispense with following Christ. But if grace becomes how I choose to live my Christian life, it means that I set out to live the Christian life in the world with all my sins justified beforehand. I can go and sin as much as I like, and rely on this "grace" to forgive me, for the world after all is justified in principle by grace.

I can therefore cling to my bourgeois secular existence and remain as I was before, but with the added assurance that the grace of God will cover me. It is under the influence of this kind of "grace" that the world has been made "Christian," but at the cost of secularizing the Christian religion as never before. The antithesis between the Christian life and the life of bourgeois respectability has vanished. The Christian life now means nothing more than living in the world and in being no different from the world; it means, in fact, being prohibited for the sake of grace from being different from the world.

The upshot of it all is that my only duty as a Christian is to escape from the world for an hour or so on a Sunday morning and go to church to be assured that my sins are all forgiven. I need no longer try to follow Christ. Cheap grace, the bitterest foe of all true discipleship, has freed me from that. Grace as the data for our calculations means grace at the cheapest price, but grace as the answer to the sum means costly grace.

It is terrifying to realize what use can be made of a genuine evangelical doctrine. In both cases—cheap grace and costly grace—we have the identical formula, "justification by faith alone." Yet misuse of the formula leads to the complete destruction of its very essence.

At the end of a lifetime spent in the pursuit of knowledge, [Goethe's] Faust has to confess: "I now do see that we can nothing know." That is the answer to a sum, the outcome of a long experience. But as Kierkegaard observed, it is quite a different matter when a freshman comes up to the university and uses the same sentiment to justify his indolence. That we can know nothing may be perfectly true as a conclusion, but as a foundational concept it is a piece of self-deception. Acquired knowledge cannot be divorced from the setting in which it is acquired.

The only man who has the right to say that he is justified by grace alone is the man who has left all to follow Christ. Such a man knows that the call to discipleship is a gift of grace, and that the call is inseparable from the grace. But those who try to use this grace as an escape from following Christ are simply deceiving themselves.

We (Lutherans) have gathered like eagles around the carcass of cheap grace,[8] and there we have drunk the poison that has killed the life of following Christ. It is true, of course, that we have paid the doctrine of pure grace divine honors unparalleled in Christendom. In fact, we have exalted that doctrine to the position of God Himself. Everywhere Luther's formula has been repeated, but its truth has been perverted into self-deception.

So long as our church holds the correct doctrine of justification, there is no doubt whatever that she is a justified church! So it was said, with the thought that we must vindicate our heritage by making this grace available on the cheapest and easiest terms. To be "Lutheran" must mean that we leave the following of Christ to Nomians [legalists], Calvinists, and Anabaptists—and all this for the sake of grace. We justified the world and condemned as heretics those who tried to follow Christ. The result was that a nation [Germany] became Christian and Lutheran, but at the cost of true discipleship. The price it was called upon to pay was all too cheap. Cheap grace won the day.

But do we also realize that this cheap grace has turned back upon us like a boomerang? The price we are now paying in the shape of the collapse of organized religion is only the inevitable consequence of our policy of making grace available at all too low a cost. We gave away the word and sacraments wholesale. We baptized, confirmed, and absolved a whole nation without asking awkward questions or insisting on strict conditions.

Our humanitarian sentiment made us give that which was holy to the scornful and unbelieving. We poured forth unending streams of grace. But the call to follow Jesus was hardly ever heard. Where were those truths which impelled the early church to institute the catechumenate, which enabled a strict watch to be kept over the frontier between the Church and the world, and afforded adequate protection for costly grace?

What happened to all those warnings of Luther against preaching the gospel in such a way as to make people feel secure in their ungodly living? Was there ever a more terrible or disastrous instance of the Christianizing of the world than this? What are those three thousand Saxons put to death by Charlemagne compared to the millions of spiritual corpses in our country today?[9] With us it has been abundantly proved that the sins of the fathers are visited upon the children unto the third and fourth generations. Cheap grace has turned out to be utterly merciless to our evangelical church.

This cheap grace has been no less disastrous to our personal spiritual lives. Instead of opening up the way to Christ, it has closed it. Instead of calling us to follow Christ, it has hardened us in our disobedience. Perhaps we had once heard the gracious call to follow Him and had even taken the first few steps along the path of discipleship, only to find ourselves confronted by the word of cheap grace. Was that not merciless and hard?

The only effect that such a word could have on us was to bar our way to progress, to seduce us to the mediocre level of the world. It quenched the joy of discipleship by telling us that we were following a way of our own choosing, that we were spending our strength and disciplining ourselves in vain—all of which was not merely useless, but extremely dangerous. After all, we were told, our salvation had already been accomplished by the grace of God. The smoking flax was mercilessly extinguished. It was unkind to speak to men like this, for such a cheap offer could only leave them bewildered and lure them from the way to which Christ had called them. Having laid hold on cheap grace, they were barred forever from the knowledge of costly grace.

Deceived and weakened, men felt that they were strong now that they were in possession of this cheap grace—whereas in fact they had lost the power to live the life of discipleship and obedience. The word of cheap grace has been the ruin of more Christians than any commandment of works.

It is becoming clearer every day that the most urgent problem besetting our church is this: How can we live the Christian life in the modern world? We are ready to admit that we no longer stand in the path of true discipleship. Although our church is orthodox as far as her doctrine of grace is concerned, we confess that we are no longer sure that we are members of a church which follows its Lord. We must therefore attempt to recover a true understanding of the mutual relation between grace and discipleship. The issue can no longer be evaded.

Happy are they who have reached the end of the road we seek to tread, who are astonished to discover the by-no-means self-evident truth that grace is costly exactly because it is the grace of God in Jesus Christ. Happy are the simple fol-

lowers of Jesus Christ who have been overcome by His grace
and are able to sing the praises of the all-sufficient grace of
Christ with humbleness of heart. Happy are they who,
knowing that grace, can live in the world without being of it,
who, by following Jesus Christ, are so sure of their heavenly
citizenship that they are truly free to live their lives in this
world. Happy are they who know that discipleship simply
means the life which springs from grace and that grace simply means discipleship. Happy are they who have become
Christians in this sense of the word. For them the word of
grace has proved a fount of mercy.

* * *

Because Jesus is the Christ, He has the authority to call and
to demand obedience to His word. Jesus summons men to
follow Him, not as a teacher or a pattern of the good life, but
as the Christ, the Son of God. To follow in His steps is something beyond defining. It gives us no intelligible program for
a way of life, no goal or ideal to strive after. The disciple simply burns his boats and goes ahead. The old life is left behind,
completely surrendered. Discipleship means Jesus Christ and
Him alone. It cannot consist of anything more than that.

When we are called to follow Christ, we are summoned
to an exclusive attachment to His person. The grace of His
call bursts all the bonds of legalism. It is a gracious call, a gracious commandment. It transcends the difference between
the law and the gospel. Christ calls, the disciple follows; that
is grace and commandment in one. "I will walk at liberty, for
I seek Your commandments."[10]

Discipleship means adherence to Christ, and because
Christ is the object of that adherence, it must take the form
of discipleship. An abstract Christology, a doctrinal system,
a general religious knowledge on the subject of grace or on
the forgiveness of sin, all render discipleship superfluous. In
fact, they positively exclude any idea of discipleship whatever.
They are essentially inimical to the whole conception of following Christ.

With an abstract idea it is possible to enter the arena of formal knowledge, to become enthusiastic about it, and perhaps even to put it into practice; but a mere abstraction can never lead to personal obedience. Christianity without the living Christ is inevitably Christianity without discipleship, and Christianity without discipleship is always Christianity without Christ. It remains an abstract idea, a myth which has a place for the Fatherhood of God, but omits Christ as the living Son. And a Christianity of that kind is nothing less than the end of discipleship.

In such a religion there is trust in God, but no following of Christ. Because the Son of God became Man, because He is the Mediator, for that reason alone the only true relation we can have with Him is to follow Him. Discipleship is bound to Christ as the Mediator, and where it is properly understood, it necessarily implies faith in the Son of God as the Mediator. Only the Mediator, the God-Man, can call men to follow Him.

Discipleship apart from Jesus Christ is a way of our own choosing. It may be the ideal way, it may even lead to martyrdom, but it is devoid of all promise. Jesus will certainly reject it.

* * *

If we would follow Jesus, we must take certain definite steps. The first step is to break away from our past. The call to follow at once produces a new situation. Levi must leave the receipt of custom and Peter his nets.[11]

One would have thought that nothing so drastic was necessary at such an early stage. Could not Jesus have initiated those who followed Him into some new religious experience and leave them as they were before? He could have done so, had He not been the incarnate Son of God. But since He is the Christ, He must make it clear from the start that His word is not an abstract doctrine, but the recreation of the whole life of man. The only right and proper way is quite literally to go with Jesus. The call to follow implies that there is only one way of believing on Jesus Christ, and that is by leaving all and going with the incarnate Son of God.

The first step places the disciple in the situation where faith is possible. But this step is not the first stage of a career. Its sole justification is that it brings the disciple into fellowship with Jesus. So long as Levi sat at the receipt of custom and Peter worked at his nets, they could both pursue their trades honestly and dutifully, and they might both enjoy religious experiences, old or new. But if they wanted to believe in God, the only way was to follow His incarnate Son.

Until that day, everything had been different. They could remain in obscurity, quietly pursuing their work in the land, observing the law and waiting for the coming of the Messiah. But now He has come, and His call goes forth. Faith can no longer mean sitting still and waiting—they must rise and follow Him.

Had Levi stayed at his post, Jesus might have been his present help in trouble, but not the Lord of his life. In other words, Levi would never have learned to believe. Peter had to leave the ship and risk his life on the sea in order to learn both his own weakness and the almighty power of his Lord.[12] If Peter had not taken the risk, he would never have learned the meaning of faith. Before he could believe, the utterly impossible and ethically irresponsible situation on the waves of the sea had to be displayed. The road to faith passes through obedience to the call of Jesus.

Discipleship is not an offer man makes to Christ. It is only the call which creates the situation. This situation never possesses any intrinsic worth or merit of its own. It is only through the call that it receives its justification.

* * *

Are you worried because you find it so hard to believe? No one should be surprised at the difficulty of faith, if there is some part of his life where he is consciously resisting or disobeying the commandment of Jesus. Is there some part of your life which you are refusing to surrender at His behest, some sinful passion, maybe, or some animosity, some hope, perhaps your ambition or your reason?

If so, you must not be surprised that you have not received the Holy Spirit, that prayer is difficult, or that your request for faith remains unanswered. Go rather and be reconciled with your brother, renounce the sin which holds you fast—and then you will recover your faith! If you dismiss the word of God's command, you will not receive His word of grace. How can you hope to enter into communion with Him when at some point in your life you are running away from Him? The man who disobeys cannot believe, for only he who obeys can believe.

The gracious call of Jesus now becomes a stern command: Do this! Give up that! Leave the ship and come to me! When a man says he cannot obey the call of Jesus, Jesus says, "First obey, perform the external work, renounce your attachments, give up the obstacles which separate you from the will of God. Do not say you have no faith. You will not have it so long as you persist in disobedience and refuse to take the first step. Neither must you say that you have faith, and therefore there is no need for you to take the first step. While you are pretending to be a humble man of faith, you are actually becoming a hardened unbeliever."

It is a malicious subterfuge to argue so, a sure sign of lack of faith, which leads in its turn to a lack of obedience. Here is the disobedience of "believers": when they are asked to obey, they simply confess their unbelief and leave it at that.[13] If you believe, take the first step: it leads to Jesus Christ. If you don't believe, take the first step all the same, for you are invited to take it. No one wants to know about your faith or unbelief; your orders are to perform the act of obedience on the spot. Then you will find yourself in the situation where faith becomes possible and where faith exists in the true sense of the word.

When people complain that they find it hard to believe, it is a sign of deliberate or unconscious disobedience. It is all too easy to put them off by offering the remedy of cheap grace. That only leaves the disease as bad as it was before and makes the word of grace a sort of self-administered consolation or a self-imparted absolution. But when this happens, the poor seeker can no longer find any comfort in the words of priestly absolution—he has become deaf to the Word of God. And even if he absolves himself from his sins a thousand times, he has lost all capacity for faith in true forgiveness, simply because he has never really known it.

Unbelief thrives on cheap grace, for it is determined to persist in disobedience. Clergy frequently come across such cases today. The usual result is that self-imparted absolution confirms the individual in his disobedience and makes him plead ignorance of the kindness as well as the commandment of God. He complains that God's commandment is uncertain and susceptible of different interpretations. At first he is well aware of his disobedience, but with his increasing hardness of heart that awareness grows ever fainter, and in the end he becomes so enmeshed that he loses all capacity for hearing God's Word, and faith becomes quite impossible.

One can imagine such a person conversing thus with his pastor:

"I have lost the faith I once had."

"You must listen to the word as it is spoken to you in the sermon."

"I do, but I cannot get anything out of it. It just falls on deaf ears as far as I'm concerned."

"The trouble is, you don't really want to listen."

"On the contrary, I do."

And here the exchange usually breaks off, because the pastor is at a loss what to say next. He remembers the first half of the proposition, "Only those who believe obey." But this does not help, for faith is just what this particular man finds impossible. The pastor feels himself confronted with the ultimate riddle of predestination. God grants faith to some and withholds it from others. So the pastor throws in the sponge and leaves the poor man to his fate.

And yet this very impasse ought to be the turning point of the interview. The pastor should give up arguing with him and stop taking his difficulties seriously. That will really be in the man's own interest, for he is only trying to hide himself behind them. It is now time for the pastor to take the bull by the horns and say, "Only those who obey believe."

Such interjection allows the pastor to continue: "You are disobedient. You are trying to keep some part of your life under your own control. That is what is preventing you from listening to Christ and believing in His grace. You cannot hear Christ because you are willfully disobedient. Somewhere in your heart you are refusing to listen to His call."

Christ now enters the lists again and comes to grips with the devil, who until now has been hiding under the cloak of cheap grace. It is all-important that the pastor should be ready with both sides of the proposition: "Only those who obey can believe, and only those who believe can obey." In the name of Christ he must exhort the man to obedience, to action, to take the first step.

He must say, "Tear yourself away from all other attachments and follow Him," for at this stage, the first step is what matters most. The strong position which the refractory sinner had occupied must be stormed and the truant dragged from his hiding place. Only then can he recover the freedom to see, hear, and believe.

Briefly, the position is this. Our sinner has drugged himself with cheap and easy grace by accepting the proposition that only those who believe can obey. He persists in disobedience and seeks consolation by absolving himself. This procedure serves to deaden his ears to the Word of God. We cannot breach the fortress so long as we merely repeat the proposition which supplies him with his self-defense. So we must make for the turning point without further ado and exhort him to obedience. Only those who obey can believe.

Will that course lead him astray and encourage him to trust in his own works? Far from it. He will the more easily realize that his faith is not genuine. He will be rescued from his entanglement by being forced to make a definite decision. In this way his ears are opened once more for the call of Jesus to faith and discipleship.

What can the call to discipleship mean today for the worker, the businessman, the squire, and the soldier? Does it not lead to an intolerable dichotomy between our lives as workers in the world and our lives as Christians? If Christianity means following Christ, is it not a religion for a small minority, a spiritual elite? Does it not mean the repudiation of the great mass of society and a hearty contempt for the weak and the poor?

Yet surely such an attitude is the exact opposite of the gracious mercy of Jesus Christ, who came to publicans and sinners,[14] the weak and the poor, the erring and the hopeless! Are those who belong to Jesus only a few, or are they many?

And if we answer the call to discipleship, where will it lead us? What decisions and partings will it require? For the answer to this question we shall need to go to Him, for only He knows the answer. Only Jesus Christ who bids us follow Him knows the end of the journey. But we do know that it will be a road of boundless mercy. Discipleship means joy.

May God grant us joy as we strive earnestly to follow [this] way. May we be enabled to say "No" to sin and "Yes" to the sinner. May we withstand our foes and yet hold out to them the word of the gospel which woos and wins the souls of men.

NOTES

1. A line from the famous hymn, "Rock of Ages," by Augustus Montague Toplady (1740-1778). The next line reads, "Thou must save, and Thou alone."
2. Matthew 13:44-46.
3. Matthew 7:7.
4. 1 Corinthians 6:20; 7:23.
5. Romans 8:32.
6. Matthew 11:30.
7. Matthew 4:19; John 21:22.
8. Matthew 24:28.
9. In A.D. 782, according to the *Encyclopedia Britannica*, 1953 edition, Charlemagne, the first "Holy Roman Emperor," put to the sword 4,500 captive Saxon warriors in one day.
10. Psalm 119:45.
11. Mark 1:16-18; 2:14.
12. Matthew 14:28-31.
13. Mark 9:24.
14. Mark 2:16.

C. S. Lewis, 1898-1963

An atheist until he turned to Christ at age twenty-nine, he sensed no divine calling to preach or evangelize, and he never attended Bible college or seminary. Yet by the sheer force of his writing this quiet, balding Britisher, who loved long walks and lived most of his life as a bachelor, may have moved more people toward and into the Christian faith than any other person in the twentieth century.

Clive Staples Lewis was a native of Belfast, Ireland, a medieval scholar, novelist, poet, and writer of children's stories. After his conversion Lewis became an active layman in the Church of England. He maintained friendships with people of many religious backgrounds, whether low churchmen, high churchmen, or nonchurchmen, and avoided his own church's internal controversies. His writings covered a kaleidoscope of topics: theology, philosophic apologetics, literary criticism, allegories, poetry, and children's classics such as the Narnia Chronicles. As a Christian, he was unusually successful in clarifying Biblical teaching for a secular and skeptical age. He spent much time discussing perennial problems such as pain, evil, suffering, immortality, prayer, miracles, and unbelief, always with a view to explaining and defending orthodox Christianity. A note of inner joy and wonder pervades all his works, not excluding his cosmic fantasies. C. S. Lewis societies are flourishing in nearly every major English-speaking city, and scores of books continue to be written about him.

After he was wounded in France during World War I, young Lewis returned to Oxford University where he taught until 1954. While he was teaching his students about saga and myth, he was also writing about the Christian faith. So well received were his Screwtape Letters *that during World War II the BBC radio asked him to deliver a series of twenty-nine broadcast talks on Christian doctrine. His nontheological approach, persuasive logic, and easy style immediately gained him immense popularity.*

In 1956 he gave up his bachelordom to marry Joy Davidman, an American divorcée facing deportation from Britain. Joy was herself a brilliant writer who became a Christian after a youthful stint as a Communist party member. Their marriage of convenience turned into genuine love. When Joy died of cancer in 1960, Jack, as he was known by intimate friends, was devastated. He poured out his feelings in a book titled A Grief Observed, *using the nom de plume of N. W. Clerk.*

When I interviewed Lewis in Cambridge three years later, his own death was just six months off. I received a clear impression that he had lost interest in life with Joy's passing and was hoping for an early departure for heaven. He was still writing on Christian themes, however, and was struggling to cope with an enormous load of correspondence.

The first excerpt is taken by permission from one of the most popular of all Lewis's theological writings, Mere Christianity, *published by Collins Publishers 1942, 1943, 1944 and 1952 C. S. Lewis Pte. Ltd. Then follows an abridgement of my personal interview with Professor Lewis in his rooms at Cambridge on May 7, 1963. The full interview first appeared in* Decision *Magazine in October and November of that year, and this excerpt is reproduced by permission.*

SEVEN

WHAT CHRISTIANS BELIEVE
by C. S. Lewis

I have been asked to tell you what Christians believe, and I am going to begin by telling you one thing that Christians do not need to believe. If you are Christian you do not have to believe that all the other religions are simply wrong all through. If you are an atheist you do have to believe that the main point in all the religions of the whole world is simply one huge mistake. If you are a Christian you are free to think that all these religions, even the queerest ones, contain at least some hint of truth.

When I was an atheist I had to try to persuade myself that most of the human race have always been wrong about the question that mattered to them most; when I became a Christian I was able to take a more liberal view. But, of course, being a Christian does mean thinking that where Christianity differs from other religions, Christianity is right and they are wrong. As in arithmetic—there is only one right answer to a sum, and all other answers are wrong; but some of the wrong answers are much nearer being right than others.

The first big division of humanity is into the majority, who believe in some kind of God or gods, and the minority who do not. On this point Christianity lines up with the majority—lines up with ancient Greeks and Romans, modern savages, Stoics, Platonists, Hindus, Mohammedans, etc., against the modern Western European materialists.

Now I go on to the next big division. People who all believe in God can be divided according to the sort of God they believe in. There are two very different ideas on this subject. One of them is the idea that He is beyond good and evil. We humans call one thing good and another thing bad. But according to some people, that is merely our human point of view. These people would say that the wiser you become, the less you would want to call anything good or bad, and the more clearly you would see that everything is good one way and bad in another, and that nothing could have been differently. Consequently, these people think that long before you got anywhere near the divine point of view, the distinction would have disappeared altogether.

We call a cancer bad, they would say, because it kills a man; but you might just as well call a successful surgeon bad because he kills a cancer. It all depends on the point of view. The other and opposite idea is that God is quite definitely "good" or "righteous," a God who takes sides, who loves love and hates hatred, who wants us to behave in one way and not in another. The first of these views—the one that thinks God beyond good and evil—is called pantheism.[1] It was held by the great Prussian philosopher Hegel and, as far as I can understand them, by the Hindus. The other view is held by Jews, Mohammedans, and Christians.

And with this big difference between pantheism and the Christian idea of God, there usually goes another. Pantheists usually believe that God, so to speak, animates the universe as you animate your body—that the universe almost is God, so that if it did not exist He would not exist either, and anything you find in the universe is a part of God.

The Christian idea is quite different. They think God invented and made the universe—like a man making a picture or composing a tune. A painter is not a picture, and he does not die if his picture is destroyed. You may say, "He's put a lot of himself into it," but you only mean that all its beauty and interest has come out of his head. His skill is not in the picture in the same way that it is in his head or even in his hands.

I expect you see how this difference between Pantheists and Christians hangs together with the other one. If you do not take the distinction between good and bad very seriously, then it is easy to say that anything you find in this world is a part of God. But, of course, if you think some things really bad, and God really good, then you cannot talk like that. You must believe that God is separate from the world and that some of the things we see in it are contrary to His will.

Confronted with a cancer or a slum the Pantheist can say, "If you could only see it from the divine point of view, you would realize that this also is God." The Christian replies, "Don't talk damned nonsense." For Christianity is a fighting religion. It thinks God made the world—that space and time, heat and cold, and all the animals and vegetables are things that God "made up out of his head" as a man makes up a story. But it also thinks that a great many things have gone wrong with the world that God made and that God insists, and insists very loudly, on our putting them right again.

And, of course, that raises a very big question. If a good God made the world why has it gone wrong? And for many years I simply refused to listen to the Christian answers to this question because I kept on feeling, "whatever you say, and however clever your arguments are, isn't it much simpler and easier to say that the world was not made by any intelligent power? Aren't all your arguments simply a complicated attempt to avoid the obvious?" But then that threw me back into another difficulty.

My argument against God was that the universe seemed so cruel and unjust. But how had I got this idea of just and unjust? A man does not call a line crooked unless he has some idea of a straight line. What was I comparing the universe with when I called it unjust? If the whole show was bad and senseless from A to Z, so to speak, why did I, who was supposed to be part of the show, find myself in such violent reaction against it? A man feels wet when he falls into water, because man is not a water animal; a fish would not feel wet.

Of course, I could have given up my idea of justice by saying it was nothing but a private idea of my own. But if I did that, then my argument against God collapsed too—for the argument depended on saying that the world was really unjust, not simply that it did not happen to please my private fancies. Thus in the very act of trying to prove that God did not exist—in other words, that the whole of reality was senseless—I found I was forced to assume that one part of reality— namely my idea of justice—was full of sense. Consequently atheism turns out to be too simple. If the whole universe has no meaning, we should never have found out that it has no meaning, just as, if there were no light in the universe and therefore no creatures with eyes, we should never know it was dark. Dark would be without meaning.

*   *   *

Very well, then, atheism is too simple. And I will tell you another view that is also too simple. It is the view I call "Christianity-and-water," the view which simply says there is a good God in Heaven and everything is all right—leaving out the difficult and terrible doctrines about sin and hell and the devil, and redemption. Both these are boys' philosophies.

It is no good asking for a simple religion. After all, real things are not simple. They look simple, but they are not. The table I am sitting at looks simple; but ask a scientist to tell you what it is really made of—all about the atoms and how the light waves rebound from them and hit my eye and what they do to the optic nerve and what it does to my brain—and, of course, you find that what we call "seeing a table" lands you in mysteries and complications which you can hardly get to the end of.

A child saying a child's prayer looks simple. And if·you are content to stop there, well and good. But if you are not— and the modern world usually is not—if you want to go on and ask what is really happening—then you must be prepared for something difficult. If we ask for something more than simplicity, it is silly then to complain that the something more is not simple.

Very often, however, this silly procedure is adopted by people who are not silly, but who, consciously or unconsciously, want to destroy Christianity. Such people put up a version of Christianity suitable for a child of six and make that the object of their attack. When you try to explain the Christian doctrine as it is really held by an instructed adult, they then complain that you are making their heads turn round and that it is all too complicated and that if there really were a God, they are sure He would have made "religion" simple, because simplicity is so beautiful, etc. You must be on your guard against these people, for they will change their ground every minute and only waste your time. Notice, too, their idea of God "making religion simple," as if "religion" were something God invented, and not His statement to us of certain quite unalterable facts about His own nature.

Besides being complicated, reality, in my experience, is usually odd. It is not near, not obvious, not what you expect. For instance, when you have grasped that the earth and the other planets all go round the sun, you would naturally expect that all the planets were made to match—all at equal distances from each other, say, or distances that regularly increased, or all the same size, or else getting bigger or smaller as you go farther from the sun. In fact, you find no rhyme or reason (that we can see) about either the sizes or the distances; and some of them have one moon, one has four, one has two, some have none, and one has a ring.

Reality, in fact, is usually something you could not have guessed. That is one of the reasons I believe Christianity. It is a religion you could not have guessed. If it offered us just the kind of universe we had always expected, I should feel we were making it up. But, in fact, it is not the sort of thing any-one would have made up. It has just that queer twist about it that real things have. So let us leave behind all these boys' philosophies—these over-simple answers. The problem is not simple, and the answer is not going to be simple either.

What is the problem? A universe that contains much that is obviously bad and apparently meaningless, but containing creatures like ourselves who know that it is bad and meaningless. There are only two views that face all the facts. One is the Christian view that this is a good world that has gone wrong, but still retains the memory of what it ought to have been. The other is the view called Dualism![2] Dualism means the belief that there are two equal and independent powers at the back of everything, one of them good and the other bad, and that this universe is the battlefield in which they fight out an endless war. I personally think that next to Christianity, Dualism is the manliest and most sensible creed on the market. But it has a catch to it.

The two powers, or spirits, or gods—the good one and the bad one—are supposed to be quite independent. They both existed from all eternity. Neither of them made the other, neither of them has any more right than the other to call itself God. Each presumably thinks it is good and thinks the other bad. One of them likes hatred and cruelty, the other likes love and mercy, and each backs its own view. Now what do we mean when we call one of them the Good Power and the other the Bad Power? Either we are merely saying that we happen to prefer the one to the other . . . or else we are saying that, whatever the two powers think about it, and whichever we humans, at the moment, happen to like, one of them is actually wrong, actually mistaken, in regarding itself as good.

Now, if we mean merely that we happen to prefer the first, then we must give up talking about good and evil at all. For good means what you ought to prefer regardless of what you happen to like at any given moment. If "being good" meant simply joining the side you happened to fancy, for no real reason, then good would not deserve to be called good. So we must mean that one of the two powers is actually wrong and the other actually right.

But the moment you say that, you are putting into the universe a third thing in addition to the two Powers—some law or standard or rule of good which one of the powers conforms to and the other fails to conform to. But since the two powers are judged by this standard, then this standard, or the Being who made this standard, is farther back and higher up than either of them, and He will be the real God. In fact, what we meant by calling them good and bad turns out to be that one of them is in a right relation to the real ultimate God and the other in a wrong relation to Him.

The same point can be made in a different way. . . . Pleasure, money, power, and safety are all, as far as they go, good things. The badness consists in pursuing them by the wrong method, or in the wrong way, or too much. I do not mean, of course, that the people who do this are not desperately wicked. I do mean that wickedness, when you examine it, turns out to be the pursuit of some good in the wrong way.

You can be good for the sake of mere goodness; you cannot be bad for the mere sake of badness. You can do a kind action when you are not feeling kind and when it gives you no pleasure, simply because kindness is right; but no one ever did a cruel action simply because cruelty is wrong—only because cruelty was pleasant or useful to him. In other words badness cannot succeed even in being bad in the same way in which goodness is good. Goodness is, so to speak, itself; badness is only spoiled goodness. And there must be something good first before it can be spoiled. We [call] sadism a sexual perversion; but you must first have the idea of a normal sexuality before you can talk of its being perverted; and you can see which is the perversion, because you can explain the perverted from the normal, and cannot explain the normal from the perverted.

Put it more simply still. To be bad [the Bad Power] must exist and have intelligence and will. But existence, intelligence and will are in themselves good. Therefore he must be getting them from the Good Power; even to be bad he must borrow or steal from his opponent. And do you now begin to see why Christianity has always said that the devil is a fallen angel? That is not a mere story for the children. It is a real recognition of the fact that evil is a parasite, not an original thing. The powers which enable evil to carry on are powers given it by goodness. All the things which enable a bad man to be effectively bad are in themselves good things—resolution, cleverness, good looks, existence itself. That is why Dualism, in a strict sense, will not work.

But I freely admit that real Christianity (as distinct from

Christianity-and-water) goes much nearer to Dualism than people think. One of the things that surprised me when I first read the New Testament seriously was that it talked so much about a Dark Power in the universe—a mighty evil spirit who was held to be the Power behind death and disease and sin. The difference is that Christianity thinks this Dark Power was created by God, and was good when he was created, and went wrong.

Christianity agrees with Dualism that this universe is at war. But it does not think this is a war between independent powers. It thinks it is a civil war, a rebellion, and that we are living in a part of the universe occupied by the rebel.

Enemy-occupied territory—that is what this world is. Christianity is the story of how the rightful king has landed, you might say landed in disguise, and is calling us all to take part in a great campaign of sabotage. When you go to church you are really listening-in to the secret wireless from our friends; that is why the enemy is so anxious to prevent us from going. He does it by playing on our conceit and laziness and intellectual snobbery.

I know someone will ask me, "Do you really mean, at this time of day, to reintroduce our old friend the devil— hoofs and horns and all?" Well, what the time of day has to do with it I do not know. And I am not particular about the hoofs and horns. But in other respects my answer is, "Yes, I do." I do not claim to know anything about his personal appearance. If anybody really wants to know him better I would say to that person, "Don't worry. If you really want to, you will. Whether you'll like it when you do is another question."

*   *   *

Christians, then, believe that an evil power has made himself for the present the Prince of this World. And, of course, that raises problems. Is this state of affairs in accordance with God's will or not? If it is, He is a strange God, you will say;

and if it is not, how can anything happen contrary to the will of a being with absolute power?

But anyone who has been in authority knows how a thing can be in accordance with your will in one way and not in another. It may be quite sensible for a mother to say to the children, "I'm not going to make you tidy the schoolroom every night. You've got to learn to keep it tidy on your own." Then she goes up one night and finds the Teddy bear and the ink and the French Grammar all lying in the grate. That is against her will. She would prefer the children to be tidy. But on the other hand, it is her will which has left the children free to be untidy. The same thing arises in any regiment, or trade union, or school. You make a thing voluntary, and then half the people do not do it. That is not what you willed, but your will has made it possible.

It is probably the same in the universe. God created things which had free will. That means creatures which can go either wrong or right. Some people think they can imagine a creature which was free but had no possibility of going wrong. I cannot. If a thing is free to be good, it is also free to be bad. And free will is what has made evil possible. Why, then, did God give them free will? Because free will, though it makes evil possible, is also the only thing that makes possible any love or goodness or joy worth having. A world of automata—of creatures that worked like machines—would hardly be worth creating. The happiness which God designs for His higher creatures is the happiness of being freely, voluntarily tied to Him and to each other in an ecstasy of love and delight compared with which the most rapturous love between a man and a woman on this earth is mere milk and water. And for that they must be free.

Of course, God knew what would happen if they used their freedom the wrong way; apparently He thought it worth the risk. Perhaps we feel inclined to disagree with Him. But there is a difficulty about disagreeing with God. He is the source from which all your reasoning comes; you could not be right and He wrong any more than a stream can rise higher than its own source. When you are arguing against

Him you are arguing against the very power that makes you able to argue at all. It is like cutting off the branch you are sitting on. If God thinks this state of war in the universe a price worth paying for free will—that is, for making a live world in which creatures can do real good or harm and something of real importance can happen, instead of a toy world which only moves when He pulls the strings—then we may take it, it is worth paying.

When we have understood about free will, we shall see how silly it is to ask, as somebody once asked me, "Why did God make a creature of such rotten stuff that it went wrong?" The better stuff a creature is made of—the cleverer and stronger and freer it is—then the better it will be if it goes right, but also the worse it will be if it goes wrong. A cow cannot be very good or very bad; a dog can be both better and worse; a child better and worse still; an ordinary man still more so; a man of genius, still more so; a superhuman spirit best—or worst—of all.

How did the Dark Power go wrong? Here, no doubt, we ask a question to which human beings cannot give an answer with any certainty. A reasonable (and traditional) guess, based on our own experiences of going wrong, can, however, be offered. The moment you have a self at all, there is a possibility of putting yourself first—wanting to be the center—wanting to be God, in fact. That was the sin of Satan; and that was the sin he taught the human race. Some people think the Fall of man had something to do with sex, but that is a mistake. (The story in the Book of Genesis rather suggests that some corruption in our sexual nature followed the Fall, and was its result, not its cause.)[3]

What Satan put into the heads of our remote ancestors was the idea that they could "be like gods"—could set up on their own as if they had created themselves—be their own masters—invent some sort of happiness for themselves outside God, apart from God. And out of that hopeless attempt has come nearly all that we call human history—money, poverty, ambition, war, prostitution, classes, empires, slavery—the long terrible story of man trying to find something other than God which will make him happy.

The reason why it can never succeed is this. God made us—invented us as a man invents an engine. A car is made to run on gasoline, and it would not run properly on anything else. Now God designed the human machine to run on Himself. He Himself is the fuel our spirits were designed to burn, or the food our spirits were designed to feed on. There is no other. That is why it is just no good asking God to make us happy in our own way without bothering about religion. God cannot give us a happiness and peace apart from Himself, because it is not there. There is no such thing.

That is the key to history. Terrific energy is expended—civilizations are built up—excellent institutions devised, but each time something goes wrong. Some fatal flaw always brings the selfish and cruel people to the top, and it all slides back into misery and ruin. In fact, the machine conks. It seems to start up all right and runs a few yards, and then it breaks down. They are trying to run it on the wrong juice. That is what Satan has done to us humans.

And what did God do? First of all He left us conscience, the sense of right and wrong; and all through history there have been people trying (some of them very hard) to obey it. None of them ever quite succeeded. Secondly, He sent the human race what I call good dreams—I mean those queer stories scattered all through the heathen religions about a god who dies and comes to life again and, by his death, has somehow given new life to men. Thirdly, He selected one particular people and spent several centuries hammering into their heads the sort of God He was—that there was only one of Him and that He cared about right conduct. Those people were the Jews, and the Old Testament gives an account of the hammering process.

Then comes the real shock. Among these Jews there suddenly turns up a man who goes about talking as if He was God. He claims to forgive sins. He says He has always existed. He says He is coming to judge the world at the end of time.

Now let us get this clear. Among Pantheists, like the Indians,⁴ anyone might say that he was a part of God, or one with God—there would be nothing very odd about it. But this man, since He was a Jew, could not mean that kind of God. God, in their language, meant the Being outside the world Who had made it and was infinitely different from anything else. And when you have grasped that, you will see that what this man said was, quite simply, the most shocking thing that has ever been uttered by human lips.

One part of the claim tends to slip past us unnoticed because we have heard it so often that we no longer see what it amounts to. I mean the claim to forgive sins—my sins. Now unless the speaker is God, this is really so preposterous as to be comic. We can all understand how a man forgives offenses against himself. You tread on my toe and I forgive you; you steal my money and I forgive you. But what should we make of a man, himself unrobbed and untrodden on, who announced that he forgave you for treading on other men's toes and stealing other men's money?

Asinine fatuity is the kindest description we should give of his conduct. Yet this is what Jesus did. He told people that their sins were forgiven, and never waited to consult all the other people whom their sins had undoubtedly injured. He unhesitatingly behaved as if He was the party chiefly concerned, the person chiefly offended in all offenses. This makes sense only if He really was the God whose laws are broken and whose love is wounded in every sin. In the mouth of any speaker who is not God, these words would imply what I can only regard as a silliness and conceit unrivaled by any other character in history.

Yet (and this is the strange, significant thing) even His enemies, when they read the Gospels, do not usually get the impression of silliness and conceit. Still less do unprejudiced readers. Christ says that He is "humble and meek," and we believe Him; not noticing that, if He were merely a man, humility and meekness are the very last characteristics we could attribute to some of His sayings.

I am trying here to prevent anyone saying the really

foolish thing that people often say about Him, "I'm ready to accept Jesus as a great moral teacher, but I don't accept His claim to be God."

That is the one thing we must not say. A man who was merely a man and said the sort of things Jesus said would not be a great moral teacher. He would either be a lunatic—on a level with the man who says he is a poached egg—or else he would be the Devil of hell.

You must make your choice. Either this man was, and is, the Son of God—or else a madman or something worse. You can shut Him up for a fool, you can spit at Him and kill Him as a demon; or you can fall at His feet and call Him Lord and God. But let us not come with any patronizing nonsense about His being a great human teacher. He has not left that open to us. He did not intend to.

*   *   *

[The following segment is from an interview I had with C. S. Lewis, held on May 7, 1963, in Professor Lewis's rooms in Magdalene College, Cambridge University, England. At the time I was serving as editor of *Decision* Magazine, published by the Billy Graham Evangelistic Association.]

Professor Lewis, if you had a young friend with some interest in writing on Christian subjects, how would you advise him to prepare himself?

I would say if a man is going to write on chemistry, he learns chemistry. The same is true of Christianity. But to speak of the craft itself, I would not know how to advise a man how to write. It is a matter of talent and interest. I believe he must be strongly moved if he is to become a writer. Writing is like a "lust" or like "scratching when you itch." Writing comes as a result of a very strong impulse, and when it does come, I for one must get it out.

Can you suggest an approach that would spark the creation of a body of Christian literature strong enough to influence our generation?

There is no formula in these matters. I have no recipe, no

tablets. Writers are trained in so many individual ways that it is not for us to prescribe. Scripture itself is not systematic. The New Testament shows the greatest variety. God has shown us that He can use any instrument. Balaam's ass, you remember, preached a very effective sermon in the midst of his "hee-haws."[5]

Should Christian writers, in your opinion, attempt to be funny?

No. I think that forced jocularities on spiritual subjects are an abomination, and the attempts of some religious writers to be humorous are simply appalling. Some people write heavily, some write lightly. I prefer the light approach because I believe there is a great deal of false reverence about. There is too much solemnity and intensity in dealing with sacred matters—too much speaking in holy tones.

But is not solemnity proper and conducive to a sacred atmosphere?

Yes and no. There is a difference between a private devotional life and a corporate one. Solemnity is proper in church, but things that are proper in church are not necessarily proper outside, and vice versa. For example, I can say a prayer while washing my teeth, but that does not mean I should wash my teeth in church.

What is your opinion of the kind of writing being done within the Christian church today?

A great deal of what is being published by writers in the religious tradition is a scandal and is actually turning people away from the church. The liberal writers who are continually accommodating and whittling down the truth of the gospel are responsible. I cannot understand how a man can appear in print claiming to disbelieve everything he presupposes when he puts on the surplice. I feel it is a form of prostitution.

I believe it was [G. K.] Chesterton who was asked why he became a member of the church, and he replied, "To get rid of my sins."

It is not enough to want to get rid of one's sins. We also need to believe in the One who saves us from our sins. Not only do we need to recognize that we are sinners; we need to believe in a Savior who takes away sin. Matthew Arnold once wrote, "Nor does the being hungry prove that we have bread." Because we are sinners, it does not follow that we are saved.

Would you say the aim of Christian writing, including your own writing, is to bring about an encounter of the reader with Jesus Christ?

That is not my language, but that is the purpose I have in view.

How can we foster the encounter of people with Jesus Christ?

You can't lay down any pattern for God. There are many different ways of bringing people into the Kingdom, even some ways that I specially dislike. I have therefore learned to be cautious in my judgment.

But we can block it in many ways. As Christians we are tempted to make unnecessary concessions to those outside the faith. We give in too much. Now, I don't mean that we should run the risk of making a nuisance of ourselves by witnessing at improper times, but there comes a time when we must show that we disagree. We must show our Christian colors, if we are to be true to Jesus Christ. We cannot remain silent or concede everything away.

There is a character in one of my children's stories named Aslan, who says, "I never tell anyone any story except his own."[6] I cannot speak for the way God deals with others; I only know how He deals with me personally. Of course, we are to pray for spiritual awakening, and in various ways we can do something toward it. But we must remember that neither Paul nor Apollos gives the increase.[7] As Charles Williams once said, "The altar must often be built in one place so that the fire may come down in another place."[8]

Do you believe the use of filth and obscenity is necessary in contemporary literature in order to establish a realistic atmosphere?

I do not. I treat this development as a symptom, a sign of a culture that has lost its faith. Moral collapse follows upon spiritual collapse. I look upon the immediate future with great apprehension.

Do you feel, then, that modern culture is being de-Christianized?

I cannot speak to the political aspects of the question, but I have some definite views about the de-Christianizing of the church. I believe that there are many accommodating preachers and too many practitioners in the church who are not believers. Jesus Christ did not say, "Go into all the world and tell the world that it is quite right." The gospel is something completely different. In fact, it is directly opposed to the world.

The case against Christianity that is made out in the world is quite strong. Every war, every shipwreck, every cancer case, every calamity contributes to making a *prima facie* case against Christianity. It is not easy to be a believer in the face of this surface evidence. It calls for a strong faith in Jesus Christ.

What do you think is going to happen in the next few years of history, Mr. Lewis?

I have no way of knowing. My primary field is the past. I travel with my back to the engine, and that makes it difficult when you try to steer. The world might stop in ten minutes; meanwhile, we are to go on doing our duty. The great thing is to be found at one's post as a child of God, living each day as though it was our last, but planning as though our world might last a hundred years.

NOTES

1. Pantheism: Any religious belief or philosophic doctrine which identifies the universe with God. *Random House Dictionary.*
2. Dualism: The doctrine that there are two independent divine beings or eternal principles, one good, the other evil. *Random House Dictionary.*
3. Cf. Genesis 3.
4. Lewis is referring to Indians of India, not to American Indians.
5. Cf. Numbers 21:21-33
6. Cf. C. S. Lewis, *The Horse and His Boy* (New York: Macmillan, 1954), chapter 11.
7. Cf. 1 Corinthians 3:7.
8. Cf. Charles Williams, *He Came Down from Heaven* (Grand Rapids: Eerdmans, 1984).

A. W. Tozer, 1897-1963

Aiden Wilson Tozer was a man who hungered and thirsted after God. He was called a mystic, but for a conscientious, hardworking North American pastor, the label seems incongruous. He was no recluse. He could be outspoken, blunt, even harsh in his judgments on contemporary western religiosity. He nevertheless will probably be remembered, not for what he said about human failings, but for what he said about his Maker.

Tozer was born on a farm in Pennsylvania and after completing the eighth grade, moved with his family to Akron, Ohio. There he went to work at age fifteen in a rubber plant. One day he heard an elderly man preach on the street. The teenager went home and prayed alone in his attic. He was the first in his family to receive and confess Christ.

After taking part in street witnessing and neighborhood prayer meetings, young Tozer joined the Locust Street Church of the Christian and Missionary Alliance. In 1918 he began holding summer evangelistic meetings in schoolhouses. Following his discharge from four months of military service, he pastored several churches until in 1928 he was called to Southside Alliance Church in Chicago, where he remained for thirty-one years.

Tozer's first published book was Wingspread, *a biography of the Presbyterian minister, A. B. Simpson, founder of the Christian and Missionary Alliance movement. He also wrote many tracts and booklets that are still widely used in evangelical churches.*

In 1950 Dr. Tozer was elected editor of the Alliance Weekly, *later to become the* Alliance Witness. *His editorials, sometimes humorous, often trenchant, attracted a widening readership; the magazine's circulation doubled. A major theme both in his preaching and writing was the Holy Spirit, who came to indwell him back in 1918 while he was at the home of his mother-in-law.* The titles of his books, Keys to the Deeper Life, The Pursuit of God, How to Be Filled with the Holy Spirit, The Root of the Righteous, Born After Midnight, *all suggest the motivating force of his entire ministry.*

It was Tozer's passionate search for God that led him to study Christian mystics and devotional writers—Fénèlon, Thomas à Kempis, Bunyan, Brother Lawrence, Tersteegen, Boehme, Tauler, Augustine, Julian of Norwich, Roger Williams, and others. "These people," he said, "know God, and I want to know what they know about God and how they came to know it." He also loved the traditional hymns of the church and on his travels often carried about a hymnal with his Bible.

In 1959, then internationally known and honored for his preaching and writing, Dr. Tozer was called to the distinguished Avenue Road Alliance Church in Toronto, Ontario, Canada, where he served until a yet higher call claimed him on a Sunday morning in May, 1963.

The name A. W. Tozer is a continuing witness to the importance of a writing ministry. It attests to the marvelous power of God that can take a young man who never saw the inside of a high school, college, or seminary, and make him into a spokesman for a mission-minded denomination that in itself became a miracle of the twentieth century.

The following excerpt is from The Knowledge of the Holy *by A. W. Tozer. Copyright 1961 by Aiden Wilson Tozer; copyright © renewed 1989 by A. W. Tozer. Reprinted by permission of HarperCollins Publishers.*

EIGHT

THE ATTRIBUTES OF GOD
by A. W. Tozer

The child, the philosopher, and the religionist have all one question: "What is God like?"

Left to ourselves we tend immediately to reduce God to manageable terms. We want to get Him where we can use Him, or at least know where He is when we need Him. We want a God we can in some measure control. We need the feeling of security that comes from knowing what God is like, and what He is like is of course a composite of all the religious pictures we have seen, all the best people we have known or heard about, and all the sublime ideas we have entertained.

If all this sounds strange to modern ears, it is only because we have for a full half century taken God for granted. The glory of God has not been revealed to this generation of men. The God of contemporary Christianity is only slightly superior to the gods of Greece and Rome, if indeed He is not actually inferior to them in that He is weak and helpless while they at least had power.

"Now acquaint yourself with Him, and be at peace."[1] These ancient words still stand after the passing of the centuries; but how shall we acquaint ourselves with One who eludes all the straining efforts of mind and heart? And how shall we be held accountable to know what cannot be known?

"Can you fathom the mysteries of God?" asks Zophar the Naamathite. "Can you probe the limits of the Almighty? They are higher than the heavens—what can you do? Deeper than Sheol—what can you know?"[2] The yearning to know what cannot be known, to comprehend the Incomprehensible, to touch and taste the Unapproachable, arises from the image of God in the nature of man. Deep calleth unto deep,[3] and though [it be] polluted and landlocked by the mighty disaster theologians call the Fall, the soul [still] senses its origin and longs to return to its Source. How can this be realized?

The answer of the Bible is simply "through Jesus Christ our Lord." In Christ and by Christ, God effects complete self-disclosure, although He shows Himself not to reason but to faith and love. Faith is an organ of knowledge, and love an organ of experience. God came to us in the Incarnation; in the Atonement He reconciled us to Himself, and by faith and love we enter and lay hold on Him.

"What is God like?" If by that question we mean "What is God like in Himself?" there is no answer. If we mean "What has God disclosed about Himself that the reverent reason can comprehend?" there is, I believe, an answer both full and satisfying. For while the name of God is secret and His essential nature incomprehensible, He in condescending love has by revelation declared certain things to be true of Himself. These we call His attributes.

It is not a cheerful thought that millions of us who live in a land of Bibles, who belong to churches and labor to promote the Christian religion, may yet pass our whole life on this earth without once having thought or tried to think seriously about the being of God. Few of us have let our hearts gaze in wonder at the I AM, the self-existent Self back of which no creature can think.

Such thoughts are too painful for us. We prefer to think where it will do more good—about how to build a better mousetrap, for instance, or how to make two blades of grass grow where one grew before. And for this we are now paying a too heavy price in the secularization of our religion and the decay of our inner lives. Perhaps some sincere but puzzled Christian may wish to inquire about the practicality of such concepts as I am trying to set forth here. We can never know who or what we are till we know at least something of what God is. For this reason the self-existence of God is not a wisp of dry doctrine; it is in fact as near our breath and as practical as the latest surgical technique.

For reasons known only to Himself, God honored man above all other beings by creating him in His own image. The divine image in man is not a poetic fancy, not an idea born of religious longing. It is a solid theological fact, taught plainly throughout the sacred Scriptures and recognized by the church as a truth necessary to a right understanding of the Christian faith.

Man is a created being, a derived and contingent self, who of himself possesses nothing, but is dependent each moment for his existence upon the One who created him after His own likeness. The fact of God is necessary to the fact of man. Think God away and man has no ground of existence. Man for all his genius is but an echo of the original Voice, a reflection of the uncreated Light. As a sunbeam perishes when cut off from the sun, so man apart from God would pass back into the void of nothingness from which he first leaped at the creative call.

Self-sufficiency

Were all human beings suddenly to become blind, still the sun would shine by day and the stars by night, for these owe nothing to the millions who benefit from their light. So, were every man on earth to become an atheist, it could not affect God in any way. He is what He is in Himself without regard to any other. To believe in Him adds nothing to His perfections; to doubt Him takes nothing away.

Almighty God, just because He is almighty, needs no support. The picture of a nervous, ingratiating God fawning over men to win their favor is not a pleasant one; yet if we look at the popular conception of God that is precisely what we see. Twentieth-century Christianity has put God on charity. So lofty is our opinion of ourselves that we find it quite easy, not to say enjoyable, to believe that we are necessary to God. But the truth is that God is not greater for our being, nor would He be less if we did not exist. That we do exist is altogether of God's free determination, not by our desert nor by divine necessity.

Probably the hardest thought of all for our natural egotism to entertain is that God does not need our help. We commonly represent Him as a busy, eager, somewhat frustrated Father hurrying about seeking help to carry out His benevolent plan to bring peace and salvation to the world. But as said the Lady Julian, "I saw truly that God doeth all-thing, be it never so little."[4] The God who works all things surely needs no help and no helpers.

Too many missionary appeals are based upon this fancied frustration of Almighty God. An effective speaker can easily excite pity in his hearers, not only for the heathen but for the God who has tried so hard and so long to save them and has failed for want of support. I fear that thousands of young persons enter Christian service from no higher motive than to help deliver God from the embarrassing situation His love has got Him into and His limited abilities seem unable to get Him out of. Add to this a certain degree of commendable idealism and a fair amount of compassion for the underprivileged, and you have the true drive behind much Christian activity today.

It is morally imperative that we purge from our minds all ignoble concepts of the Deity and let Him be the God in our minds that He is in His universe. That God exists for Himself and man for the glory of God is the emphatic teaching of the Bible.

In His love and pity God came to us as Christ. This has been the consistent position of the church from the days of the apostles. It is fixed for Christian belief in the doctrine of the Incarnation of the Eternal Son. In recent times, however, this has come to mean something different from, and less than, what it meant to the early church.

The Man Jesus as He appeared in the flesh has been equated with the Godhead and all His human weaknesses and limitations attributed to the Deity. The truth is that the Man who walked among us was a demonstration, not of unveiled deity but of perfect humanity. The awful majesty of the

Godhead was mercifully sheathed in the soft envelope of human nature to protect mankind.

Christians today appear to know Christ only after the flesh. They try to achieve communion with Him by divesting Him of His burning holiness and unapproachable majesty, the very attributes He veiled while on earth but assumed in fullness of glory upon His ascension to the Father's right hand. The Christ of popular Christianity has a weak smile and a halo. He has become Someone-up-There who likes people, at least some people, and these are grateful but not too impressed. If they need Him, He also needs them.

Eternity

Because God lives in an everlasting now, He has no past and no future. When time-words occur in the Scriptures, they refer to our time, not to His. Since God is uncreated, He is not Himself affected by that succession of consecutive changes we call time.

God dwells in eternity but time dwells in God. He has already lived all our tomorrows as He has lived all our yesterdays. An illustration offered by C. S. Lewis may help us here.[5] He suggests that we think of a sheet of paper infinitely extended. That would be eternity. Then on that paper draw a short line to represent time. As the line begins and ends on that infinite expanse, so time began in God and will end in Him.

Time is known to us by a succession of events. It is the way we account for consecutive changes in the universe. Changes take place not all at once but in succession, one after the other, and it is the relation of "after" to "before" that gives us our idea of time. We wait for the sun to move from east to west or for the hour hand to move around the face of the clock, but God is not compelled so to wait. For Him everything that will happen has already happened.

We who live in this nervous age would be wise to meditate on our lives and our days long and often before the face of God and on the edge of eternity. For we are made for eternity as certainly as we are made for time, and as responsible moral beings we must deal with both.

"He has set eternity in their heart," said the Preacher,[6] and I think here he sets forth both the glory and the misery of men. All within us cries for life and permanence, and everything around us reminds us of mortality and change. Yet that God has made us of the stuff of eternity is both a glory and a prophecy, a glory yet to be realized and a prophecy yet to be fulfilled.

Infinity

The world is evil, the times are waxing late, and the glory of God has departed from the church. The God of Abraham has withdrawn His conscious Presence from us, and another god whom our fathers knew not is making himself at home among us. This god we have made, and because we have made him we can understand him; because we have created him he can never surprise us, never overwhelm us, nor astonish us, nor transcend us.

Of all that can be thought or said about God, His infinity is the most difficult to grasp. Since the word *infinite* describes what is unique, it can have no modifiers. We do not say "more unique" or "very finite." Before infinity we stand silent. Even to try to conceive of it would appear to be self-contradictory. Yet we must try, for the Holy Scriptures teach that God is infinite. This means that His being has no limits. Therefore there can be no limit to His presence. He is omnipresent. In his infinitude He surrounds the finite creation and contains it. There is no place beyond Him for anything to be.

God is our environment as the sea is to the fish and the air to the bird. "God is over all things," wrote Hildebert of Lavardin, "under all things, outside all; within but not enclosed; without but not excluded, above but not raised up, below but not depressed; wholly above, presiding; wholly beneath, sustaining; wholly within, filling."[7]

When we say that God is infinite, we mean that He knows no bounds. Whatever God is and all that God is, He is without limit. Novatian wrote, "All our thoughts about Him will be less than He, and all our loftiest utterances will be trivialities in comparison with Him."[8] Again, to say that God is infinite is to say that He is measureless. Measurement is the way created things have of accounting for themselves. It describes limitations and imperfections, and cannot apply to God. Weight describes the gravitational pull of the earth; distance describes intervals between bodies in space; length means extension in space.

Is it not plain that all this does not and cannot apply to God? It is the way we see the works of His hands, but not the way we see Him. He is above all this, outside of it, beyond it. There are no degrees in God. All that He is, He is without growth or addition or development. He is what He is in Himself, without qualifying thought or word. He is simply God.

Because God's nature is infinite, everything that flows out of it is infinite also. We poor human creatures are constantly being frustrated by limitations imposed upon us from without and within. The days of the years of our lives are few, and swifter than a weaver's shuttle. Life is a short and fevered rehearsal for a concert we cannot stay to give. Just when we appear to have attained some proficiency, we are forced to lay down our instruments. There is simply not time enough to think, to become, to perform what the constitution of our natures indicates we are capable of.

How completely satisfying to turn from our limitations to a God who has none. For Him time does not pass, it remains; and those who are in Christ share with Him all the riches of limitless time and endless years. God never hurries. There are no deadlines against which He must work. Only to know this is to quiet our spirit and relax our nerves. For those out of Christ, time is a devouring beast; before the sons and daughters of the new creation time crouches and purrs and licks their hands. The foe of the old human race becomes the friend of the new, and the stars in their courses fight for the man God delights to honor.

But there is more. God's gifts in nature have their limitations, but the gift of eternal life in Christ Jesus is as limitless as God. The Christian possesses God's own life and shares infinity with Him. The life of God returns upon itself and ceases never. And this is life eternal, to know the only true God, and Jesus Christ whom He has sent.

Wisdom

When Christian theology declares that God is wise, it means vastly more than it says or can say, for it tries to make a comparatively weak word bear an incomprehensible plenitude of meaning. "His understanding is infinite," says the psalmist.[9] The idea of God as infinitely wise is at the root of all truth.

Without the creation, the wisdom of God would have remained forever locked in the boundless abyss of the divine nature. God brought his creatures into being that He might enjoy them and they rejoice in Him. "And God saw every thing that he had made, and behold, it was very good."[10]

We rest our hope in the only wise God, our Savior, and wait with patience the slow development of His benign purposes. In spite of tears and pain and death, we believe that the God who made us all is infinitely wise and good. As Abraham staggered not at the promises of God through unbelief, but was strong in faith, giving glory to God, and was fully persuaded that what He had promised He was able to perform, so do we base our hope in God alone and hope against hope till the day breaks. We rest in what God is. I believe that this alone is true faith. Any faith that must be supported by the evidence of the senses is not real faith.

The testimony of faith is that no matter how things look in this fallen world, all God's acts are wrought in perfect wisdom. Atonement was accomplished with the same flawless skill that marks all of God's acts. However little we understand it all, we know that Christ's expiatory work perfectly reconciled God and men and opened the Kingdom of Heaven to all believers. Our concern is not to explain but to proclaim. Indeed, I wonder whether God could make us understand all that happened there at the cross. According to the Apostle Peter not even angels know, however eagerly they may desire to look into these things.

The operation of the gospel, the new birth, the coming of the divine Spirit into human nature, the ultimate overthrow of evil, and the final establishment of Christ's righteous Kingdom—all these have flowed and do flow out of God's infinite fullness of wisdom. Most of us go through life praying a little, planning a little, jockeying for position, hoping but never being quite certain of anything, and always secretly afraid that we will miss the way.

There is a better way. It is to repudiate our own wisdom and take instead the infinite wisdom of God. God has charged Himself with full responsibility for our eternal happiness and stands ready to take over the management of our lives the moment we turn in faith to Him. He constantly encourages us to trust Him in the dark. With the goodness of God to desire our highest welfare, the wisdom of God to plan it, and the power of God to achieve it, what do we lack? Surely we are the most favored of all creatures.

Goodness

When Christian theology says that God is good, it is not the same as saying that He is righteous or holy. The holiness of God is trumpeted from the heavens and reechoed on earth by saints and sages wherever God has revealed Himself. However, we are not at this time considering His holiness but His goodness, which is quite another thing.

The goodness of God is that which disposes Him to be kind, cordial, benevolent, and full of good will toward mankind. He is tenderhearted and of quick sympathy, and His unfailing attitude toward all moral beings is open, frank, and friendly. By His nature He is inclined to bestow blessedness, and He takes holy pleasure in the happiness of His people.

That God is good is taught or implied on every page of the Bible and must be received as an article of faith as impregnable as the throne of God. It is a foundation stone for all sound thought about God and is necessary to moral sanity. To allow that God could be other than good is to end in the negation of every moral judgment. If God is not good, then there can be no distinction between kindness and cruelty. Heaven can be hell and hell, Heaven. The goodness of God is the drive behind all the blessings He daily bestows upon us. God created us because He felt good in His heart, and He redeemed us for the same reason.

Julian of Norwich, who lived six hundred years ago, saw clearly that the ground of all blessedness is the goodness of God. Chapter 6 of her *Revelations of Divine Love* begins, "This showing was made to learn our souls to cleave wisely to the goodness of God."[11] She saw that all our religious activities and every means of grace, however right and useful they may be, are nothing until we understand that the unmerited, spontaneous goodness of God is back of all and underneath all His acts.

Divine goodness, as one of God's attributes, is self-caused, infinite, perfect, and eternal. Since God is immutable, He never varies in the intensity of His lovingkindness. He has never been kinder than He is now, nor will He ever be less kind. He is no respecter of persons but makes His sun to shine on the evil as well as on the good, and sends His rain on the just and the unjust. The cause of His goodness is in Himself; the recipients of His goodness are all His beneficiaries without merit and without recompense.

Always God's goodness is the ground of our expectation. There can be no merit in human conduct, not even in the purest and the best. Repentance, though necessary, is not meritorious but a condition for receiving the gracious gift of pardon which God gives of His goodness. Prayer is not in itself meritorious. It lays God under no obligation nor puts Him in debt to any. He hears prayer because He is good, and for no other reason. Nor is faith meritorious; it is simply confidence in the goodness of God, and the lack of it is a reflection upon God's holy character.

The whole outlook of mankind might be changed if we could all believe that we dwell under a friendly sky and that the God of Heaven, though exalted in power and majesty, is eager to be friends with us.

But sin has made us timid and self-conscious, as well it might. Years of rebellion against God have bred in us a fear that cannot be overcome in a day. The captured rebel does not enter willingly the presence of the king he has so long fought unsuccessfully to overthrow. But if he is truly penitent he may come, trusting only in the lovingkindness of his Lord, and the past will not be held against him. Meister Eckhart encourages us to remember that when we return to God, even if our sins were as great in number as all mankind's put together, still God would not count them against us, but would have as much confidence in us as if we had never sinned.[12]

Now someone who in spite of his past sins honestly wants to become reconciled to God may cautiously inquire, "If I come to God, how will He act toward me? What kind of disposition has He? What will I find Him to be like?"

The answer is that He will be found to be exactly like Jesus. "He that has seen me," said Jesus, "has seen the Father."[13] Christ walked with men on earth that He might show them what God is like and make known the true nature of God to a race that had wrong ideas about Him. The greatness of God rouses fear within us, but His goodness encourages us not to be afraid of Him. To fear and not be afraid—that is the paradox of faith.

Mercy

There is nothing in God's justice which forbids the exercise of His mercy. God is never at cross-purposes with Himself. No attribute of God is in conflict with another. God's compassion flows out of His goodness, and goodness without justice is not goodness. God spares us because He is good, but He could not be good if He were not just.

Mercy is an attribute of God, an infinite and inexhaustible energy within the divine nature which disposes God to be actively compassionate. Both the Old and New Testaments proclaim the mercy of God, but the Old Testament has more than four times as much to say about it as the New.

If we could remember that the divine mercy is not a temporary mood but an attribute of God's eternal being, we would no longer fear that it will someday cease to be. Mercy never began to be, but from eternity was; so it will never cease to be. It will never be more since it is in itself infinite, and it will never be less because the infinite cannot suffer diminution. Nothing that has occurred or will occur in Heaven or earth or hell can change the tender mercies of our God. Forever His mercy stands, a boundless, overwhelming immensity of divine pity and compassion. Mercy is the goodness of God confronting human suffering and guilt.

"Kyrie eleison! Christe eleison!" (Lord, have mercy. Christ, have mercy) the church has pleaded through the centuries, but if I mistake not, I hear in the voice of her pleading a note of sadness and despair. Her plaintive cry, so often repeated in that tone of resigned dejection, compels one to infer that she is praying for a boon she never actually expects to receive. Her plea for mercy sounds like a forlorn hope and no more, as if mercy were a heavenly gift to be longed for but never really enjoyed.

It is not enough to believe that [God] once showed mercy to Noah or Abraham or David and will again show mercy in some happy future day. We must believe that God's mercy is boundless, free and, through Jesus Christ our Lord, available to us now in our present situation. We may, if we will, lay hold on the mercy of God by faith, enter the [banquet] hall, and sit down with the bold and avid souls who will not allow diffidence and unbelief to keep them from the feast prepared for them.

Grace

In God mercy and grace are one, but as they teach us they are seen as two, related but not identical.

As mercy is God's goodness confronting human misery and guilt, so grace is His goodness directed toward human debt and demerit. It is by His grace that God imputes merit where none previously existed and declares no debt to be where one had been before.

Grace is the good pleasure of God that inclines Him to bestow benefits upon the undeserving. Grace takes its rise far back in the heart of God, in the awful and incomprehensible abyss of His holy being, but the channel through which it flows out to men is Jesus Christ, crucified and risen. The Apostle Paul, who beyond all others is the exponent of grace in redemption, never dissociates God's grace from God's crucified Son. John also in the Gospel that bears his name identifies Christ as the medium through which grace reaches mankind. "For the law was given by Moses, but grace and truth came by Jesus Christ."[14]

No one was ever saved other than by grace, from Abel to the present moment. Grace indeed came by Jesus Christ, but it did not wait for His birth in the manger or His death on the cross before it became operative. Christ is the Lamb slain from the foundation of the world.[15] The grace of God is infinite and eternal. As it had no beginning, so it can have no end; and being an attribute of God, it is as boundless as infinity.

Love

The phrase "God is love" means that love is an essential attribute of God. We do not know, and we may never know what love is, but we can know how it manifests itself, and that is enough for us here. First we see it showing itself as good will. Love wills the good of all and never wills harm or evil to any.

A child lost in a crowded store is full of fear because it

sees the strangers around it as enemies. In its mother's arms a moment later all the terror subsides. The known good will of the mother casts out fear.

The world is full of enemies, and as long as we are subject to the possibility of harm from these enemies, fear is inevitable. The effort to conquer fear without removing the cause is altogether futile. The heart is wiser than the apostles of tranquility. As long as we must trust for survival to our ability to out-think or out-maneuver the enemy, we have every good reason to be afraid. And fear has torment.

To know that love is of God and to enter into the secret place leaning upon the arm of the Beloved—this and only this can cast out fear. Let a man become convinced that nothing can harm him, and instantly for him all fear goes out of the universe. The nervous reflex, the natural revulsion to physical pain may be felt sometimes, but the deep torment of fear is gone forever. God is love and God is sovereign.

The love of God is one of the great realities of the universe, a pillar upon which the hope of the world rests. But it is a personal, intimate thing, too. God does not love populations; He loves people. He loves not masses, but men. He loves us all with a mighty love that has no beginning and can have no end.

[It is] characteristic of love that it takes pleasure in its object. God enjoys His creation. The Apostle John says frankly that God's purpose in creation was His own pleasure. God is happy in His love for all that He has made. We cannot miss the feeling of pleasure in God's delighted references to His handiwork. "The glory of the Lord shall endure forever; the Lord shall rejoice in his works."[16]

The Lord takes peculiar pleasure in His saints. Many think of God as far removed, gloomy, and mightily displeased with everything; but this is to think erroneously. True, God hates sin and can never look with pleasure upon iniquity, but where men seek to do God's will He responds in genuine affection. In Christ all believing souls are objects of God's delight. "The Lord your God is with you, he is mighty to save. He will take great delight in you, he will quiet you with his love, he will rejoice over you with singing."[17]

In Christian experience there is a highly satisfying love content that distinguishes it from all other religions and elevates it to heights far beyond even the purest and noblest philosophy. This love content is more than a thing; it is God Himself in the midst of His church singing over his people. True Christian joy is the heart's harmonious response to the Lord's song of love.

Sovereignty

God's sovereignty is the attribute by which He rules His entire creation, and to be sovereign God must be all-knowing, all-powerful, and absolutely free. Were He less than free, He must be less than sovereign.

While a complete explanation of the origin of sin eludes us, there are a few things we do know. In His sovereign wisdom God has permitted evil to exist in carefully restricted areas of His creation, a kind of fugitive outlaw whose activities are temporary and limited in scope. In doing this God has acted according to His infinite wisdom and goodness. More than that no one knows at present, and more than that no one needs to know. The name of God is sufficient guarantee of the perfection of His words.

Another real problem created by the doctrine of the divine sovereignty has to do with the will of man. If God rules His universe by His sovereign decrees, how is it possible for man to exercise free choice? And if he cannot exercise freedom of choice, how can he be held responsible for his conduct? Is he not a mere puppet whose actions are determined by a behind-the-scenes God who pulls the strings as it pleases Him?

The attempt to answer these questions has divided the Christian church neatly into two camps which have borne the names of two distinguished theologians, Jacobus Arminius and John Calvin.[18] Most Christians are content to get into one camp or the other and deny either sovereignty to God or free will to man. It appears possible, however, to reconcile these two positions without doing violence to either.

Here is my view: God sovereignly decreed that man should be free to exercise moral choice, and man from the beginning has fulfilled that decree by making his choice between good and evil. When he chooses to do evil, he does not thereby countervail the sovereign will of God but fulfils it, inasmuch as the eternal decree decided not which choice the man should make but that he should be free to make it. Man's will is free because God is sovereign. A God less than sovereign could not bestow moral freedom upon His creatures.

Perhaps a homely illustration might help us to understand. An ocean liner leaves New York bound for Liverpool. Its destination has been determined by proper authorities. Nothing can change it. This is at least a faint picture of sovereignty. On board the liner are several scores of passengers. They are not in chains, neither are their activities determined for them by decree. They are completely free to move about as they will. They eat, sleep, play, lounge about on the deck, read, talk altogether as they please, but all the while the great liner is carrying them steadily toward a predetermined port.

Both freedom and sovereignty are present here, and they do not contradict each other. So it is, I believe, with man's freedom and the sovereignty of God. The mighty liner of God's sovereign design keeps its steady course over the sea of history. God moves undisturbed and unhindered toward the fulfillment of those eternal purposes which He purposed in Christ Jesus before the world began. We do not know all that is included in those purposes, but enough has been disclosed to furnish us with a broad outline of things to come and to give us good hope and firm assurance of future well-being.

We must all choose whether we will obey the gospel or turn away in unbelief and reject its authority. Our choice is our own, but the consequences of the choice have already been determined by the sovereign will of God, and from this there is no appeal.

Conclusion

To know God is at once the easiest and the most difficult thing in the world. It is easy because the knowledge is not won by hard mental toil, but is something freely given. As sunshine falls free on the open field, so the knowledge of the holy God is a free gift to men who are open to receive it. But this knowledge is difficult because there are conditions to be met, and the obstinate nature of fallen man does not take kindly to them. Let me present a summary of these conditions as taught by the Bible.

First, we must forsake our sins. Second, there must be an utter committal of the whole life to Christ in faith. Third, there must be a reckoning of ourselves to have died to sin and to be alive to God in Christ Jesus, followed by a throwing open of the entire personality to the inflow of the Holy Spirit. We must practice whatever self-discipline is required to walk in the Spirit and trample under our feet the lusts of the flesh. Fourth, we must boldly repudiate the cheap values of the fallen world. Fifth, we must practice the art of long and loving meditation upon the majesty of God. Sixth, as the knowledge of God becomes more wonderful, greater service to our fellow men will become for us imperative. Any intensified knowledge of God will soon begin to affect those around us in the Christian community.

There is a glorified Man on the right hand of the Majesty in heaven faithfully representing us there. We are left for a season among men; let us faithfully represent Him here.

NOTES

1. Job 22:21.
2. Job 11:7-8.
3. Psalm 42:7.
4. Julian of Norwich (1342-1413), *Revelations of Divine Love* (London: Methuen, 1911).

5. Cf. C. S. Lewis, "Time and Beyond Time" in *Mere Christianity* (New York: Macmillan, 1967).
6. Cf. Ecclesiastes 3:11 (NIV).
7. H. L. Mencken, *A New Dictionary of Quotations* (New York: Alfred A. Knopf, 1942).
8. Novatian (d. 258), *On the Trinity* (New York: Macmillan, 1919).
9. Psalm 147:5.
10. Genesis 1:31.
11. Julian, *op.cit.*
12. Meister Eckhart (c. 1260-1327), Dominican mystic. No reference given.
13. John 14:9.
14. John 1:17.
15. Revelation 13:8.
16. Psalm 104:31.
17. Zephaniah 3:17 (NIV).
18. Jacobus Arminius (1560-1609), Dutch theologian, expounded the doctrine of free will. John Calvin (Jean Cauvin, 1509-1564), French reformer, defended determinism and predestination.

Corrie ten Boom, 1892-1982

Without question Cornelia Arnolda Johanna ten Boom ranks as one of the twentieth century's outstanding women. Plunged into a long night of horror, she came out singing. A lifelong spinster who was early frustrated in love, she found a Love far greater. It enabled her to endure an incredible prison ordeal that robbed her of her father and sister; but because she shared this new Love, she became an inspiration to millions. "Corrie," as she was known everywhere, gave three decades of her life to a magnificent worldwide ministry, lifting up the name of Jesus whom she rejoiced to call "the Victor."

The story of Ravensbruck, told in these pages, provides a vivid look at the curse the Nazi movement laid on the people of Europe during the years 1933-1945, and particularly after World War II began in 1939. Cornelia was delivered from the concentration camp, but her sister was not. What makes the story so memorable is the release of spiritual power that enabled the whole ten Boom family to reach out to their persecuted Jewish neighbors, to give them shelter, and then after being arrested for their "crime," to rise above the common levels of hate and revenge to forgiveness and love.

Corrie ministered in sixty-three countries around the world during the postwar years, becoming in her own words a "tramp for the Lord." Fulfilling a vow she made at Ravensbruck, she set out virtually alone at the age of fifty-three to tell the world about Jesus. She lived out of a suitcase for the next thirty years, visiting the prisons of Africa, picking her way through the muddy war zones of Vietnam, carrying Bibles behind the iron curtain, and sleeping at times in the palaces of royalty, always on the move, always talking up her Lord, and always with a twinkle in her clear blue eyes.

Her dozen books, translated into scores of languages, have been read by millions. She appeared in five motion pictures. She was honored by kings and queens, by presidents, by Indian chiefs, by the government of Israel, by civic leaders, by publishers, by schools, by churches, and by ordinary people in nation after nation, including Germany.

In 1977, thirty-three years to the day after Corrie's arrest for harboring Jews in an upper room of the family home, she moved into a house of her own in southern California. Here, at eighty-five years of age, she engaged in an active ministry, counseling by telephone, writing books, publishing a magazine, visiting prisons, supporting her missionary programs, and turning out films.

It was not to last. In July, 1978, in Denver, Colorado, people from all over the world paid tribute to Corrie, who was guest of honor at the annual Christian Booksellers' Convention. One month later she suffered a severe stroke. A second stroke made it impossible for her to speak. For nearly five years she remained bedridden until the Lord called her to Himself on her ninety-first birthday in 1982. But even in the long silences Corrie ten Boom retained the faith and serenity that had sustained her to the very gates of hell and back, and which she in turn bequeathed to so many people around the world. Hers was the peace of Jesus, the Victor.

The following pages are reproduced by permission from her book The Hiding Place, *written with John and Elizabeth Sherrill, first published in 1971 by Chosen Books, Inc., Chappaqua, New York 10514.*

NINE

RAVENSBRUCK
by Corrie ten Boom
with John and Elizabeth Sherrill

The small freight car was getting crowded. We were being shoved against the back wall; and still the soldiers drove women over the side, cursing, jabbing with their guns. Shrieks rose from the center of the car as the press increased. Thirty or forty people were all that could fit in; but it was only when eighty women were packed inside that the door thumped shut and we heard iron bolts driven into place.

It was hours before the train gave a sudden lurch and began to move. Almost at once it stopped, then again crawled forward. The rest of the day and into the night it was the same, stopping, starting, slamming, jerking. At dawn someone called out that we were passing through the border town of Emmerich.

We had arrived in Germany.

For two more incredible days and two more nights we were carried deeper and deeper into the land of our fears. Occasionally one of the loaves of bread was passed from hand to hand. But not even the most elementary provision had been made for sanitation, and the air in the car was such that few could eat.

Gradually, more terrible than the crush of bodies and the filth, the single obsession was—something to drink. Two or three times when the train stopped, the door was slid open a few inches and a pail of water passed in. But we had become animals, incapable of plan or system. Those near the door got it all.

At last, the morning of the fourth day, the train stopped and the door was opened its full width. Like infants, on hands and knees, we crawled to the opening and lowered ourselves over the side. In front of us was a smiling blue lake. On the far side, among sycamore trees, rose a white church steeple. The stronger prisoners hauled buckets of water from the lake. We drank through cracked and swollen lips. Only a handful of soldiers, some of them looking no older than fifteen, were there to guard a thousand women. No more were needed. We could scarcely walk, let alone resist.

After awhile they got us into straggly columns and marched us off. For a mile the road followed the shore of the lake, then left it to climb a hill. I wondered if [my sister] Betsie could make it to the top, but the sight of trees and sky seemed to have revived her and she supported me as much as I her. From the crest of the hill we saw it, like a vast scar on the green German landscape—a city of low gray barracks surrounded by concrete walls on which guard towers rose at intervals. In the very center a square smokestack emitted a thin gray vapor into the sky.

Ravensbruck!

Like a whispered curse the word passed back through the lines. This was the notorious women's extermination camp whose name we had heard even in Haarlem. That squat concrete building, that smoke disappearing in the bright sunlight—no! I would not look at it. As Betsie and I stumbled down the hill, I felt the Bible bumping between my shoulder blades. God's good news. Was it to this world that He had spoken it?

Now we were close enough to see the skull-and-crossbones posted at intervals on the walls to warn of electrified wiring along the top. The massive iron gates swung in; we marched between them. Acres of soot-gray barracks stretched ahead of us. Just inside the wall was a row of waist-high water spigots. We charged them, thrusting hands, arms, legs, even heads under the streams of water, washing away the stench of the boxcars. A squad of women guards in dark blue uniforms rushed at us, hauling and shouting, swinging their short, hard crops.

At last they drove us back from the faucets and herded us down an avenue between barracks. This camp appeared far grimmer than the one we had left. At least, in marches about Vught, we had caught sight of fields and woods. Here every vista ended in the same concrete barrier; the camp was set down in a vast man-made valley rising on every side to those towering wire-topped walls.

At last we halted. In front of us a vast canvas tent-roof— no sides—covered an acre or more of straw-strewn ground. Betsie and I found a spot on the edge of this area and sank gratefully down. Instantly we were on our feet again. Lice! The straw was literally alive with them. We stood for awhile, clutching blankets and pillowcases well away from the infested ground. But at last we spread our blankets over the squirming straw and sat on them.

Some of the prisoners had brought scissors from Vught; everywhere beneath the huge tent women were cutting one another's hair. A pair was passed to us. Of course we must do the same; long hair was folly in such a place. But as I cut Betsie's chestnut waves, I cried.

Toward evening there was a commotion at one end of the tent. A line of SS guards was moving across it, driving women out from under the canvas. We scrambled to our feet and snatched up our blankets as they bore down upon us. Perhaps a hundred yards beyond the tent the chase stopped. We stood about, uncertain what to do. Whether a new group of prisoners had arrived or what was the reason for driving us from the tent, no one knew. Women began spreading their blankets on the hard cinder ground. Slowly it dawned on Betsie and me that we were to spend the night here where we stood. We laid my blanket on the ground, stretched out side by side and pulled hers over us.

"The night is dark and I am far from home." Betsie's sweet soprano was picked up by voices all around us. "Lead thou me on . . . "

We were awakened some time in the middle of the night by a clap of thunder and a deluge of rain. The blankets soaked through, and water gathered in puddles beneath us. In the morning the field was a vast sodden swamp; hands, clothes, and faces were black from the cinder mud.

We were still wringing water from our blanket when the command came to line up for coffee. It was not coffee but a thin liquid of approximately the same color, and we were grateful to get it as we shuffled double-file past the makeshift field kitchen. There was a slice of black bread for each prisoner, too, then nothing more until we were given a ladle of turnip soup and a small boiled potato late in the afternoon.

In between we were kept standing at rigid attention on the soggy parade ground where we had spent the night. We were near one edge of the huge camp here, close enough to the outer wall to see the triple row of electric wires running along the top. Two entire days we spent this way, stretching out again the second night right where we stood. It did not rain again, but ground and blankets were still damp. Betsie began to cough. I took Nollie's blue sweater from my pillowcase, wrapped it around her, and gave her a few drops of the vitamin oil. But by morning she had agonizing intestinal cramps. Again and again throughout that second day she had to ask the impatient woman monitor at the head of our row for permission to go to the ditch that served as sanitary facility.

It was the third night as we were getting ready to lie down again under the sky when the order came to report to the processing center for new arrivals. A ten-minute march brought us to the building. We inched along a corridor into a huge reception room, and there under the harsh ceiling lights we saw a dismal sight. As each woman reached a desk where some officers sat, she had to lay her blanket, pillowcase, and whatever else she carried onto a growing pile of these things. A few desks further along she had to strip off every scrap of clothes, throw them onto a second pile, and walk naked past the scrutiny of a dozen SS men into the shower room.

Coming out of the shower she wore only a thin prison dress and a pair of shoes. Nothing more.

But Betsie needed that sweater! She needed the vitamins! Most of all, we needed our Bible. How could we live in this place without it? But how could I ever take it past so many watchful eyes without the overalls covering it? We were almost at the first desk. I fished desperately in my pillowcase, drew out the bottle of vitamins, and closed my fist around them. Reluctantly we dropped the other things on the heap that was fast becoming a mountain. "Dear God," I prayed, "You have given us this precious Book. You have kept it hidden through checkpoints and inspections. You have used it for so many—"

I felt Betsie stagger against me and looked at her in alarm. Her face was white, her lips pressed tight together. A guard was passing by; I begged him in German to show us the toilets. Without so much as a glance, he jerked his head in the direction of the shower room. Timidly Betsie and I stepped out of line and walked to the door of the big, dank-smelling room with its row on row of overhead spigots. It was empty, waiting for the next batch of fifty naked and shivering women to be admitted.

"Please," I said to the SS man guarding the door, "where are the toilets?"

He did not look at me either. "Use the drain holes," he snapped, and as we stepped inside he slammed the door behind us. We stood alone in the room where a few minutes later we would return stripped even of the clothes on our backs. Here were the prison things we we were to put on, piled just inside the door. From the front and back of each otherwise ordinary dress a large "X" had been cut out and replaced with cloth of another color. And then we saw something else—stacked in the far corner, a pile of old wooden benches. They were slimy with mildew, crawling with cockroaches, but to me they seemed the furniture of heaven itself.

"The sweater! Take off the sweater!" I hissed, fumbling with the string at my neck. Betsie handed it to me, and in an instant I had wrapped it around the Bible and the vitamin bottle and stuffed the precious bundle behind the benches. And so it was that when we were herded into that room ten minutes later we were not poor, but rich. Rich in new evidence of the care of Him who was God even of Ravensbruck.

We stood beneath the spigots as long as the flow of icy water lasted, feeling it soften our lice-eaten skin. Then we clustered dripping wet around the heap of prison dresses, holding them up, looking for approximate fits. I found a loose long-sleeved dress for Betsie that would cover the blue sweater when she would have a chance to put it on. I squirmed into another dress for myself, then reached behind the benches and shoved the little bundle quickly inside the neck. It made a bulge you could have seen across the Grote Markt. I flattened it out as best I could, pushing it down, tugging the sweater around my waist, but there was no real concealing it beneath the thin cotton dress. And all the while I had the incredible feeling that it didn't matter, that this was not my business, but God's. That all I had to do was walk straight ahead.

As we trooped back through the shower room door, the SS men ran their hands over every prisoner, front, back, and sides. The woman ahead of me was searched three times. Behind me, Betsie was searched. No hand touched me.

At the exit door to the building was a second ordeal, a line of women guards examining each prisoner again. I slowed down as I reached them, but the Aufseherin in charge shoved me roughly by the shoulder. "Move along! You're holding up the line!"

And so Betsie and I arrived at Barracks 8 in the small hours of the morning, bringing not only the Bible, but a new knowledge of the power of Him whose story it was. Three women were already asleep in the bed assigned to us. They made room for us as best they could, but the mattress sloped and I kept sliding to the floor.

At last all five of us lay sideways across the bed and managed to get shoulders and elbows arranged. The blanket was a poor threadbare affair compared with the ones we had given up, but at least the overcrowding produced its own warmth. Betsie had put on the blue sweater beneath her long-sleeved dress, and as she was wedged now between me and the others, her shivering gradually subsided and she was asleep. I lay awake awhile longer, watching a searchlight sweep the rear wall in long regular arcs, hearing the distant calls of soldiers patrolling the walls. . . .

* * *

Morning roll call at Ravensbruck came half an hour earlier than at Vught. By 4:30 a.m. we had to be mustered outside in the black predawn chill, standing at parade attention in blocks of one hundred women, ten wide, ten deep. Sometimes after hours of this we would gain the shelter of the barracks only to hear the whistle.

"Everybody out! Fall in for roll call!"

Barracks 8 was in the quarantine compound. Next to us—perhaps as a deliberate warning to newcomers—were located the punishment barracks. From there all day long and often into the night came the sounds of hell itself. They were not the sounds of anger or of any human emotion, but of a cruelty altogether detached—blows landing in regular rhythm, screams keeping pace. We would stand in our ten-deep ranks with our hands trembling at our sides, longing to jam them against our ears to make the sounds stop.

At the instant of dismissal we would mob the door of Barracks 8, stepping on each other's heels in our eagerness to get inside, to shrink the world back to understandable proportions.

It grew harder and harder. Even within these four walls there was too much misery, too much seemingly pointless suffering. Every day something else failed to make sense, something else grew too heavy. "Will you carry this too, Lord Jesus?"

But as the rest of the world grew stranger, one thing became increasingly clear, and that was the reason the two of us were here. Why others should suffer we were not shown. As for us, from morning until lights-out, whenever we were not in ranks for roll call, our Bible was the center of an ever-widening circle of help and hope. Like waifs clustered around a blazing fire, we gathered about it, holding out our hearts to its warmth and light. The blacker the night around us grew, the brighter and truer and more beautiful burned the word of God.

"Who shall separate us from the love of Christ? Shall tribulation, or distress, or persecution, or famine, or nakedness, or peril, or sword? . . . Nay, in all these things we are more than conquerors through him that loved us."[1]

I would look about us as Betsie read, watching the light leap from face to face. " More than conquerors." It was not a wish. It was a fact. We knew it, we experienced it minute by minute—poor, hated, hungry. We are more than conquerors. Not "we shall be." We are! Life in Ravensbruck took place on two separate levels, mutually impossible. One, the observable, external life, grew every day more horrible. The other, the life we lived with God, grew daily better, truth upon truth, glory upon glory.

Sometimes I would slip the Bible from its little sack with hands that shook, so mysterious had it become to me. It was new; it had just been written. I marveled sometimes that the ink was dry. I had believed the Bible always, but reading it now had nothing to do with belief. It was simply a description of the way things were—of hell and heaven, of how men act and how God acts. I had read a thousand times the story of Jesus' arrest—how soldiers had slapped Him, laughed at Him, flogged Him. Now such happenings had faces and voices.

Fridays—the recurrent humiliation of medical inspection. The hospital corridor in which we waited was unheated, and a fall chill had settled into the walls. Still we were forbidden even to wrap ourselves in our own arms, but had to maintain our erect, hands-at-sides position as we filed slowly past a phalanx of grinning guards. How there could have been any pleasure in the sight of these stick-thin legs and hunger-bloated stomachs I could not imagine. Surely there is no more wretched sight than the human body unloved and uncared for. Nor could I see the necessity for the complete undressing. When we finally reached the examining room, a doctor looked down each throat; another (a dentist presumably) at our teeth, a third in between each finger. And that was all. We trooped again down the long, cold corridor and picked up our X-marked dresses at the door.

It was one of these mornings while we were waiting, shivering in the corridor, that yet another page in the Bible leapt into life for me.

He hung naked on the cross.

I had not known—I had not thought . . . The paintings, the carved crucifixes showed at the least a scrap of cloth. But this, I suddenly knew, was the respect and reverence of the artist. But oh, at the time itself, on that other Friday morning—there had been no reverence. No more than I saw in the faces around us now.

I leaned toward Betsie, ahead of me in line. Her shoulder blades stood out sharp and thin beneath her blue-mottled skin.

"Betsie, they took His clothes too."[2]

Ahead of me I heard a little gasp. "Oh, Corrie. And I never thanked Him . . . "

Each day the sun rose a little later, and the bite took longer to leave the air. It will be better, everyone assured everyone else, when we move into permanent barracks. We'll have a blanket apiece. A bed of our own. Each of us painted into the picture her own greatest need. For me it was a dispensary where Betsie could get medication for her cough. "There'll be a nurse assigned to the barracks." I said it so often that I convinced myself.

The move to permanent quarters came the second week in October. We were marched ten abreast along a wide cinder avenue and then into a narrower street of barracks. Several times the column halted while numbers were read out— names were never used at Ravensbruck. At last Betsie's and mine were called: "Prisoner 66729, Prisoner 66730." We stepped out of line with a dozen or so others and stared at the long gray front of Barracks 28. Half its windows seemed to have been broken and replaced with rags. A door in the center let us into a large room where two hundred or more women bent over knitting needles. On tables between them were piles of woolen socks in army gray.

On either side doors opened into two still larger rooms—by far the largest dormitories we had yet seen. Betsie and I followed a prisoner-guide through the door at the right. Because of the broken windows the vast room was in semi-twilight. Our noses told us, first, that the place was filthy; somewhere plumbing had backed up. The bedding was soiled and rancid. Then as our eyes adjusted to the gloom we saw that there were no individual beds at all, but great square piers stacked three high and wedged side by side and end to end with only an occasional narrow aisle slicing through.

We followed our guide single file (the aisle was not wide enough for two) fighting back the claustrophobia of these platforms rising everywhere above us. The tremendous room was nearly empty of people; they must have been out on various work crews. At last she pointed to a second tier in the center of a large block. To reach it we had to stand on the bottom level, haul ourselves up, and then crawl across three other straw-covered platforms to reach the one that we would share with—how many? The deck above us was too close to let us sit up. We lay back, struggling against the nausea that swept over us from the reeking straw. We could hear the women who had arrived with us finding their places.

Suddenly I sat up, striking my head on the cross-slats above. Something had pinched my leg.

"Fleas!" I cried. "Betsie, the place is swarming with them!"

We scrambled across the intervening platforms, heads low to avoid another bump, dropped down to the aisle, and edged our way to a patch of light.

"Here! And here another one!" I wailed. "Betsie, how can we live in such a place?"

"Show us. Show us how." It was said so matter of factly that it took me a second to realize she was praying. More and more the distinction between prayer and the rest of life seemed to be vanishing for Betsie. "Corrie!" she said excitedly, "He's given us the answer. Before we asked, as He always does. In the Bible this morning. Where was it? Read that part again!"

I glanced down the long dim aisle to make sure no guard was in sight, then drew the Bible from its pouch. "It was in 1 Thessalonians," I said. We were on our third complete reading of the New Testament since leaving Scheveningen. In the feeble light I turned the pages. "Here it is, 'Comfort the frightened, help the weak, be patient with everyone. See that none of you repays evil for evil, but always seek to do good to one another and to all.'"[3] It seemed written expressly to Ravensbruck.

"Go on," said Betsie, "that wasn't all."

"Oh yes, '. . . to one another and to all. Rejoice always, pray constantly, give thanks in all circumstances; for this is the will of God in Christ Jesus.'"[4]

"That's it, Corrie! That's His answer. 'Give thanks in all circumstances!' That's what we can do. We can start right now to thank God for every single thing about this new barracks."

I stared at her, then around me at the dark, foul-aired room.

"Such as?" I asked.

"Such as being assigned here together."

I bit my lip. "Oh, yes, Lord Jesus!"

"Such as what you're holding in your hands."

I looked down at the Bible. "Yes! Thank you, dear Lord, that there was no inspection when we entered here. Thank you for all the women here in this room who will meet you in these pages."

"Yes," said Betsie. "Thank you for the very crowding here. Since we're packed so close, that many more will hear!" She looked at me expectantly. "Corrie!" she prodded.

"Oh, all right. Thank you for the jammed, crammed, stuffed, packed, suffocating crowds."

"Thank you," Betsie went on serenely, "for the fleas and—"

The fleas! This was too much. "Betsie, there's no way even God can make me grateful for a flea."

"'Give thanks in all circumstances,'" she quoted. "It doesn't say, 'in pleasant circumstances.' Fleas are part of this place where God has put us."

And so we stood between piers of bunks and gave thanks for fleas. But this time I was sure Betsie was wrong.

*   *   *

They started arriving soon after six o'clock, the women of Barracks 28, tired, sweat-stained, and dirty from the long forced-labor details. The building, we learned from one of our platform mates, had been designed to hold four hundred. There were now fourteen hundred quartered here with more arriving weekly as concentration camps in Poland, France, Belgium, Austria as well as Holland were evacuated toward the center of Germany.

There were nine of us sharing our particular square, designed for four, and some grumbled as they discovered they would have to make room for Betsie and me. Eight acrid and overflowing toilets served the entire room; to reach them we had to crawl not only over our own bedmates but over those on the other platforms between us and the closest aisle, always at the risk of adding too much weight to the already sagging slats and crashing down on the people beneath. It happened several times that first night. From somewhere in the room would come a splintering sound, a shriek, smothered cries.

Even when the slats held, the least movement on the upper platforms sent a shower of dust and straw over the sleepers below, followed by a volley of curses. In Barracks 8 most of us had been Dutch. Here there was not even a common language, and among the exhausted, ill-fed people quarrels erupted constantly.

There was one raging now as the women sleeping nearest the windows slammed them shut against the cold. At once scores of voices demanded that they be raised again. Brawls were starting all up and down that side of the room. We heard scuffling, slaps, sobs. In the dark I felt Betsie's hands clasp mine. "Lord Jesus," she said aloud, "send your peace into this room. There has been too little praying here. The very walls know it. But where You come, Lord, the spirit of strife cannot exist. . . . "

The change was gradual but distinct. One by one the angry sounds let up.

"I'll make you a deal." The voice spoke German with a strong Scandinavian accent. "You can sleep in here where it's warmer, and I'll take your place by the window."

"And add your lice to my own. No thanks." But there was a chuckle in the answer.

"I'll tell you what." The third voice had a French burr. "We'll open them halfway. That way we'll only be half-frozen and you'll be only half-smothered."

A ripple of laughter widened around the room at this. I lay back on the sour straw and knew there was one more circumstance for which I could give thanks. Betsie had come to Barracks 28.

Roll call came at 4:30 A.M. here as it had in quarantine. A whistle roused us at 4:00 when, without even shaking the straw from clothes and hair, the stampede began for the ration of bread and coffee in the center room. Lastcomers found none.

The count was made in the Lagerstrasse, the wide avenue leading to the hospital. There we joined the occupants of the other barracks—some 35,000 at that time—stretching out of sight in the pale glow of the street lamps, feet growing numb on the cold cinder ground.

After roll call, work crews were called out. For weeks Betsie and I were assigned to the Siemens factory. This huge complex of mills and railroad terminals was a mile and a half from the camp. The "Siemens Brigade," several thousand of us, marched out the iron gate beneath the charged wires into a world of trees and grass and horizons. The sun rose as we skirted the little lake; the gold of the late fall fields lifted our hearts.

The work at Siemens, however, was sheer misery. Betsie and I had to push a heavy handcart to a railroad siding where we unloaded large metal plates from a boxcar and wheeled them to a receiving gate at the factory. The grueling workday lasted eleven hours. At least, at noontime we were given a boiled potato and some thin soup; those who worked inside the camp had no midday meal. Returning to camp, we could barely lift our swollen and aching legs. The soldiers patrolling us bellowed and cursed, but we could only shuffle forward inches at a step. I noticed again how the local people turned their eyes another way.

Back at the barracks we formed yet another line to receive our ladle of turnip soup in the center room. Then as quickly as we could for the press of people, we made our way to the rear of the dormitory room where we held our worship "service." Around our own platform area there was not enough light to read the Bible, but back here a small light bulb cast a wan yellow circle on the wall, and here an ever larger group of women gathered.

They were services like no others, these times in Barracks 28. A single meeting might include a recital of the Magnificat in Latin by a group of Roman Catholics, a whispered hymn by some Lutherans, and a sotto-voce chant by Eastern Orthodox women. With each moment the crowd around us would swell, packing the nearby platforms, hanging over the edges, until the high structures groaned and swayed.

At last either Betsie or I would open the Bible. Because only the Hollanders could understand the Dutch text, we would translate aloud in German. Then we would hear the life-giving words passed back along the aisles in French, Polish, Russian, Czech, and back into Dutch. They were little previews of heaven, these evenings beneath the light bulb. I would think of Haarlem, each substantial church set behind its wrought-iron fence and its barrier of doctrine. And I would know again that in darkness God's truth shines most clearly.

At first Betsie and I called these meetings with great

timidity. But as night after night went by and no guard ever came near us, we grew bolder. So many now wanted to join us that we held a second service after evening roll call. There on the Lagerstrasse we were under rigid surveillance, guards in their warm wool capes marching constantly up and down. It was the same in the center room of the barracks; half a dozen guards or camp police always present. Yet in the large dormitory room there was almost no supervision at all. We did not understand it.

* * *

Call-ups for the Siemens factory ceased, and we speculated that it had been hit in one of the bombing raids that came within earshot almost nightly now. Betsie and I were put to work leveling some rough ground just inside the camp wall. This too was backbreaking labor. Sometimes as I bent to lift my load my heart cramped strangely; at night spasms of pain gripped my legs.

But the biggest problem was Betsie's strength. One morning after a hard night's rain we arrived to find the ground sodden and heavy. Betsie had never been able to lift much; today her shovelfuls were microscopic and she stumbled frequently as she walked to the low ground where we dumped the loads.

"*Schneller!*" a guard screamed at her. "Can't you go faster?"

As I sank my shovel into the black muck I wondered, why must they scream? Why couldn't they speak like ordinary human beings?

"Loafer! Lazy swine!" The guard snatched Betsie's shovel from her hands and ran from group to group of the digging crew, exhibiting the handful of dirt that was all Betsie had been able to lift.

"Look what Madame Baroness is carrying! Surely she will overexert herself!"

The other guards and even some of the prisoners laughed. Encouraged, the guard threw herself into a parody of Betsie's faltering walk. A male guard was with our detail today, and in the presence of a man the women guards were always animated. As the laughter grew, I felt a murderous anger rise. The guard was young and well-fed—was it Betsie's fault that she was old and starving? But to my astonishment, Betsie too was laughing.

"That's me all right," she admitted. "But you'd better let me teeter along with my little spoonful, or I'll have to stop altogether."

The guard's plump cheeks went crimson. "I'll decide who's to stop!" And snatching the leather crop from her belt, she slashed Betsie across the chest and neck.

Without knowing I was doing it, I seized my shovel and rushed at her. Betsie stepped in front of me before anyone had seen. "Corrie!" she pleaded, dragging my arm to my side. "Corrie, keep working!" She tugged the shovel from my hand and dug it into the mud. Contemptuously the guard tossed Betsie's shovel toward us. I picked it up, all in a daze. A red stain appeared on Betsie's collar, a welt began to swell on her neck.

Betsie saw where I was looking and laid a bird-thin hand over the whip mark. "Don't look at it, Corrie. Look at Jesus only." She took away her hand: it was sticky with blood.

*   *   *

One evening I got back to the barracks late from a wood-gathering foray outside the walls. A light snow lay on the ground, and it was hard to find the sticks and twigs with which a small stove was kept going in each room. Betsie was waiting for me, as always, so that we could wait through the food line together. Her eyes were twinkling.

"You're looking extraordinarily pleased with yourself," I told her.

"You know we've never understood why we had so much freedom in the big room," she said. "Well—I've found out."

That afternoon, she said, there'd been confusion in her

knitting group about sock sizes, and they'd asked the super-visor to come and settle it. "But she wouldn't. She wouldn't step through the door and neither would the guards. And you know why?" Betsie could not keep the triumph from her voice. "Because of the fleas! That's what she said, 'That place is crawling with fleas!'"

I remembered Betsie's bowed head, and remembered her thanks to God for creatures I could see no use for.

*   *   *

On December 31, 1944, Corrie ten Boom was discharged from Ravensbruck concentration camp through a clerical error. She later learned that one week after her departure, all women prisoners her age were taken to the gas chambers. The death toll at Ravensbruck under the Nazis is estimated at 96,000.

NOTES

1. Romans 8:35-37.
2. Luke 23:34.
3. 1 Thessalonians 5:14-15.
4. 1 Thessalonians 5:16-18.

Carl F. H. Henry, 1913-

For the past forty-some years Carl Ferdinand Howard Henry has been striding across the religious landscape in seven-leagued boots. He was and is, without doubt, the most important living evangelical theologian in the world. A strapping, engaging, convincing defender of the orthodox faith, he has cut his own swath between the marshes of liberalism and the gravel pits of extreme fundamentalism. Yet for all that, he has maintained an irenic posture toward both sides even while denying or decrying some of their dearest assumptions.

The eldest son of German immigrants, Carl Henry was born in New York City and grew up in Central Islip, Long Island. By age nineteen he had become editor of his county's largest weekly newspaper, and for the rest of his life would combine the roles of journalist and scholar. After his conversion in 1933 and his subsequent academic studies, which culminated in a doctor of philosophy degree from Boston University, Henry became a brilliant communicator of Christian truth. Whether from the pulpit, lecture platform, or in print, he has shown an amazing ability to take any theological subject, such as the attributes of God, for example, and present it in clear, understandable terms.

But Henry was more than an able interpreter of the evangelical position in a highly skeptical postwar world. A creative thinker, he had some questions of his own regarding the American church scene, and in 1946 began writing some articles that asked whether the evangelical community was interested only in self-circumscribed, ingrown salvation, or whether it really delineated and implemented a consistent world-life view. Eerdmans published them the following year as chapters *in a small book priced at one dollar under the title* The Uneasy Conscience of Modern Fundamentalism.

Today that small book is recognized as the turning point in the development of an evangelical social conscience, although in 1947 it was bitterly attacked for its challenge to fundamentalism. Henry shortly afterward became one of four original faculty members at the newly opened Fuller Theological Seminary in Pasadena, California. In 1956 his newspaper background, his Biblical and philosophical training, and his strong personal Christian convictions admirably qualified him to be editor of a new national, evangelical publication founded by Billy Graham, to be known as Christianity Today.

Ten inches of type are required in Who's Who in the World *to list the positions, writings, and honors that have come to Carl Henry since those early days. He married and reared a family, traveled the world, published major works in theology, chaired international consultations, and taught thousands of students. He continues today to be in demand on every continent. His wisdom, imbued by the Spirit of God, has settled many a theological difference among believers.*

The following reflections on the resurrection of Jesus Christ are gathered by permission from Carl Henry's published works: New Strides of Faith *(Chicago: Moody Press, 1972);* God, Revelation and Authority, *volume 3 (Waco, TX: Word, 1979);* Christian Countermoves in a Decadent Culture *(Portland, OR: Multnomah Press, 1986); and from a magazine article,* "Christ's Resurrection and Human Destiny," *copyrighted by* Christianity Today, *April 27, 1973.*

TEN

THE SIGNIFICANCE OF THE RESURRECTION
by Carl F. H. Henry

The resurrection of Jesus Christ is the turning point of the New Testament narratives and the heart of the Christian faith. The entire New Testament was written from the perspective of Jesus' resurrection from the dead. Without faith that the crucified Christ is alive, the Christian church would never have come into being, nor would we have the New Testament writings. The rise of the Christian movement can be adequately explained in only one way, that Jesus' followers personally saw the risen Lord and considered His resurrection from the tomb conclusive evidence that he was truly the Messiah of Old Testament promise.

Over half a century ago, on Long Island, when I was a young newspaper reporter and editor, I moved with those who shrugged off spiritual priorities. Joking about Christian realities and profaning Christ's name were commonplace. I had read the resurrection narratives much as Saul heard the same story in the first churches. I disbelieved, yet all the time was disturbed by the shadow of Christ's resurrection. But something happened in the summer of 1933 when I took Christ at His word. The crucified and risen Lord became undeniably real to me.

Instead of first examining what ancient believers said and what modern theologians and unbelievers say about Jesus' resurrection, let us begin with what the opponents of Jesus conceded. The sources of information we have about

Jesus' life provide two vital lines of knowledge about how adversaries of the Christian movement viewed the claims made for the bodily resurrection of Jesus Christ. One line of testimony relates to the desecration or nondesecration of the tomb in which the body of Jesus was placed. The other relates to the factuality or nonfactuality of Jesus' so-called resurrection appearances.

By assigning an official military guard to the site where the slain Jesus was entombed, the powerful Jewish Sanhedrin had in place what would not have interested the disciples, that is, a day-and-night, round-the-clock watch at the burial place.[1] The sepulcher itself, as a burial place that originally belonged to Joseph of Arimathea, a wealthy Jew, was obviously a highly secure gravesite. Afraid that the disciples might remove the body and thus give credence to Jesus' sporadic remarks about a resurrection, the Jewish Council took care from the very first moments of Jesus' burial to guarantee the inviolability of the gravesite.

A sharp earthquake thrust open the tomb and disclosed to the erstwhile slumbering soldiers that Jesus' body was missing.[2] The problem that now vexed Jesus' enemies was how to explain the empty tomb. Almost from the very first, the astonished disciples insisted that Jesus had risen bodily, that He now encountered them personally, and by repeated resurrection appearances gave proof of his identity.

These facts are the only primary evidence we have of what happened. Had it wished to do so, the Hebrew council could have explained the empty tomb as a figment of the heightened imagination of Jesus' followers. But instead, and deliberately so, it claimed that the disciples had stolen the body of Jesus.[3] In short, the council officially admitted that the tomb was empty; it attributed the violation of the tomb to illegal entry by Jesus' disciples and charged them with removing the corpse.

We sometimes overlook the fact that for one fleeting moment even some of Jesus' followers thought at first that His body had been stolen from the tomb. Mary Magdalene, shocked to discover the tomb apparently desecrated, hurriedly protested to Peter and John: "They have taken the Lord from the tomb, and we don't know where they have placed him."[4] She suspects that Jesus' enemies—surely not his friends—have removed the body. This possibility may likewise have haunted Peter and John as they raced to the tomb during those anxious moments before John, seeing the discarded graveclothes, "believed" that Christ was raised even before the risen Jesus appeared to the women and then to the other disciples.[5]

Although the Sanhedrin along with the disciples acknowledged that the tomb was empty, it promptly insisted that it did not have the body of Jesus. Otherwise it could and would have displayed the body to demoralize the apostles and to discredit their preaching of the resurrection. Instead the Sanhedrin charged the disciples with removing and concealing the dead body of Jesus.

Meanwhile, however, one and another of the disciples, then small groups of them, and finally all of them, were exchanging reports not about a decomposing corpse but about the risen Jesus' unpredictable personal appearances that turned their despair over His death into boundless joy.[6] Almost coincidentally with the discovery of the empty tomb, they proclaimed a resurrection reality that could hardly have been grounded in a lie and a fraud. Since it had ordered and maintained the soldiers' guard at the tomb, the Sanhedrin was in a special position to ascertain the actuality of the empty tomb, if there was any doubt about its emptiness. As it was, the Sanhedrin openly and unhesitatingly conceded that the tomb was empty.

The explanation of the soldiers [was] that Jesus' disciples had stealthily removed his body while the official guard slept. [This] has always elicited a cynical smile deserved by those who confidently profess to discern historical actualities while they themselves are sound asleep. The fact that the Sanhedrin bribed the soldiers' watch to circulate this explanation as an official version surely indicates something. It would seem that the soldiers themselves were not personally comfortable with such a hypothesis. Either the theory clashed with what they suspected to be a more factual explanation (cf. Matthew 28:2-4), or it involved them in giving an explanation for which they had no conscious evidence, or perhaps both.

The four Gospels without exception testify to the fact of the empty tomb. In addition the Fourth Gospel records the eyewitness report of that empty tomb and its abandoned graveclothes by Peter and John.[7] Even John A. T. Robinson grants that the evidence in the Gospels concerning the empty tomb "is in substance unanimous"; none of the divergences, he adds, is of the kind that "impugns the authenticity of the narrative."[8]

The Gospel representations of the empty tomb have sometimes been questioned by Biblical critics. They dismiss them as merely an inference from supposed resurrection appearances, or as a projection of the early church for apologetic purposes, or as grounded in the human error of distraught disciples who mistook an unused tomb for the actual burial place of Jesus.

But the empty tomb could not have been an inference from supposed resurrection appearances, whether these appearances be interpreted as encounters with an invisible spirit or as subjective hallucinatory experiences. The Jews meant by resurrection bodily resurrection, whether they were Sadducees who disbelieved in resurrection or Pharisees who affirmed it. Without the empty tomb any claim for Jesus' resurrection was meaningless.

If the apostles or their successors invented the empty tomb story for apologetic purposes, moreover, they would hardly have affirmed, as do all four Gospels, that the discovery was first made by the women, since the testimony of women was not accepted in a Jewish court of law. And if the disciples went to the wrong tomb, why did the Sanhedrin, which knew the precise location of the authentic burial place, publicly concede that the tomb was empty? Why did it not exhibit the corpse of the crucified Jesus and thus silence forever the resurrection message of the early church?

The Sanhedrin refused to share the view of the meaning and mission of Jesus of Nazareth that was held not only by the disciples generally but also by two of its very own members, Joseph of Arimathea and Nicodemus. Even so, it was compelled to admit openly that the tomb guarded by a contingent of imperial soldiers had assuredly lost its crucified occupant. From the technically qualified representatives of the Hebrew Sanhedrin, from the military watch surrounding the grave of the entombed crucified Jesus—from them the God of history in His divine providence elicited the candid, unreserved confession and open acknowledgment that the tomb was empty.

For another reason the testimony of the enemies of the Christian movement touching the resurrection of Jesus is highly important. This is summed up in a conclusion insistently forced on the Sanhedrin yet resisted by that most prestigious and responsible body of Jewish religious leaders. We have just indicated how these men formulated their polemic against the Christian community in regard to the empty tomb. We must reckon also with the mission and final verdict of Saul of Tarsus.

This gifted student of the revered rabbi Gamaliel was specially selected by the Sanhedrin, we are informed, for an inquisitorial and ambassadorial role in destroying what it considered to be a deluded Christian movement.[9] As a representative of the Sanhedrin, Saul must have shared the official Jewish view that the tomb was empty because Jesus' followers had stolen the body. In the battle against Christian claims, Saul served the Sadducees no less than the Pharisees; both denied the resurrection of Jesus, whatever else may have been their differences. Saul's unrelenting pursuit of the Christians may well have been expedited by the assumption that if he probed far and deep enough, he himself would expose the culprits who had allegedly stolen the body of Jesus and would uncover the deteriorating remains for all to see.

At first Saul of Tarsus was unidentified with the Christian movement and wholly disinterested in it. Soon he became critical and contemptuous of it. Next he became dedicated to persecuting and even eliminating its adherents. Officially designated prosecutor and persecutor on an international level, he was dispatched in the service of the supreme Jewish council as an intelligence agent or spy. He was an authorized deprogrammer (a Ted Patrick before our time), equipped by the religious hierarchy with all the necessary means to punish and destroy both men and women.

He was turned from this task of terror at the height of his career, so to speak, when confronted on the Damascus road by "Jesus the Nazarene, whom you are persecuting"— this is how he echoes the voice from heaven. Just as "this Way" was Paul's contemptuous term for the Christians, so "the Nazarene" was the usual Jewish designation for Jesus. Paul was himself later called "a ringleader of the Nazarenes."[10] Paul likens his Damascus road experience to the calling of the prophets and the apostles, a divine confrontation which made him at once a Christian, an apostle, and specifically the apostle to the Gentiles.

To summarize these two lines of testimony relevant to the resurrection that come from enemies of the Christian movement, one might say two things: First, the Sanhedrin was forced to acknowledge the empty tomb because of and through its officially designated representatives who were stationed in round-the-clock operations at the scene of action. Second, the Sanhedrin must have been stunned when Saul, its investigator and persecutor, repudiated the notion that the disciples had stolen the crucified body. He became instead a worshiper and servant of the risen Jesus even, as it developed, to the death, and moreover exhorted all Jewry and the whole Gentile world to worship Him.

It is a remarkable irony of the New Testament that whereas the Sanhedrin took precautions lest Jesus' cryptic references to his resurrection might become the basis of a hoax, the disciples themselves were thrown into utter despair by his crucifixion.[11] There is little doubt that Jesus Himself anticipated His violent death, that He anticipated His resurrection, and that He shared these expectations on numerous occasions with His disciples. The disciples freely acknowledge occasions when they totally missed the point of Jesus' open and clear teaching, especially about His impending death and resurrection. "The gospel writers are quite frank to admit," comments Bernard Ramm, that Jesus' predictions of His death and resurrection "did not penetrate their minds till the resurrection was a fact."

The Gospels are therefore unanimous on several facts, however adversely these facts may reflect on the disciples. One, Jesus on numerous occasions during His three-year public ministry spoke clearly and even earnestly of His approaching death and deliverance. Two, the disciples neither comprehended what He meant nor did they expect His crucifixion and resurrection. Three, only after Jesus' actual resurrection did His earlier references make sense to the disciples. The disciples were in fact so dispirited by the crucifixion of Jesus that they questioned even the report of the women that the tomb was empty.[12]

We have seen how separate representatives of the Sanhedrin conceded the empty tomb on the one hand and the reality of the resurrection on the other. And we have heard Jesus' disciples confess that the resurrection of the Crucified One surprised and even perplexed them. Thus John: "At first his disciples did not understand all this," and Luke: "The disciples did not grasp this."[13] Luke seems to imply that God in some way veiled the meaning; God designed, purposed, willed the disciples' lack of perception.

We believe that this design lay in the need to understand Jesus' crucifixion and resurrection in the context of Old Testament prophecy. The resurrection of Jesus Christ cannot be properly understood as simply an isolated phenomenon of brute power thrust by surprise upon an unsuspecting human race. If it were only such a phenomenon, then the resurrection appearances would be like the uninvited emergence from nowhere of a mysterious anthropoid from the moon or from Mars or from who knows where aboard a flying saucer.

From the very first Easter, however, the resurrection of the crucified Jesus was quickly recognized as something far different from an isolated wonder, a bizarre phenomenon of power having no intelligible links to the past and no relationship to history and nature. Only John, when he glimpsed the empty tomb and the abandoned graveclothes, claims to have believed the reality of Jesus' resurrection before the risen Christ's first resurrection appearances. The clear implication is that Peter, who had raced with him to the burial place, did not believe until he was personally confronted by the risen Lord. But never were the disciples without an intelligible context in which to evaluate the phenomenon of the resurrection. Jesus makes very plain that it is the inspired Old Testament writers who are the basic source; it is Moses and the prophets who speak incontrovertibly and definitively of Messiah's crucifixion and resurrection.

In summary, the most qualified representatives of the foes of Jesus conceded that the tomb was empty and that they did not have the crucified body of Jesus. The officially appointed investigator and persecutor conceded that Jesus is alive in a resurrection body and named him the promised Messiah. The most intimate followers of Jesus admitted that they were inexcusably dull to Jesus' forewarnings of his crucifixion and resurrection. Their failure to grasp its significance lay in their neglect of Old Testament prophecies of which Jesus had constantly reminded them.[14]

Long-range, the resurrection of Jesus had its setting in the eschatological resurrection of all mankind and the redemptive suffering of Messiah foretold by the prophets. Short-range, the physical and spiritual marks of personal identification linked the Risen One indubitably with the crucified teacher and master whom the disciples loved.

The resurrection of Christ stands firm against all objections rooted in the so-called uniformity of nature or the analogies of history, because it is rooted instead in the sovereign purpose of the living God, the God of redemptive promise and fulfillment. All modern objections to the resurrection stem from metaphysical requirements arbitrarily imposed by those who cannot, apart from revelation, know either the entire course of history or the whole secret of the cosmos. Yet they presume to tell us, if not what absolutely must be in the future, at least what must invariably have been the truth about the empty tomb, even if this means discrediting the only historical witnesses. But the resurrection violates neither nature nor history, because Jesus was raised from the dead by the very God of nature and history.

To anyone unfamiliar with the Scriptural context of divine promise and fulfillment in which the events of the first Easter occurred, the historical resurrection of the promised Messiah can signal only that human life and history are firmly in God's sovereign hands for final judgment. That is hardly a message of joy for sinners, past or present.

Why then, for the disciples of Jesus, did the resurrection morning mean incomparable joy?[15] For them the resurrection of the Crucified One was not an inexplicable oddity. Its meaning was clear: "Christ died for our sins according to the Scriptures; and . . . was buried, and . . . rose again the third day according to the Scriptures, and . . . was seen. . . ."[16] Resurrection morning was the dawn of a continuing moral and spiritual relationship with the risen Messiah and coming King.

The New Testament does not exhibit Jesus' resurrection as merely a prelude to some distant future. For regenerate believers, the resurrection is a present reality known and anticipatively experienced in daily fellowship with the risen Jesus. From the ascended Christ His followers received the indwelling Spirit poured out at Pentecost; so too they still receive from Him the Spirit's daily filling, and by the Spirit they taste even now the powers of the age to come and are daily sampling their coming inheritance.

The fact of the resurrection remains fully as decisive for human destiny today as it was in Paul's day. Secular philosophers in both ancient and recent times who affirmed the reality of an afterlife on the basis of other considerations have failed to make their case. The rationalistic notions of immortality are today totally discredited. Like the classic Greek idealists and the Roman stoics, modern philosophers and theologians believed the mind of man to be secretly divine and hence indestructible, while they resigned the body to destruction and scorned the doctrine of resurrection. These thinkers were confident that the human spirit on its own would survive death.

The whole tide of modern history has upset and challenged the notion that the spirit of man is essentially divine. Freud's recognition that dark subconscious drives motivate man as we now know him; the barbaric actions of Hitler and the Nazis and other totalitarian tyrants in their wanton devastation of men and nations; the yielding of the most brilliant achievements of scientific reasoning to destructive pursuits—such considerations make it wholly impossible to accept the myth that man is inherently divine and immortal. Every passing hour simply carries the whole man—spirit and body alike—nearer to a destiny of cosmic dust and ashes unless, indeed, Jesus Christ is risen from the dead.

A new development in modern thought, in the area of psychology, likewise disputes the idea that man's spirit will survive death apart from bodily relationships of some kind. For the Greeks man was essentially a mind; the body was a dispensable prison. For modern psychology the human being is a "psychosomatic" entity; you cannot have a man without a body. Mind and body are a unitary whole. Modern naturalism or materialism interprets this to mean that death terminates the existence of both the human spirit and the body.

The normative psychology of the Bible also views the human self as a unitary whole, a composite of soul and body. But Biblical theology has a far more profound understanding, for in the light of the resurrection we are promised a new body fit for the eternal order. The factuality of Christ's resurrection has implications for the final destiny of every last human being.

We Americans bury our dead, as anthropologists are driven to comment, in a way that gives them a final semblance of being alive. That is not the only indication of our refusal to yield to the final reality of death. We are now reaching for a pseudo-immortality—maybe even a doubling of man's present life span—through the continual replacement of human organs. Science is being looked upon as the giver of immortality in this body.

On the surface, modern science and the Bible strike similar notes on the incompleteness of men without bodies. On a deeper level their underlying bases for the assertion are completely different. One place this difference shows up is in ethics. Science does not raise questions concerning the goodness or the wickedness of the person it helps. The Bible sets human destiny in this life and in the life to come in a moral and spiritual context. Each man's personal relationship to Jesus Christ is decisive.

The factuality of Christ's bodily resurrection is a foundational doctrine, one that distinguishes Christianity from speculative religions. There is a basic difference, however, between reanimating a body not yet fully decomposed, even if disintegration has begun, and transforming the very nature of a body. The resurrection of Jesus was not merely revivification such as occurred with Lazarus and others who were called back to earthly life. It involved rather resurrection from death to unending life in a new bodily mode.

The body in which Jesus arose, while continuous with the body that had been placed in the tomb, was in evident ways released from material conditions. It was human nature manifested by Jesus of Nazareth that God approvingly raised from the dead, and the divine declaration of a future universal resurrection is given in the context of His victory over sin as well as over death.

Jesus' contemporaries had associated the resurrection with the final end of history and the beginning of the eschatological age. Jesus' resurrection in history's mid-course gave mankind a public preview of the end-time and its moral implications. The risen Jesus is unveiled in advance as the future judge of the whole human race.

These truths, then, are finalities of the resurrection: (1) that Jesus exemplifies in a new bodily mode the afterlife to which mankind is destined; (2) that Jesus mirrors the quality of humanity that God approves in the eternal order; (3) that Jesus was raised after His crucifixion in a divine identification of the coming judge of the human race; (4) that your destiny and mine turn on a cosmic conflict of sin and righteousness that involves two different destinies for mankind in the life to come.

After some two thousand years Jesus Christ still leaves His mark upon men, even in their rebellion. We are still secretly embarrassed by the resurrection. For all modern man's break with the supernatural and the eternal world, he seems unable to reconcile himself to any conviction that he is merely a temporary creature whose threescore years and ten are a prelude to mere nothingness. And our deepest longing for personal immortality has a Christian anchorage—Christ's resurrection. It is that ever-present, ever-embarrassing resurrection which drives us to the point of decision for or against Christ and provides us with our only glimmer of hope for a future life.

After the philosophic hope of the Greeks and Romans for immortality has faded, after the pantheism of Hegel has withered, the resurrection of the crucified Jesus remains the only firm basis for two of mankind's cardinal concerns—our personal survival of death, and a life fit for eternity. By eternal life the New Testament does not mean simply an endless existence after death; it means life *now* of a new quality, a new kind, given from above by the indwelling of the Holy Spirit. Death does not put an end to any man's existence; rather it puts an end to the opportunity for life sheltered by the grace of God, for a life fit for eternity, for life on speaking terms with God, for life unshadowed by the judgment of God.

What significance has the resurrection of Jesus of Nazareth from the dead for us today? I have met worldwide a fellowship of joyous persons whose outlook and character are shaped by the reality and power of Christ's resurrection, and who even now have special access to the Risen One. They are men and women who rejoice in the redemption and the renewal Christ offers, a company of believers of every race and color on every continent and of every walk of life. All have this in common: whereas like Saul of Tarsus they were once unbelievers who considered Christians a strange lot even if they did not openly persecute them, now like C. S.

Lewis they declare themselves "surprised by joy," a match-less, incomparable joy.

Jesus Christ is the first to bring immortality to light. He becomes lord over death by annihilating it. Death itself is broken by Christ's triumph over it. This made the new community of faith alive with a sense of victory. The subjective spiritual and moral experience of New Testament believers gains profound reorientation from His resurrection. Not only the fear of physical death, but also the sting of spiritual death is removed. The life of the Spirit has a new dynamic through the resurrection and Pentecost. The redeemed enjoy in this life a spiritual and moral union with the exalted Redeemer. "Students of antiquity," wrote Bishop Henson, "have dwelt frequently on the note of despondency, even of despair. . . . Against this background of diffused and dominant pessimism, the profession of Christianity presented an arresting spectacle of jubilant hope. . . . The secret of the difference lay in the Christian belief that by his resurrection Christ had validated the human effort."[17] Since the resurrection . . . the ascended Christ in and by the Spirit has been personally present in believers as a life-transforming power. Christian morality therefore has about it an element of buoyant Easter joy sustained by the risen Jesus as our eternal Contemporary.

Jesus' resurrection bears witness to all the generations that one dramatic exception exists to the universal clutch of sin and death upon beleaguered mankind, and that singular exception is Jesus of Nazareth. It is His human nature alone that God approves and commends going into the eternal future. Speak as we may at times of Christians as "little Jesuses," we are far less than that even at our best. Nobody but Jesus has marched into the world of death and defanged it, marched through it and left it in disarray, stripped away its sting and triumphed over it. The exclusivity of Jesus' resurrection speaks to all human beings of the supreme righteousness of God manifest in the risen Redeemer.

We are not dealing with literary fiction and intellectual conjecture—with myths—when we speak of the incarnation, crucifixion, and resurrection of Jesus of Nazareth. The resurrection confirms that Christianity is about God who is active in nature and history, and in saving sinners who turn to Him for grace. The Bible has as its climax the person of Jesus Christ—the centrality of his incarnation, crucifixion, and resurrection as the promised Messiah, who took on Himself our human nature, lived a perfect life, died an atoning death, and rose in triumph over the tomb.

The Jesus People once distributed a cartoon that showed several tombs holding the remains of founders of the great world religions. Underneath was the line: "Will the real Messiah please stand up?" Only one of those tombs was empty—the tomb of Jesus. The others were still in the grip of death. The risen Jesus controls the sluice gates of eternity; the founders of nonbiblical religions will be answerable to Him in the life to come.

The resurrection of Jesus is more than a standing invitation to personal faith in the risen Redeemer; it is an incentive to service. It is a guarantee that our good deeds have eternal significance and worth. Christ's resurrection spurs the church to the evangelistic proclamation of personal salvation, and also to the promotion of world justice. The victory over injustice and evil that Jesus won in his own conquest over sin and death He wishes to extend through the church, of which He has become the living and exalted head.

The church is not simply to preach personal salvation, but is to publish the criteria by which Christ will judge the world and even now judges it, and to affirm God's interest in the whole person and the whole world. The church is to live as the new society within a rebellious world, and is to challenge and call humanity to authentic life and hope, and to exhibit what it means to live by the standards of the returning King.

The resurrection therefore strips away all racial, national, economic and cultural distinctions; it is not bounded by differences of color and culture, of race and rank. It reminds us that the God of the eternal future is the God of creation and redemption who discriminates not on the basis of pigment, but on the basis of justice and mercy, of purity and penitence.

The risen Christ not only embodies that quality of humanity in which God delights, but also by His character provides an ongoing challenge to men, enabling all to anticipate the meaning and nature of God's coming judgment. The Christian therefore is to be God's man or God's woman among the masses of people, salt of the earth, light of the world, a mirror of that humanity which in both public and private affairs brings delight to God. This unique fraternity of the resurrection enfleshes the only enduring hope of a spiritually depleted race.

According to the New Testament, the quality of our future resurrection at the consummation of all things depends and turns upon our present relationship to Jesus Christ. This relationship offers us moreover a special anticipation or sample of the resurrection, for even now we have moral and spiritual life, a life that anticipates eternity.

Finally, the visible resurrection of Jesus is the pledge that Jesus will return personally and visibly to consummate His kingdom in triumphant power and glory. He came and left in person as the incarnate and crucified Logos;[18] now he is the risen and returning Lord. The Apostle John writes that when the risen Jesus returns, "every eye will see him, even those who pierced him."[19] Remember the ascension morning testimony when the risen Jesus returned to the Father and resumed the glory that was His before the world began: "This same Jesus, who has been taken from you into heaven, will come back in the same way you have seen him go into heaven."[20] We shall behold Him—either as the Judge before whom mankind cowers, or as the Redeemer whose return the people of God cherish.

That Jesus is risen attests that His teaching has firm anchorage in eternity—that in Jesus, God has already welcomed to Himself the one and only bearer of a sinless humanity, that Jesus was not holden of death but died voluntarily, that the gospel is not literary myth but is rooted in historical redemptive acts and in divinely revealed truth, that the rulers of the nations and founders of nonbiblical religions must yet appear at Jesus' throne, that salvation remains today an option even for persecutors like Saul of Tarsus, that our Christian service and dedication to good works has a guaranteed survival value, that the church of which the risen Lord is head is to extend His victory over injustice and evil, and that Christ will return as King in power and glory to consummate His Kingdom.

Only if the New Testament hope holds firm is there a sure prospect of personal life beyond the grave. But the New Testament doctrine of the afterlife does not stand alone; it is part and parcel of the comprehensive Christian view of God and humanity. It involves a distinctive view of origins and of the created dignity of men and women. It involves a distinctive view of sinners in revolt against the holy Lord of the universe. It involves a distinctive view of redemption, involving God's self-revelation, the gift of His Son, Christ's atoning death, and His bodily resurrection. This is the glory of Easter. It involves the offer of new life, a new birth, and a new character with a will transformed and a mind for the things of God.

NOTES

1. Matthew 27:65-66.
2. Matthew 28:2.
3. Matthew 28:12-15.
4. John 20:2.
5. John 20:8.
6. Luke 24:32.
7. John 20:6-7.
8. John A. T. Robinson, quoted in Henry, *God, Revelation and Authority*, vol. 3, (Waco, TX: Word Books, 1979), pp. 147 ff.
9. Acts 9:1-2.
10. Acts 24:5.
11. Luke 24:37, 41.
12. Luke 24:11.
13. Luke 9:45.
14. Luke 24:27.
15. John 20:20.
16. 1 Corinthians 15:3-5.
17. Herbert Hensley Henson (1863-1947) served as bishop of Durham, England, from 1920 to 1939.
18. The word *logos* is usually translated "Word." Cf. John 1:1.
19. Revelation 1:7.
20. Acts 1:11.

Billy Graham, 1918-

The son of a Carolina dairy farmer and grandson of a Confederate soldier wounded at Gettysburg, Evangelist William Franklin (Billy) Graham has become perhaps the best-known religious figure of the twentieth century, surpassing even saints, popes, imams, and lamas. Among other unusual records, he has preached the gospel of Jesus Christ to more people personally and electronically than any other human being.

Born in Charlotte, North Carolina, in 1918, he was converted to Christ at an evangelistic meeting shortly after his sixteenth birthday. He was educated at Bob Jones College, Florida Bible Institute, and Wheaton College, Illinois. His leadership potential soon became apparent. After a brief pastorate in a Chicago suburb, he became vice-president of the newly formed Youth for Christ International and began his lifelong itinerant evangelistic ministry.

Between his early travels Graham served four years as president of Northwestern College, Minneapolis. He came to national attention during a 1949 evangelistic campaign in Los Angeles, and the following year he founded the Billy Graham Evangelistic Association with headquarters in Minneapolis. His earnest delivery and compelling manner made a lasting impression on Britain during his 1954 meetings in London; years later fifty Anglican clergymen traced their conversion to those days. Queen Elizabeth II invited him to preach at Windsor Castle.

In the decades that followed, Graham ranged the continents with a growing team of associates, preaching to throngs in remote African villages, and in metropolitan areas to as many as a million people who gathered one Sunday afternoon on an island outside of Seoul, Korea. Multiple academic honors came to him. Heads of state sought his counsel. He formed his own motion picture company and sought to harness modern technology to the proclamation of the gospel.

Graham's global vision led him to sponsor world congresses on evangelization in Berlin (1966), Lausanne (1974), and Amsterdam (1983, 1986). His books, beginning with Peace With God *(1952) have been perennial best sellers. His magazine* Decision, *of which I was the first editor, reached a circulation of five million copies and appears in six languages. Graham also founded the magazine* Christianity Today. *Through his daily newspaper column and weekly radio broadcasts, his telecasts, his interviews, and other uses of the media, Graham's witness to new life in Jesus Christ has had worldwide impact. Thousands trace their faith in Christ to his preaching.*

Observers credit him with a significant role in the 1989-90 political thaw in Eastern Europe. Amid the scandals that rocked the American religious scene in the late 1980s, Billy Graham's integrity was never questioned. Over the years his charitable and relief undertakings to alleviate human suffering have been generous and widespread. His personal winsomeness, humility, and exemplary family life, moreover, have made him one of the world's most admired personalities.

It is characteristic of his graciousness that he granted permission to include three of his evangelistic messages in this volume in the form in which they appeared in Decision *Magazine.*

ELEVEN

WHY YOU SHOULD COME TO CHRIST
by Billy Graham

Conversion

"Unless you are converted and become as little children, you will by no means enter the kingdom of heaven." (Matthew 18:3)

Mahatma Gandhi, the man who led India to independence, once received a group of Christian ministers at 6:30 in the morning. After a breakfast of goat's milk in which sweet lime leaves had been boiled, they went up on the roof of his house for a private conference. Mr. Gandhi was dressed in a loincloth and carried a dollar watch in a pocket of it.

The ministers asked the mahatma about conversion, and he said, "I believe in Christian conversion if it is genuine. On the other hand there is nothing worse than being something on the outside that you are not on the inside. If a man has really found God through discovering Jesus Christ, then he must be baptized and show the world that he is a follower of Jesus, or else he will be a living lie."[1]

When I began my ministry of evangelism, I had not read a single book on the subject of conversion. However, I had experienced conversion myself as a young, rebellious student, aged sixteen. Now, over half a century later, the brilliance and wonder of that encounter with Jesus Christ remains unabated.

Today throughout the scientific, theological, and intellectual world there is an increasing discussion of the subject of conversion. A British psychiatrist said not long ago, "Man is so psychologically constituted that he needs converting." Another remarked, "If the church does not get back to converting the people, we psychiatrists are going to have to do it."

This word *conversion* is being used almost everywhere. Advertisers employ it in trying to get people to switch from one product to another. Finance uses it to describe the exchanging of one type of security for another. Forestry uses it to describe the changing of one type of forest to another. The military world uses it to explain the transfer from propeller-driven aircraft to jet aircraft, or from conventional weapons to nuclear weapons.

Just as *conversion* is a word used constantly in almost every realm, so it is used in the spiritual. Webster defines conversion as "turning from one position or direction to another; passing from one side to another."

Let us turn to the Scriptures and learn what the Bible has to say about conversion. The word *convert* or some form of it occurs fourteen times in the New Testament. It simply means "stopping and turning." The idea of "turning" in this word is basic. Sometimes it is said of an individual that he turns himself, sometimes that he is turned. The word was the subject of the Apostle Peter's powerful message on the day of Pentecost, in which he warned his listeners, "Repent, therefore, and be converted."

Conversion, then, is that voluntary change in the mind of a sinner in which he turns from sin and to Jesus Christ. Conversion is the human side of the tremendous transformation that takes place which, as viewed from the divine side, is called in the Bible "the new birth" or "regeneration." It is simply man's turning from sin to Christ.

While the Scripture teaches that God turns men and women to Himself, those same persons are also exhorted to turn themselves to God. While God is represented as the author of the new heart and the new spirit, men and women are also commanded in each case to make for themselves a new heart and a new spirit. It is the old problem of grace and free will.

No one can be converted except by the grace of God, for we are too weak to turn ourselves, unaided; and we turn only in response to some stimulus provided outside ourselves. But no one can be converted except with the consent of his own free will, because God does not override human choice. We may not be free to choose, because sin weakens our power of moral choice; but we are free to refuse. We can refuse to be chosen.

This combination of divine calling and human responsibility, which commands a "yes" or "no" response, runs throughout the Bible and characterizes all of God's dealings with men and women. The Bible confronts us with our moral independence within ourselves and our spiritual dependence upon God.

In the picturesque words of Psalm 18:29 the psalmist says, "By my God I can leap over a wall." No one can leap over walls except by his own will and effort, but some walls are so high that they need more than this. The psalmist knew such walls. They could be leaped over only with the help of his God. God does not lift him over. God helps him when he leaps. Man does the leaping—God does the helping.

It is like this with conversion. There is a resolve, a sheer act of will within the sphere of an individual's power of choosing and deciding. But this resolve is also a response to a stimulus from outside himself, which he did not prompt or cause or perhaps expect. The Bible says, "For by grace are you saved through faith; and that not of yourselves, it is the gift of God; not of works, lest any man should boast."[2]

The grace is God's; the faith is ours, but the free will with which we choose is God's gift, and the capacity to believe and trust is God's gift also. Therefore within every conversion there is the working of the divine and the human; but their relation to each other remains a mystery. It has been my privilege to see thousands converted to Christ, and I still do not understand the mystery of God's grace and man's faith. But I know that both are involved.

On the one hand Jesus said, "The one who comes to me I will by no means cast out."[3] And on the other hand he said, "No one can come to me unless the Father who sent me draws him."[4]

I am convinced that the Bible teaches the necessity of conversion. I am absolutely certain of my own conversion. I am equally convinced of the genuineness of the conversion of thousands of people in many parts of the world.

The great Augustine of Hippo once described his own conversion in a famous passage in his *Confessions*. He said, "In some way, I'm not just sure how, I flung myself down under a fig tree and gave free course to my tears. I sent up these sorrowful cries, 'How long, how long? Tomorrow and tomorrow? Why not now? Why not this very hour make an end to my uncleanness?' I was saying these things and weeping in the most bitter contrition of my heart, when suddenly I heard the voice of a boy or a girl—I know not which—coming from the neighboring house, chanting over and over again, 'Take up and read, take up and read.'

"Immediately I ceased weeping and began to ask whether it was usual for children in some kind of game to sing such a song, for I could not remember ever having heard the like. I got to my feet, since I could not but think that this was a divine command to open the Bible and read the first passage I should light upon. I quickly returned to the bench where Alypius was sitting, for there I had put down the apostle's book when I had left.

"I snatched it up, opened it and in silence read the passage on which my eyes first fell: 'Let us conduct ourselves becomingly as in the day; not in reveling and drunkenness, not in debauchery and licentiousness, not in quarreling and jealousy; but put on the Lord Jesus Christ, and make no provision for the flesh, to gratify its lusts.' I wanted to read no further, nor did I need to. For instantly, as the sentence ended, there was infused in my heart something like the light of full certainty, and all the gloom of doubt vanished away."[5]

Before this moment Augustine was an immoral man. In no sense could he be called Christian. He was cultured and civilized, but he was still a pagan. As a result of this one experience he became one of the greatest Christian theologians of all time.

John Wesley describes his conversion experience. He was born into a Christian home, the son of the rector of Epworth parish; he was devoutly religious at Oxford, the leader of the "Holy Club," given to prayer and good works, always eager from his earliest days to lead others to Christ. He went to the colony of Georgia in 1735 as a missionary. From all outward appearances he seemed to be a Christian.

Despite all of these good works he had never been truly converted to Jesus Christ until May 24, 1738, when he had an experience like that of the Apostle Paul on the Damascus road and that of Augustine in an Italian garden. He writes in his journal:

"In the evening I went very unwillingly to a society in Aldersgate, where one was reading Luther's *Preface to the Epistle to the Romans.* About a quarter before nine, while he was describing the change which God works in the heart through faith in Christ, I felt my heart strangely warmed. I felt I did trust in Christ, Christ alone, for salvation, and an assurance was given me that he had taken away my sins, even mine, and saved me from the law of sin and death."[6]

In reading the rest of Wesley's journal, I noted that he always looked back to that moment as the hour of his conversion.

Both of these conversions were sudden, though in both cases there had been a considerable period of restlessness beforehand. A sudden conversion does not preclude a good many preparatory incidents one way or another. Both of the above were prompted by hearing the voice of the living God through a passage of Scripture. The Word of God touched them. In both cases the experience produced an immediate change in life and attitude and a sense of release from sin and guilt.

This is the great need of the world: the conversion of sinners to Christ. In God's balances one soul weighs more than the entire world of material things. New Testament conversion applies God's remedy to the need of the world. Our world is sick unto death, our culture is in chaotic confusion, and our civilization is in peril. The good news of the gospel of Christ offers the only satisfying remedy. There is nothing else, nothing better and nothing beyond. The evangel of the redeeming Christ is the ultimate. We cannot improve upon this gospel that can transform the lives of individuals. The good news of the gospel solves the problem of human destiny, the most fundamental problem of human existence. It solves the anthropological problem. It solves the philosophical problems of where we came from, why we are here, and where we are going.

There are many people who are frustrated, confused, and empty. They have a sense of sin and guilt upon their consciences; yet somehow they feel inadequate to solve the innermost problems of the soul, heart, and mind. Are you one of them? Are you searching for an answer? The true answer is simply this:

First, we must recognize that we are sinners. The Bible says, "All have sinned and come short of the glory of God."[7] We do not like to admit that we are wrong. It is not easy to do. But God requires that we not only admit that we are wrong, but that we turn from our sin. This is where our own human will comes in. We may not have the ability to turn from sin, but we must will to turn from sin. And when we are willing, God will help us.

Second, we must recognize that Christ died and rose again for our sins. His death was not an accident. It was in the plan of God that He should pour out his blood on the cross for our sins. We do not like to come to a cross where blood is shed. To some people that is odious. That is one reason why we have a cross—to show us how repugnant sin is in the sight of a holy God.

If the cross is offensive to us, how much more was it to

God, as indicated when Christ prayed on the cross, "My God, my God, why have you forsaken me?"[8] In that terrible moment He had grappled with sin, hell, and the grave. But thank God, the resurrection attested that He had conquered. The cross and the grave are empty. Christ is alive, able to save to the uttermost those who put their trust in Him.

Third, God requires that we receive His Son by faith. "As many as received him, to them he gave the right to become children of God, even to those who believe in his Name."[9] This is a simple act of faith. Jesus said, "Unless you turn and become like children, you will never enter the kingdom of heaven."[10] The moment you receive Christ by repentance and faith, regeneration takes place and you become a new creation in Christ. The Scripture teaches that old things will pass away, and all things will become new.

A distinguished scientist once said, "I am a Christian by the laboratory method of experimentation." I ask you today, have you by "experimentation" come to know Christ? You have heard about Christ, but have you ever truly received Him? Are you a Christian "by the laboratory method"?

Newton had his dynamics of matter and motion. Einstein had his dynamics of relativity. But Jesus Christ has His dynamics of the Spirit. In chemistry, under given conditions, hydrogen and oxygen combine to form water. So repentance and faith in Christ always produce a new life.

Yes, Christian conversion is real. You need the experience of conversion! Take Christ now as your own personal Savior.

From *Decision* Magazine, November 1969. © 1969 Billy Graham Evangelistic Association. Used by permission.

* * *

Excuse Me, Please

"A certain man was preparing a great banquet and invited many guests. At the time of the banquet he

sent his servant to tell those who had been invited,
'Come, for everything is now ready.'

"But they all alike began to make excuses. . . .
The servant came back and reported this to his master.
Then the owner of the house became angry and
ordered his servant, 'Go out quickly into the streets
and alleys of the town and bring in the poor, the crip-
pled, the blind, and the lame. . . .'"

Luke 14:16-21

I would like to show you a picture of Jesus Christ. He is
going up and down the countryside doing good. He makes
the blind to see, the deaf to hear, the dumb to speak, and the
lame to walk. He feeds the hungry multitude with five loaves
and two fishes. Jesus had compassion on people. He loved
people. He was interested in people. And everywhere He
went He taught as one having authority.

The Scripture says that people were amazed at His learning. He never went to college or to the university. He never
saw the inside of a seminary. Yet when He spoke, He spoke
as one having authority.[11] He did not say, "I suppose so," or
"I hope so." He said there was one way to heaven, and
explained, "I am the way."[12]

On one occasion during His ministry Jesus went to dinner at the home of one of the religious leaders of the city, a
chief Pharisee. And He mingled with worldly people; He did
not withdraw from the world. There are many modern-day
Pharisees who like to pull their self-righteous robes around
them and adopt a holier-than-thou attitude. They go about
sniffing like theological bloodhounds to see if anyone is off
the track a little bit. They may be quick to get angry, to spread
gossip, to slander a neighbor, to act proud and yet would
never rub shoulders with the world.

Jesus did not become a part of the world. He never par-
took of the sins of the world. But He went out into the high-
ways and byways and ate with sinners in order to win them.
He had a motive. We who are His followers should be going

into every area of social life in order to testify concerning Christ by the way we live and the way we talk.

While He was eating with this prominent Pharisee, Jesus told an appropriate story about a feast. He said that the host of the feast had sent out invitations to the people. In the Orient such an invitation was really a command. To refuse it was a very serious thing indeed.

Jesus used the story to illustrate the spiritual need of man. Whether we realize it or not, we need a gospel feast. We are hungry, we are thirsty, we need God. And God is saying to all of us, "Come. Come. Come. Come, I want to forgive you. I want to make you My child. I want to open your spiritual eyes. I want to give you the assurance that when you die, you will go to heaven. I am a God of love and mercy and grace, and I want you to come."

God offers us pardon and new life. He tells us to come and partake of Christ, to partake of eternal life. It is an invitation. The whole gospel is an invitation. Come and receive the Savior! Come to the cross! That is the invitation that Jesus gives as He hangs on the cross for our sins, His two arms outstretched to a lost world. "Come to me that you may have life, and have it more abundantly!"[13]

But do you know, when these people in Jesus' story were invited to the feast, they began to make excuses. One of them said, "Would you kindly excuse me, sir; I have bought a piece of ground and I have to go look it over."

What a silly excuse. The land would be there the next morning. He was more interested in the things of this world and in building a large estate than he was in his own soul. He was giving preference to the body over the soul, to the things of time above those of eternity. Many of us would not want to miss heaven, but we are saying by our attitude, "Lord, excuse me. I am building an estate."

Jesus said, "Seek ye first the kingdom of God and his righteousness."[14] But we seek our own security, our own jobs, our own appetites, our own pleasures first. It is we first and God second. We are glad to be Christians if it doesn't bother us too much. If it is a matter of one hour on Sunday, all right. Otherwise—"Excuse me."

Another man said, "I have bought five yoke of oxen, and I'm going out to plow with them to see how they work." Think of that! Those oxen were going to be with him probably for several years, but he couldn't come to the feast; he had to go out and plow now. Such a little thing kept him from the Kingdom of God. It was a lawful thing that he wanted to do, but it proved a fatal hindrance to his coming to Christ.

Many things we do are lawful, but we put them ahead of Christ. We may put television before Christ, or money-making or pleasure or good food or recreation or athletics. I tell you that Christ must be first.

Then another fellow said, "I have married a wife, and therefore I cannot come." Now I think that man had some excuse! But do you know what Jesus said? "If any man come to me, and hate not his own father, and mother, and wife, and children, and brothers, and sisters, yes, and his own life also, he cannot be my disciple."[15]

You say, "That's pretty hard." Of course it's hard. Whoever said it was easy to follow Jesus? This modern, twentieth-century religion that we have in the West, that we call Christianity, would hardly be recognized in New Testament times. Jesus said we have to put Him before our family. The family is no excuse. You give an excuse as to why you don't come to Christ and the Bible thunders back, "There is no excuse!"

What is your excuse? "Well," some fellow says, "I would like to come to Christ, but I have committed too many sins to come now. I don't feel worthy. Let me clean up a bit." That man will never come, because we cannot clean up. We cannot become righteous. We can improve ourselves intellectually, morally, physically, yes! But we cannot become righteous. According to Scripture, all our righteousnesses are as "filthy rags" in the sight of God, for no matter how good we think we are, we have fallen below God's standards. We cannot make ourselves acceptable to Him except through Christ.

Someone else says, "I would like to come to Christ, but

there are too many hypocrites in the church." I agree, there are a lot of hypocrites in the church. But that is no excuse to keep you from Christ. Suppose you refused the help of a good doctor because there are so many quacks, or refused to buy any more groceries because there are hypocrites in the grocery business, or refused to drink milk because there are hypocrites in the dairy business. To cry, "hypocrites in the church!" is just an excuse to cover up an unwillingness to receive Christ.

Others will say, "If I come to Christ I will have to give up too much." It is true, you will have to give up something. You will have to give up your sins. Those things that are wrong: the lying, the cheating, the pride, the jealousy. Yes, it will cost you something. And yet, a man will practice a golf swing until his fingers bleed in order to become a champion. A man will ruin his health to make money.

Still others will say, "I would become a Christian, but I don't understand it all." I would like to confess something to you: I don't understand it all either. I don't think anyone does. I cannot understand why Christ died for me, or why God said that the only way to heaven is through the cross. But I believe it because God said it. I accept it by faith, and I am going to do what God said.

I don't understand how a black cow can eat green grass and give white milk that makes yellow butter. When I stand before a microphone, I don't understand what makes an amplification system work, but I know it works. That's enough. I know Christ works. He has worked in my life. He has changed the lives of thousands of people in our generation.

And yet others say, "Excuse me, please, but I've tried it before and I just can't make it." Hundreds of people have been baptized or confirmed or have gone forward in evangelistic meetings, and they find nothing has happened—the total result seems to have been a dismal failure. But if you were walking down the road and fell into the ditch, would you say, "I'm going to stay here—I've tried walking and I've failed"? No, you would not.

People tell me, "I can't hold out." But you don't have to "hold out" or "hold on" or "turn loose" or "look for a light." It is not a matter of effort or of some vision or special feeling to come to Christ. We simply come by faith, turning our lives over to Him, trusting Him, and Christ helps us to live the Christian life. In fact, He lives it in us.

There are others who say, "I intend to become a Christian, but not now. Some other time." This is a deceitful wile of the devil. He does not care how deeply convicted we may be of sin if he can just get us to wait another day before we make our decision to come to Christ. You see, nobody knows what tomorrow may bring forth. The Bible says that today is the day of salvation! Don't put it off. God is calling.

Finally there are people who say, "Well, I would come, but I don't know how. What do you want me to do?" The Bible says that first we must acknowledge our sins to God. We are to say, "O God, I confess that I have sinned. I have broken Your laws. I am guilty."

Second, we are to turn from our sins and receive Jesus Christ as Savior and Lord. We are to trust Him and commit our lives to Him. You can do that right now, at this moment. You might ask, "Can a little thing like going forward in a meeting change my life?" No. It is Christ who changes us. He meets us when we are willing to meet Him. And when we come to Him openly, surrendering our lives, confessing Him before men and saying, "I will," then He enters into our hearts and gives us a new dimension of living, a new dynamic, a new power, and we become children of God.

At the end of his story Jesus cautioned that those who do not come when they are bidden will not taste of His feast. He warned of judgment ahead.

Will you come? Or what is your excuse?

From *Decision* Magazine, September 1967. © 1967 Billy Graham Evangelistic Association. Used by permission.

*   *   *

Only One Thing Wrong

> "As Jesus started on his way, a man ran up to him and fell on his knees before him. 'Good teacher,' he asked, 'what must I do to inherit eternal life?' . . .
>
> "Jesus answered, 'You know the commandments: "Do not murder, do not commit adultery, do not steal, do not give false testimony, do not defraud, honor your father and mother."'
>
> "'Teacher,' he declared, 'all these I have kept since I was a boy.'
>
> "Jesus looked at him and loved him. 'One thing you lack,' he said. 'Go, sell everything you have and give to the poor, and you will have treasure in heaven. Then come, follow me.'
>
> "At this the man's face fell. He went away sad, because he had great wealth."
>
> Mark 10:17-22

Here was a young man who "had it all." He was courageous, clean, ambitious, handsome, rich—and religious. Isn't that a combination? What more could you ask for? He had everything "going for him" that young people would like to have for themselves today.

And yet the Bible tells us that the young ruler came to Jesus and then turned away from him "crestfallen," to use the expression of J. B. Phillips in his translation. Why?

I want you first to see that this young man came running to Christ. It is splendid to see young people enthusiastic for the Lord Jesus Christ. People go to a football game today and shout their heads off or go to a circus and cheer act after act. They become enthusiastic about everything conceivable, but when it comes to spiritual matters, they think we are supposed to become sober and quiet, and wear black, and never have a good time or enjoy a religious event at all.

David did not feel that way. He says, "In thy presence is fullness of joy; at thy right hand there are pleasures forevermore."[17] And I believe one of the desperate needs among Christian young people is exuberance and vitality in their loyalty to Christ. If we would put our heart into Christ's service the way we put ourselves into a football game, the world would know it.

Notice also that this young man had courage. He came to the Lord in the daytime, whereas another familiar Bible character, Nicodemus, a leading Pharisee, came by night![18] I like people with courage. I don't like to see a young person clam up or sputter and turn red when Jesus Christ is mentioned on the college campus or in high school. I believe that if the thousands of young Christians in our cities and towns would set about witnessing—"gossiping" about Jesus—they would see a change in our world beyond anything imaginable.

This young fellow was also ambitious. He showed a deep interest in spiritual things. He wanted the most out of life. He didn't want God's second best. I like ambitious young people, too—not show-offs, not ambitious to put themselves in the spotlight, but ambitious for the things of the Lord Jesus Christ.

Furthermore, our young ruler was a man of high principles. He lived up to the light he had and kept the commandments. I wonder how many of us have done so? This fellow was religious. Today he would have been a deacon or a Sunday school teacher. In a day of increasing moral degradation, I say to young people, "Live clean for Christ." The Apostle Paul, writing to young Timothy, said, "Flee youthful lusts."[19] You know what he was talking about.

And then notice something else: he was a wealthy young fellow. Now, there is nothing wrong with money, if money comes after Christ. But Christ has to be first. I think the young man must have been handsome. Rich, handsome, courageous, clean, religious, filled with enthusiasm, a contagious personality—a wonderful young fellow. And yet he was unhappy! There was something lacking, something still unsatisfied in the depths of his being, something he did not have for which his soul cried out.

I want you to see that this young man came to the right person to get an answer to the problem he had. He came to

Christ. I don't care what your problem is, young people, whether it be physical or philosophical or spiritual, the Son of God has an answer. Whether it be a marital problem, or a problem of puppy love (which is real to the puppy!) or a problem of finances, or a problem of sin—bring it to Christ.

Now, the young man asked the right question of Jesus. He asked what he should do to gain eternal life. He wanted to find a reason for his existence. Would it just end in a blank—a question mark? Would he wink out and that would be all?

Many young people today are troubled about finding a meaning or purpose in what they are doing. They have no philosophy of life. They are asking, "Where did we come from? Why are we here? Where are we going?" Others are obsessed by the problem of sex. Sex might be called the major problem of youth today. What can a young person do with this tremendous creative power? How can he dedicate it to that which will keep him from destroying himself?

Will you invite Jesus Christ into your life to work out these problems? Will you let Him find solutions that will lift these burdens? Tell me, has He become absolutely all and wonderful and glorious to you? If not, you can accept Him right now.

This young ruler not only came to the right person; he came with the right attitude. He ran to Jesus. That's the attitude for us to take today, for the Scripture says, "Now is the accepted time; today is the day of salvation."[20] And not only did this young man run to Christ, but he came in an attitude of humility. Notice how he knelt before Jesus, recognizing that there was a lack in his life. Before we ever come to Christ, we must realize that we are sinners. The Bible says, "All have sinned," and, "The wages of sin is death."[21]

Jesus loved this young man. He told him that he lacked but one thing to inherit eternal life—just one simple thing, but it made the difference between heaven and hell. What was it? Jesus told him to sell all he had and give the money to the poor, and then take up his cross and follow him.

"What?" exclaimed the young man, "Sell everything I

have and take up a cross? Jesus, I am very rich. Surely you don't mean that you want all—everything? Why, Jesus, I'll give you half of it, as Zacchaeus did, and I'll do anything else; but not all my riches. Not everything. Jesus, I want something for myself."

Do you know what Jesus was doing? He was putting His finger on the one problem in that young man's life that kept him from coming all the way for Jesus Christ. One problem, that's all: he loved his money too much. What about you? Is that your problem? Or is it some habit, or a secret desire, or an ungodly alliance? Jesus was pinpointing the thing in that youth's life that stood between him and God, and He was saying, "Young man, I must be Lord and Master. I must have control of every phase of your personality and life and being."

But Satan came to that rich young ruler and whispered to him. What did he say? We don't know. Perhaps it was, "Put it off for a while and I will show you a good time." Perhaps it was, "Don't give up your money, you might starve to death." Whatever it was, the young man listened and turned away from Jesus, and the lines of his face took on—perhaps unconsciously—a sorrowful aspect. He started away from the Lord, down the broad road that leads to destruction.

I can see the Lord Jesus standing with heavy heart and watching him as the youth made his decision to walk that road. He made his choice to live another life, possibly even a good life, but a life without Jesus Christ.

It is true that we can have a good time outside of Christ. The Scripture speaks of the "pleasures of sin."[22] We can kick up our heels and sow our wild oats and have a fine time. But the Scripture adds that the "pleasures of sin" are "for a season." The end of that kind of life is destruction and hell.

Jesus tells us that it is very easy to take the broad turnpike that leads to destruction and very hard to travel the narrow way that leads to eternal life, and that few find the narrow way. There is a lot of trouble along the narrow way, but there is also real joy. It was "for the joy that was set before him" that Jesus "endured the cross, despising the shame."[23]

Let poverty come! Let disaster strike! The Christian knows he is safe; that he is sure of going to be with Christ.

When the rich young man went away, he may have told Jesus that he would "think it over for a while." But the Bible does not record that he ever got another chance to give his allegiance to the Savior. And we see that type of person again in the Bible as an old man, proud and cold and hard and very well-to-do. As he walks through his huge fields he says, "Soul, take your ease.[24] Eat, drink and be merry. Enjoy life and retire." Then he goes to bed. And at midnight there is a scream. The servants cry, "It is from the master's room," and they find him there, dying, with his hands clenched in a strange manner—as though he had been holding something and it got away.

God calls him a "fool." He does not use the expression often, but he does so label a man who lets his money stand between him and his soul's welfare. Notice that the rich young ruler, as his story is told in the Gospels, came to the right person. He came at the right time, when he was young. He came with the right attitude. He came with the right principles. He asked the right question. He got the right answer. But he did the wrong thing.

He had one foot almost within the Kingdom of God. He was so close to the Kingdom, and yet he missed it by a million miles. Some of you are also very close to the Kingdom of God. Like the young man, you are asking, "How can I find life?"

Don't let what happened to him happen to you. Don't let anything block your path. Down deep in your soul you know what it is that is keeping you from God. You know that you are a sinner, and that you need to give your heart and life to Jesus Christ. Come to Him now!

From *Decision* Magazine, October 1968. © 1968 Billy Graham Evangelistic Association. Used by permission.

NOTES

1. Mohandas K. Gandhi (1869-1948), the Hindu leader, made many statements about Christianity. The source of this one is not identified.
2. Ephesians 2:8-9.

3. John 6:37.
4. John 6:44.
5. Cf. Augustine (354-430), *Confessions*, tr. by Sherwood Wirt as *Love Song* (New York: Harper & Row, 1971), pp. 117-18.
6. *The Heart of John Wesley's Journal*, ed. P. L. Parker (Old Tappan, NJ: Fleming H. Revell, n.d.), pp. 43-44.
7. Romans 3:23.
8. Mark 15:34.
9. John 1:12.
10. Matthew 18:3.
11. Matthew 7:29.
12. John 14:6.
13. John 10:10.
14. Matthew 6:33.
15. Cf. Matthew 10:37; Luke 14:26.
16. Luke 14:24.
17. Psalm 16:11.
18. John 3:2.
19. 2 Timothy 2:22.
20. 2 Corinthians 6:2.
21. Romans 6:23.
22. Hebrews 11:25.
23. Hebrews 12:2.
24. Luke 12:19.

Francis A. Schaeffer, 1912-1984

In the years since Francis August Schaeffer died of lymphatic cancer in Rochester, Minnesota, evangelical Christians have differed about the significance of his work. Millions who have read his books regard him as a superb teacher and one of the most influential thinkers of the twentieth century.

There are also those who consider themselves evangelicals, but find Schaeffer's doctrinal orthodoxy and his insistence on Biblical inerrancy too restrictive for their taste. Still others, disturbed by his comments on art and culture, challenge his competence in some of the subjects he addresses. Where one finds Schaeffer loving, another finds him harsh. Where some find him somber, others point to his statement, "God means Christianity to be fun!"[1] Those who knew him best remember him as a warm human being who loved Jesus and who was devoted to building hope into people in despair.

In the years since his death, five large volumes of Schaeffer's collected works, hours upon hours of his tape recordings, and hundreds of reels of his narrated films have continued to circulate among Christian churches and institutions around the world. The L'Abri Fellowship, which he and his wife, Edith, founded in Switzerland as an international study center, now has branches in several countries. Among educated lay Christians in the English-speaking world, it could be said that Francis Schaeffer remains a household word.

Schaeffer's early life gave little hint of his future ministry. Brought up in a nominally Lutheran working-class family in Philadelphia, he was disillusioned by liberal preaching to the point of becoming an agnostic in his teenage years. When he was converted to Christ, new Christian friends encouraged him to

227

drop out of his engineering program and enroll at Hampden Sidney College, Virginia. He graduated in 1935, and two years at Westminster Theological Seminary followed. Schaeffer found himself caught up in a theological controversy that caused him to move to a new school, Faith Seminary, Wilmington, Delaware, where he received his bachelor of divinity degree. He subsequently pastored Bible Presbyterian churches in Grove City and Chester, Pennsylvania, and St. Louis, Missouri.

In 1948, now married, Schaeffer took his growing family to Europe where he served several years under an independent Presbyterian mission board in an outreach program called "Children for Christ." Three years later he faced a spiritual crisis in his own life, caused partly by his conviction that he could find little reality of Christian joy in the lives of orthodox Christians. His studies in philosophy and his friendship with European students in Switzerland, where he was living, brought into being the L'Abri Fellowship in the Swiss town of Huemoz.

As an informal community of intellectual seekers, L'Abri grew by attracting students from many countries. Lectures and tapes became the basis for discussion. An article in Time Magazine about the Schaeffers was followed by the publication of his first book, The God Who Is There, in which he blamed the cultural malaise of his time on secular humanism. He soon was in demand as an international lecturer. He began accumulating honorary degrees. In 1978, learning he had cancer, he returned to the States and in his final years became active in social causes. This excerpt is taken from Schaeffer's book Death in the City, vol. 4 of his Complete Works (Wheaton, IL: Crossway Books) by permission of Edith Schaeffer.

TWELVE

LIVING BY FAITH
by Francis A. Schaeffer

The Apostle Paul says in his letter to the Romans that the just shall live by faith.[2] That is, they shall live existentially by reliance on God and faith in Him. We turn now to see what living by faith means in our twentieth-century world.

We who live in the second half of our century live in an increasingly complicated universe—much more complicated for us than for people just a few years ago. Our telescopes see farther, and we speak of light-years running up into huge numbers. The very magnitude of those numbers tends to confuse us. On the other hand, our physicists work with smaller and smaller particles, and as mass retreats into energy and energy into formulae, reality seems to slip through our fingers. We look and shrink away.

Or, as we examine the tiny particles, we grow like Alice in Wonderland. But our size doesn't help us here because we tend to become uncomfortable as we observe material reality reduced to sets of mathematical formulae and energy particles dashing about at furious speed. Yet we must understand, if we would live as Christians, that while these phenomena are indeed complicated and confusing, nevertheless from the Biblical viewpoint the universe is simple.

Let me illustrate this. Imagine that the room where you are now sitting has the curtains drawn and the doors locked. Let us suppose that this room is the only universe that God has made. Now that would be possible; God could have made such a universe. So let us say that the only universe that exists is this room with the doors locked and the curtains drawn. There is nothing outside, absolutely nothing. We are in a universe that can be seen with one look around the room.

Now let us go further. Suppose we have two chairs in this room and that sitting on these chairs are two persons, the only two persons in the universe. As we consider them, we find that they differ. One is a totally consistent materialist. As far as he is concerned, the universe is made up of nothing but mass, energy, and motion; that's all there is to it. On the other chair sits a Christian who lives in the light of the teaching of the Bible as the propositional revelation of God. And these two sit facing each other in a universe in which they are alone.

After they have looked at each other awhile, the materialist says, "Now I'm going to explore our universe."

And the Christian says, "That's fine."

So the materialist begins to study the universe, and it takes him a long time. He goes through all the scientific procedures that we now use to examine our own universe. He uses the sciences of chemistry, biology, physics, and so on. He reaches back of the periodic table to the atom. He examines everything from the paint on the wall to the more basic particles. All of this takes him years.

Finally as an older man he comes to the Bible-believing Christian, bringing with him a large set of books. He says, "Here are some books, nicely bound, that give in great detail a description of our universe." So the Christian takes a number of months, even years, to study those books with care.

At last the Christian turns to the materialist and says, "Well, this is a tremendous work. You have told me a great deal about my universe that I wouldn't otherwise have known. However, my friend, while it is all very instructive, it is woefully incomplete."

You can imagine this materialist, who has spent his lifetime pouring his heart into all the measuring and weighing, being suddenly taken aback. He says to the Christian, "Well, now, I'm shocked that you would tell me it's not all here. What have I missed?"

The Christian then responds somewhat like this: "I have a book here, the Bible, and it tells me things that you do not know. It tells me the origin of the universe. Your scientific investigation by its very nature cannot do that. It says nothing about where you and I as persons came from. You have examined us because we, like the paint on the wall, are phenomena in the universe. You have studied something of our physiology and psychology and have presented me with several volumes on the subject, but you have not told me how we came to be here. In short, you don't know the origin either of the universe or of us.

"Furthermore," the Christian continues, "I know from this book that there is more to the universe than you have described. There is an unseen portion as well as a seen portion, and there is a cause-and-effect relationship between them. They are not mutually exclusive, but are parts of one reality. It's as if you had taken an orange, sliced it in half, and only concerned yourself with one of the halves. To understand reality in our universe, you have to consider both halves—both the seen and the unseen."

In this sense *supernatural* is not a good word to describe the unseen portion. We must understand that the unseen portion of the universe is just as natural and as real as the seen portion. The seen and the unseen are not totally separated. When we do certain things, it makes a difference in the unseen world, and things in the unseen world make a difference in the seen world.

The Christian would say to the materialist, "Your volume on the philosophy of history does not hang together. The reason is that you are only looking at half of what is there. You are only looking at half of history; you do not take into account the unseen portion. Consequently your philosophy of history will never be sound."

He is right. Nobody has ever produced a satisfactory philosophy of history beginning with the materialistic viewpoint. There is too much in the world that does not make sense when taken as if it were all that there is. One cannot produce a philosophy of history based on only half of history.

Now, what happens next? These two persons look at each other rather askance because their two primary views of the universe are set one against the other. The materialist replies, "You're out of your mind. You are talking about things you can't see."

The consistent Christian responds, "Well, you may say that I am a mental case because I am talking about things I cannot see, but your position is completely unbalanced. You know only half of your own universe."

Let us notice something extremely important: these two views can never be brought into synthesis. One man is not a little right and the other a little right, so that a synthesis would be better than both. These are two mutually exclusive views. One is right and the other is wrong. If you say less, you reduce Christianity to a psychological crutch, a glorified aspirin. That doesn't mean the Christian cannot glean much detail from the materialist's observations. But as far as the comprehensive view of the universe is concerned, there can be no synthesis. Either this person is right and that person is wrong, or that person is right and this person is wrong. It is a total antithesis.

Let me pursue their situation further. Suppose that hanging on the wall of our room is a large clock. All of a sudden it stops ticking. The two men turn and look at it and say, "What a pity. The clock has stopped."

The materialist adds, "This will never do, and because only you and I are in this universe, one of us must clamber up the wall and start the clock. There's nobody else to do it."

The Christian replies, "Now, wait a moment. Yes, it is possible for one of us to climb up and start the clock, but there is another possibility. I may talk to the One who made this universe—One who is not in the universe in the sense of it merely being an extension of His essence—and He can start the clock."

Here is a tremendous difference in attitude. You can imagine the reaction of the materialist. "Now I know you are out of your mind. You are talking about someone we can't see starting a material clock." Anyone who has been engaged in modern twentieth-century thought will recognize the relevance of his reaction. I also think we may see here why so many Christians have no sense of God's reality. They are not certain that it is possible for the God who made the universe to "start the clock" when a Christian talks to Him.

Allow me to give you an illustration from experience. Once I was flying at night over the North Atlantic. The year was 1947, and I was coming back from my first visit to Europe. Our airplane, one of those old DC4s with twin engines on each wing, was within two or three minutes of the middle of the Atlantic. Suddenly the two engines on one wing stopped functioning. I had already flown a good bit and could sense that the aircraft was in trouble.

I remember thinking, *If I'm about to go down into the ocean, I had better get my coat.* As I did so, I spoke to the flight attendant and told her, "There's something wrong with the engines."

She was a bit snappy and said, "You people always think there's something wrong with the engines."

So I shrugged my shoulders, but put on my coat. I had no sooner sat down than the lights came on, and a very agitated copilot appeared. "We're in trouble," he said. "Hurry and put on your life jackets."

So down we went; we fell and fell, until in the middle of the night with no moon we could actually see the waves breaking under us in the darkness. As we were making our descent, I prayed. Interestingly enough, a radio message had gone out, a MAYDAY that was picked up and broadcast immediately all over the United States. The flash announcement said, "A plane is having engine trouble in the middle of the Atlantic." My wife, Edith, heard about the announcement, and immediately gathered our three little girls together and knelt and began to pray. They were praying in St. Louis, Missouri, while I was praying on the plane. Meanwhile we were going down and down.

Then, as we were watching the waves breaking beneath us and everybody was ready for the ditching, suddenly the two engines started up, and we went on to Gander airport in Newfoundland. After we landed I looked up the pilot and asked him what had happened.

"Well," he said, "It's a strange thing, something we can't explain. Only rarely do two engines shut down on one wing, but when they do, you can make it a rule that they don't start again. We don't understand it."

I said to him, "I can explain it."

He looked at me. "How?"

I said, "My Father in heaven started them because I was praying."

That pilot had the strangest look on his face as he turned away. I'm sure he was the man sitting in the materialist's chair.

Here is the point: there is no distinction between the clock starting and those engines starting. Is it or is it not possible for the God who made the mechanistic portion of the universe to start the clock or start the engines? The materialist must say "No"; the Bible-believing Christian says "Yes."

Let us now get away from our small universe of a single room and suddenly throw wide the curtains, open the doors, push out the walls, the ceiling and the floor, and have the universe as it is in its full size, as it has been created by God. Instead of two persons, there are many people in the universe, but they are still represented by these two. What we must see is that no matter how deeply we get into the particles of matter and energy, or how much we learn by our telescopes and radiotelescopes about the vastness of the created universe, in reality the universe is no more complicated than the room we have been describing. It is only larger, that's all. Looking at the entire universe, we either see it as the materialist sees it or as the Christian sees it. We see it with one set of presuppositions or with the other.

However, what one must realize is that seeing the world as a Christian does not mean simply saying, "I am a Christian. I believe in the supernatural world." It is possible to be saved through faith in Christ and then spend much of our lives in the chair of the materialist. We can say we believe in a supernatural world, and yet live as though there were no supernatural in the universe at all. It is not enough merely to say that we believe in such a supernatural environment; we must ask, "Which chair am I sitting in at this existential moment?"

Christianity is not just mental assent to the truth of certain doctrines. That is only the beginning. It would be like a starving man sitting in front of great heaps of food and saying, "I believe the food exists. I believe it is real," and yet never tasting it. It is not enough merely to say, "I am a Christian," and then in practice to live as if present contact with the supernatural were something far-off and strange. Many Christians I have known seem to act as though they came into contact with the supernatural just twice—once when they were justified and became Christians, and again when they died. The rest of the time they acted as though they were sitting in the materialist's chair.

The difference between a Christian who is being supernatural in practice, and one who says he is a Christian but lives like a materialist, can be illustrated by the difference between a storage battery and a light plug. There are Christians who seem to think that when they are born again, they become a self-contained unit like a storage battery. From then on until they die, they have to operate under their own power and pep. But this is wrong. After we are justified once for all through faith in Christ, we are to live in supernatural communion with the Lord every moment. We are to be like lights plugged into an electric current.

The Bible makes it plain that our joy and spiritual power depend on a continuing relation to God. If we do not love and draw on the Lord as we should, the plug is pulled from its socket, and the spiritual power and spiritual joy cease. The Apostle Paul wrote to the Corinthians, "The grace of the Lord Jesus Christ, and the love of God, and the communion of the Holy Spirit, be with you all."[3] The reality of the communication of the Holy Spirit, who lives within us and who is the agent of the whole Trinity, is to be a continuing reality in the Christian's life.

Let us be more specific. The Bible says that Jesus Christ rose physically from the dead. It implies that if you had been there that day, you would have seen Christ stand up and walk away in a space-time, observable episode of true history.

The materialist says, "No, I don't believe it. Christ was

not raised from the dead." That is unbelief. Liberal theology is also unbelief because it says either that Jesus was not raised from the dead in history, or that maybe He was and maybe He wasn't, because who knows what's going to happen in this world in which you can't be sure of anything? The historic resurrection of Christ doesn't really matter, says this theology; what matters is that the church got a big push from thinking He was raised in history. They understand the psychological importance of the resurrection, and they may even leave open the door to an actual resurrection, since we live in a universe that we cannot be sure of. I would say that the old liberalism, the new liberalism, and materialism are basically the same. To all of them the same word finally applies: *unbelief*.

Now, we are Bible-believing Christians. We stand and say, "No, I'm not going to accept that. I'm going to speak out against the materialist and against the old and the new liberalism. Jesus Christ was raised from the dead, and He did ascend with the same body His disciples saw and touched. Between His resurrection and His ascension, He appeared and disappeared many times. He often went back and forth between the seen and the unseen world in those forty days. And then finally He took an official departure at the Mount of Olives."

But the Bible says that if Christ is raised from the dead, we are supposed to act upon it in our moment-by-moment lives. Its importance lies not just in past history. So the Bible-believing Christian says, "Well, I believe it!" The materialist says, "I don't believe it!" and sits in unbelief. But what about the person who says, "I believe it, I believe it," but then doesn't act upon this in faith in his daily life? What shall we say about him? I have made up a word for it. I call it *unfaith*.

The unbelieving person says, "Well, the resurrection—I really don't believe it." The Christian says, "I do believe it." But surely, shouldn't I [as a Christian] call it *unfaith* if I am not acting upon [my belief] and letting Christ, whom I say is raised from the dead, bring forth His fruit through me?

With this in mind, let's look at prayer. I feel that the

determinism of our own generation has infiltrated us as evangelical Christians so that we tend not to be praying people. We must understand what prayer is. Prayer according to the Bible is speaking to God. The reason why we can speak to God is that He exists. He is personal, and we are made in His image. Since we are made in His image, it shouldn't be surprising that we can be in communication with Him, even though He is infinite and we are finite.

When our guilt is removed through the finished work of Christ, communication with God is to be expected. You and I communicate in a horizontal direction with each other through verbalization. In fact, many anthropologists say that verbalization more than anything else distinguishes man from nonman. God too communicates to us in verbalization in Scripture, and we communicate to God in verbalization by prayer. It's as simple and as profound as that.

How then does prayer fit into the Biblical view of the universe? God made the universe. It is external to Himself, not spatially, but in the sense that it is not an extension of His essence. There is, of course, a machine portion of the universe, but neither God nor man is caught in the machine. There is a uniformity of natural causes, but not in a closed system. The course of nature can be changed—can be reordered—just as I through a choice of the will can interrupt something, for example, by reaching over and turning off a light. This act of my will reorders the natural flow of cause and effect. It is in this setting that the Bible sets forth its teaching about prayer.

To return therefore to the airplane: I prayed, my family was praying, and God started the airplane engines. In this case He did. The distinction is that the Christian knows it is not absurd to think God can "start the engines." To think or act otherwise is for the Christian to be in the place of unfaith.

This is prayer, this is what it is supposed to be. God as well as man can start the engines in the space-time world. Without the true orthodox doctrine of God and man, prayer is just nonsense. You have to understand that there is a personal God and that He has created the universe.

But let us notice that this emphasis must not be just a matter of doctrine. We must really sit in the supernaturalist's chair and pray. If a Christian does not pray, if he does not live in an attitude of prayer, then no matter what he says about his doctrine, no matter how many naughty names he calls the unbelieving materialist, the Christian has moved over and is sitting in the materialist's chair. He is living in unfaith if he is afraid to act upon the supernatural in the present life.

Unfaith turns Christianity into a mere philosophy. Of course Christianity is a philosophy, though not a rationalistic one because we have not worked it out for ourselves. Rather, God has told us the answers. In this sense it is the true philosophy, for it gives the right answers to man's philosophic and intellectual questions. However, while it is the true philosophy, our Father in heaven did not mean it to be only theoretical or abstract. He meant it to tell us about Himself—how we can get to heaven, but equally how we can live right now in the universe as it is, with both the seen and the unseen portions standing in equal reality.

If Christians just use Christianity as a matter of mental assent between conversion and death, if they use it simply to answer intellectual questions, it is like using a silver spoon for a screwdriver. I can believe that a silver spoon makes a good screwdriver at certain times, but it is meant for something else. To take the silver spoon that is meant to feed you moment by moment and keep it in your toolbox to use only as a screwdriver is silly.

Let us look further at the Christian living in unfaith. If the Bible-believing Christian has moved over and is in practice sitting in the materialist's chair, he is living as though the universe were something different than it is. He is out of step with the universe and is in practice living as though he is more ignorant than a pagan in a remote jungle.

Suppose three men were sitting together in a jet airliner, one against the window, one against the aisle, and one in the middle. In the window seat is a pagan who hasn't a clue as to how the airplane flies. He is terrified as it takes off. The man on the aisle, by contrast, knows every nut and bolt in this type of airplane; he designed it. But he does not believe in any supernatural at all.

You, as a Christian, are sitting in the middle.

Which of the other two men would, in your view, best understand the universe? The pagan doesn't have a clue about the aircraft, but he knows that there is a seen and an unseen portion in the universe because he worships demons. The man on the aisle knows all about the plane, and he doesn't worship demons, but he is unaware that there is any unseen portion at all. The pagan is less ignorant of reality than the engineer, for the latter is living in only half of the universe. But what about you as a Christian? If you say that the universe has a spiritual dimension and yet do not live as if it did, you are acting as though you know less than the pagan.

Perhaps now we will begin to see why in the evangelical church we often have a feeling of dustiness, unreality, and abstraction. I think the reason is that many are functioning as though they knew less about the universe than the pagan knows. They have moved over into unfaith and are living as though the universe is naturalistic. No wonder there is a dustiness! In such a case the evangelical church is a museum of dead artifacts representing what once was living practice of the doctrine we still say we believe.

If courses in a Christian college are being taught as though the professor is sitting in the materialist's chair, is it any wonder that there is unreality? It is possible to teach our subjects that way. We can carry on our church life that way. We can carry on our evangelism that way. And our children then look at us, shake their heads, and think, *"Well, certainly there is something very unreal and musty in what I see in my teacher's, my pastor's, and my parents' Christian lives." If we sit in the chair of unfaith, that is the result we should expect.*

But let us take note: there are only two chairs, not three. And at this present moment we are sitting either in one or the other. Unfaith is just the Christian sitting in the materialist's chair. At every moment, existentially, as Christians, the two chairs are before us. I am either yielding my life to the living

Christ at a given moment or I am not. I am either in one chair or the other.

Which chair are we in? How do we live our lives? What is the "set of the sail" in the way we live? None of us is perfect, it is true. All of us sometimes find ourselves in the materialist's chair. But is this where we habitually sit? Is this how we usually teach our subjects? Is this the way we usually study? Is it even the way we do what we call "the Lord's work"? Are we sitting in the chair of unfaith while we are trying to present the doctrines of belief?

Being a Bible-believing Christian, then, not only means believing with our heads, but in this present moment acting through faith on that belief. True spirituality is acting at the given moment upon the doctrines which one as a Christian says he believes.

We must fight the Lord's battles with the Lord's weapons in faith, sitting in the chair of belief. Only then can we have any part in the real battle. If we fight the Lord's battles merely by duplicating the way the world does its work, we are like little boys playing with wooden swords, pretending they are in the battle while their big brothers are away at war in some distant and bloody land.

The Lord will not honor with power the way of unfaith in His children, because it does not give Him the honor. He is left out. That is true in Christian activities, in missionary work, in evangelism, in anything you name. Living supernaturally does not mean doing less work; nor does it mean less work getting done, but more. Who can do more? We, with our own energy and wisdom, or the God who created heaven and earth? Who can work in space-time history with a power which none of us has?

God exists. And if we through faith stay in the Bible-believing chair moment by moment in practice and do not move into the chair of unfaith, Christ will bring forth His fruit through us. The fruit will differ with each of us, but it will be His fruit.

*   *   *

Our generation is overwhelmingly naturalistic. There is an almost complete commitment to the concept of the uniformity of natural causes in a closed system. This is its distinguishing mark. If we are not careful, even though we say we are Biblical Christians and supernaturalists, the naturalism of our generation tends to come in upon us. It may infiltrate our thinking without our recognizing its coming, like a fog creeping in through a window opened only half an inch. As soon as this happens, Christians begin to lose the reality of their Christian lives.

As I travel about, I am impressed with the number of times I am asked by Christians about the loss of reality in their lives. It tends to get covered by the barnacles of naturalistic thought. I suppose this is one of half a dozen questions that are most often presented to me by young people from Christian backgrounds: where is the reality? Where has it gone? I have heard it asked in honest, open desperation by fine young Christians in many countries. As the ceiling of the naturalistic comes down upon us, as it invades by injection or by connotation, reality gradually slips away.

Surely this is one of the greatest, and perhaps the greatest reason for a loss of reality—that while we say we believe one thing, we allow the spirit of the naturalism of the age to creep into our thinking unrecognized. All too often the reality is lost because the ceiling is down too close upon our heads. It is too low.

Now the Christian's spirituality does not stand alone. It is related to the unity of the Bible's view of the universe. That means we must understand—intellectually, with the doors open—that the universe is not what our generation says it is. It is seeing only the naturalistic universe. We are to love God enough to say, "Thank you," even in the midst of the battle. We must immediately understand, as we say this, that our saying it has no meaning whatsoever unless we live in a personal universe in which there is a personal God who objectively exists.

In the normal perspective it is very difficult to say "no" to things and to self, in the things-mentality and the self-men-

tality of men, especially in the twentieth century. But on the
Mount of Transfiguration we are brought face to face with a
supernatural universe. Here we find Moses and Elijah speaking to Christ as He is glorified;[4] and we observe that this
supernatural universe is not a far-off universe. Quite the contrary. There is a perfect continuity with normal life.

So the day after these things had occurred, Jesus and the
disciples went down the mountain and entered into the normal activities of life.[5] Indeed, the normal sequence was continuing while they were on the mountain. Here is a perfect
example of the temporal and spatial relationship. As they
climbed the mountain, there was no place where they passed
into the philosophic "other." If they had had watches upon
their wrists, those watches would not have stopped at some
point; they would have ticked away. And when they came
down, it was the next day and the normal sequence had proceeded. Here we find the supernatural world in relationship
to the normal sequence and spatial relationships of this
present world.

When one refers to the supernatural, immediately the
naturalistic man is determined to get rid of it. He is determined to argue that it is not there. That is why liberal theology, which is naturalistic, tries to make a theology that will
stand when there is nothing left but anthropology. Here is
really where the battle of truth is being fought throughout the
world. But if we see this, then we have thrust upon us the
necessity, the high calling and the duty to live in the light of
the existence of the two parts of the universe, the seen and the
unseen parts, in the realization that the "heavenlies" are not
far off. They are about us here.

Christ tells us us that when a sinner repents, the angels
in heaven rejoice.[6] This is, in twentieth-century language, a
cause-and-effect relationship. There is a cause upon the earth,
and in the unseen world there is an effect. The supernatural
world is not a long way off, and our part is not unimportant,
because we are observed; and more than that, there is a cause-
and-effect relationship with the real battle in the "heavenlies"
on the basis of our living the Christian life or not.

If we keep in mind 1 Corinthians 4:9, in which we are told that we are "on the stage" before men and angels, we must also note what Paul says in 1 Corinthians 2:4, "And my speech and my preaching were not with enticing words of man's wisdom, but in demonstration of the Spirit and of power." In demonstration before whom? In the light of Paul's remarks in chapter 4, it is surely not only a demonstration before the lost world, or before the church, but a demonstration before the angels as well.

What Paul is saying here is that the preaching of the gospel to simple or more "complicated" people fails in both cases if it does not include a demonstration of the Christian life, if it does not include the work of the Holy Spirit. The fact that Christ as the Bridegroom brings forth fruit through me as the bride, through the agency of the indwelling Holy Spirit by faith—this fact opens the way for me as a Christian to begin to know in the present life the reality of the supernatural.

This terrain is where the Christian is to live. Doctrine is important, but it is not an end in itself. Moment by moment there is to be an experiential reality. And the glory of the experiential reality of the Christian, as opposed to the bare existential experience or the religious experiences of the East, is that we can do it with all the intellectual doors and windows open. We do not need a dark room; we do not need to be under the influence of hallucinatory drugs; we do not need to be listening to a certain kind of music; we can know the reality of the supernatural here and now.

This experiential result is not just an experience of bare supernaturalism, one without content, which we are unable to describe and communicate. It is much more. It is a moment-by-moment, increasing, experiential relationship with Christ and the whole Trinity. The doors are open now— the intellectual doors and also the doors to reality.

So this is the "how." This is how to live a life of freedom from the bonds of sin—not perfection, for that is not promised to us in this life. But this is how to have freedom in the present life not only from the bonds of sin, but also from the results of those bonds. This is the way we may exhibit the reality of the supernatural to a generation which has lost its way. This is the Christian life, and this is true spirituality. In the light of the unity of the Bible's teaching about the supernatural nature of the universe, the "how" is the power of the crucified and the risen Christ, through the agency of the indwelling Holy Spirit, by faith.

NOTES

1. Francis A. Schaeffer, *Complete Works* (Wheaton, IL: Crossway Books,1982), vol. 3, p. 355
2. Romans 1:17.
3. 2 Corinthians 13:14.
4. Mark 9:4.
5. Mark 9:14.
6. Luke 15:10.

Charles W. Colson, 1931-

Why would a convicted felon, a Watergate conspirator, be included in a collection of outstanding Christian writers of the twentieth century? Have we such a dearth of articulate religious leaders that we must resort to those whose lives have been touched by scandal?

Were we to follow such critics, we would have to delete from the Bible David's psalms, Moses' prayers, and Paul's letters; for before these men turned to God, they too broke the law.

Charles Wendell Colson was born in 1931 in Boston, Massachusetts, the son of a distinguished Episcopalian family. After being graduated from Brown University, he served in the U. S. Marine Corps and later attended the law school of George Washington University. He filled several minor federal government positions, joined a Washington law firm, and in 1969 was appointed special counsel to President Richard Nixon. In the years that followed he became known as the "White House hatchet man."

The story of the Watergate break-in and subsequent cover-up is well known and does not belong here. Colson was convicted for his role in obstructing justice, a role that included the disseminating of derogatory information. He served seven months in two federal prisons. After his release in 1975, he wrote Born Again, *a book that describes his conversion to Jesus Christ during the Watergate era.*

A year later Colson formed an organization called Prison Fellowship, which seeks to aid victims of America's overcrowded penal system. By 1990 Prison Fellowship had established a network of some 30,000 volunteers who work in over 500 prisons in the United States. More than 250,000 prisoners and their families have benefited from the Fellowship's programs, which include among other things in-prison seminars, Bible studies, and discipleship training. The organization now functions with similar programs in over forty countries worldwide. Colson's license to practice law has been restored.

Justice Fellowship, which was launched in 1983, provides assistance to government officials who deal with criminal justice issues and urges alternative punishments to imprisonment, such as restitution and community service. The latest expansion of the ministry has established an assistance program for victims of crime.

Besides Born Again, Colson has authored several books, including Life Sentence, Loving God, Who Speaks for God?, Kingdoms in Conflict, and Against the Night. Now a Southern Baptist, he has been the recipient of many honors and honorary degrees and is much sought after as a lecturer. He has been called a prophet of our day. He has, in fact, developed into one of the leading exponents of evangelical Christianity in the latter part of our century.

Some of the very people who condemned Colson for his Watergate involvement are now endorsing the man and his ministry. Referring to his conversion, Bob Woodward of the Washington Post, who was one of the first to expose the Watergate cover-up, has stated, "I think it's genuine. I salute him. I think he is one of the people who, after Watergate, went on really to redeem himself and do something important."

The two excerpts from Colson's writings are taken by permission from Born Again (Revell, 1976) and Kingdoms in Conflict (Zondervan/Morrow, 1987).

THIRTEEN

SIGNS OF THE KINGDOM
by Charles W. Colson

My transfer to Holabird Prison in Baltimore [from Maxwell air base prison camp in Alabama] came unexpectedly in mid-November, 1974. Once again I was to be a witness, this time in the Watergate trial of Bob Haldeman, John Ehrlichman, and John Mitchell.

I left Maxwell with strangely mixed feelings, hating the place but loving so many of the people. We had been through a lot together. We cared about each other. On Christmas Eve my heart was so heavy for the men at Maxwell in their lonely outpost that I spent much of the evening writing Paul [Kramer] and the others.

Since we had been denied the privilege to attend midnight services at a local church in Baltimore, the four Watergate prisoners [John Dean, Herbert Kalmbach, Jeb Magruder and myself] assembled in Dean's room. Jeb and I read aloud from the Scriptures about the birth of Christ. We prayed quietly for each other and our families, and in the silence I asked an extra blessing for the men at Maxwell.

It was while the jury was still out in the Watergate trial after Christmas that serious rumors began trickling out about our imminent release. As is standard practice the four of us had filed motions asking for reduction of sentence; normally they are routinely rejected. But the judges had not yet acted on them. They were waiting for something, we knew, perhaps the trial's end. Our hopes grew as the speculation became epidemic.

Jeb and I became the activists, suggesting that we peti-

tion the Justice Department, flood President Ford with letters, file new motions with the judges. Dean, too, was map-
ping his campaign. Kalmbach was the first of us eligible for
parole, but his application had been ensnarled in red tape. He
had the most legitimate reason to be impatient. Instead he was
the steadiest of the four.

"Look, fellows," Herb said one evening just after New
Year's. "I've done what I can do; my lawyers are doing everything. I'm just going to trust the lawyers"—he paused, staring at
me—"and the Lord."

Herb was right; his words were like dashing cold water
on my face. I had slipped back into trying to do things my
way. How easy it is to fall on your face in the Christian walk.
Harold [Senator Harold Hughes] had brought me up short
on this very point in December. "Look, Chuck, until you surrender this to the Lord, really put your whole trust in Him,
you are simply punishing yourself. Just thank Him for everything. Turn it all over to Him, trust Him, and you'll be set
free."

"Sure," I snapped back. "It's easy enough for you to say
that. You'll be home tonight. I go on day after day—the
dreary endless sameness, the closed-in, trapped feeling. It is
hell." Harold was right. I knew it. But so desperately did I
want my freedom that I was fighting again.

On January 8 I was in Washington for more interroga-
tion on other cases at the prosecutor's office. Our meeting
was interrupted midmorning by an emergency phone call.
Dean's lawyer calling me. He explained that John was at
Holabird and could not call me but had asked him to do so.
John wanted me to hear it from him first.

"What is it?" I asked impatiently.

"John Dean has been released today by Judge Sirica,"
the lawyer said. "He wanted to be sure you heard it from him,
not over the radio."

"Why?" I asked. "It's great news."

"Well—it is for John," he replied, "and for Jeb and Herb,
too, but it's kind of tough on you."

For a long moment I couldn't believe the words pounding into my ears. Magruder, Kalmbach, and Dean, all sentenced by Judge Sirica, were set free. I was not. Because I'd been sentenced by a different judge, Gerhard Gesell, my future was still much in doubt.

By the time I arrived back at Holabird, John, Herb, and Jeb had already left for home. A heavy pall hung over the ramshackle barracks that night. I walked down the hall and stared into Dean's room where each night the four of us had met. There was nothing but the bed, its dirty mattress bare, two chairs, and the small desk. It was quiet—an eerie silence. On my desk I found a hand-scribbled note:

> Dear Chuck,
>
> It is difficult to know what to say, other than I know you will soon be freed. Rest assured that I will be calling for your freedom when I'm first confronted by the press. Also I will be in touch with you soon to talk about it all. My prayers are with you, and my actions will do whatever I can to help.
>
> Your friend,
> John

The evening television news highlighted the release of the three men with scenes of the jubilant homecoming in the Magruders' front yard, neighbors gathered for the welcome, interviews with the families. For Patty, watching it was nearly unbearable. Each week end she had visited with the other families. Patty, Gail Magruder, and Mo Dean were friends, enjoying the dubious camaraderie of being prison widows together.

The next morning I stayed in my room reading the Scriptures, waiting for the phone to ring on the marshal's desk with the news that I felt had to come. Fittingly, the lesson in my devotional literature, "Our Daily Bread," for this gloomy day, January 9, was entitled "The Philosophy of Patience." The key Scripture passage: "Rest in the Lord, and wait patiently for him . . . " (Psalm 37:7).

The only call that day was from Dave Shapiro [a former law partner, now representing me]. "No news," he said, "and the scuttlebutt from the courthouse ain't good. Gesell doesn't like to have anyone think he's being forced to follow Sirica's lead. Hang tough, my boy."

Time seemed to stand still. I stared out of my little room at the prickly strands of barbed wire, tried to read and write, but my mind wandered. The marshals were sympathetic, dropping almost all barriers between captor and captive. A lean, rawboned southerner named Jack, an all-out believer, was the most helpful. "The Lord will handle this," he said confidently.

The visiting hours were precious now, but hard, too, as I watched Patty suffering the agony of the vigil, our hopes fading each day as freedom and our own homecoming seemed to be slipping further and further away. Our prayers together, more fervent now, sustained us.

On January 20 the Virginia Supreme Court announced that I was disbarred. It should not have been the shock it was. Most of the lawyers implicated in Watergate were targets of ceaseless cries for reform: "Clean up the bar—purge the scoundrels." The Ervin committee had sent to every State Bar Association computer printouts of every allegation, proven or not, affecting each of us.

I had built false hopes. Although I was unable to attend the hearing before the Supreme Court in Virginia, the members seemed sympathetic, according to [the lawyers] who argued for me. We had asked for a delay until I could appear personally, but now it was denied.

Two days later I was summoned to the prison office. "It's your attorney," the duty marshal told me as he handed me the phone. The trip-hammer went off inside me again. Stupidly I still believed every call would be the one telling me I was free.

"Chuck, are you ready for a tough one?" The voice on the other end was Ken Adams. *How many tough ones are left?* I wondered. "Go ahead, Ken."

"Your son Christian has been arrested for narcotics possession. He's in jail, but we'll have him out on bail in a few hours."

I couldn't reply; my stomach went again as if someone had kicked me in the middle. Chris, now a freshman at the University of South Carolina, had never caused us any trouble, hardly any worry. He had the kind of personality everybody loved. We'd talked about drugs, Chris and I, and I was certain he never used them. But it was all too true. Chris had taken school board money advanced to him during Christmas vacation and invested $150 in fifteen ounces of marijuana. He hoped to sell it for a quick profit and use the proceeds to replace his old car with one in better condition.

I thought I had been through all the tribulations one person could take. My son in prison seemed the worst blow of all. I knew that Chris had been soured by all that had happened to me, but I never dreamed that it might lead him to do this.

"Now you've got both of us," Chris told the arresting officer in a quote that made the front pages of the papers. It was the frustrated outburst of an eighteen-year-old boy, embittered over what had happened to his dad. That I couldn't be at my son's side made the pain intense.

I never once thought, however, that God had forsaken me. More testing, yes, and more teaching from Him. I knew all the Scriptural references which tell us to praise Him no matter what, but alone by my bunk that cold, bleak January night I simply couldn't bring myself to do it. Surely God could not expect me to praise Him for my son's life being ruined!

And how long must the agony continue? My license to practice law was gone, my son imprisoned, my dad gone, my compatriots freed, and over two years of a three-year sentence still staring me in the face. Though I knew I could not give up, those next days were the most difficult of any that I had spent in prison, probably the most difficult of my life.

Word filtered through that during the first week of February I would be returned to Maxwell, that Holabird was to be closed. It would be good to be with my brothers there

again, but I was deeply concerned now for Patty who had
been through so much the past two years. How would she
take many months of commuting to Alabama? Her sweet,
gentle nature was near the breaking point.

Charlie Morin had nearly abandoned his law practice,
visiting me several times a week and organizing a campaign
to ask President Ford to pardon me. Ken Adams spent full
time on motions and procedures for early parole. Both men
visited often. The mail poured in, too, from warmhearted
people across the country sympathizing that the others were
freed and I was still imprisoned. Their encouragement helped
sustain me.

The brothers at Fellowship House rallied to my aid. On
Tuesday, January 28, Al Quie called: "Chuck, I've been thinking about what else we can do to help you. All of us today
signed a letter to the President appealing for mercy, but is
there anything else?" The voice at the other end didn't sound
like Al; the words came slowly and seemed laden with sadness.

"Al, you guys are doing everything possible," I told
him, "and I love you for it. I just don't know what else you
can do."

"There's got to be something else, Chuck. I have been
thinking—" There was a long pause. "There's an old statute
someone told me about. I'm going to ask the President if I can
serve the rest of your term for you."

Stunned, I could only stammer a protest. Al Quie with
twenty years in Congress, was the sixth-ranking Republican
in the House, senior minority member of the Education and
Labor Committee, and one of the most respected public
figures in Washington. He could not be serious.

"I mean it, Chuck," he said. "I haven't come to this decision lightly."

"I won't let you," I said.

"Your family needs you, and I can't sleep while you're
in prison. I think I'd be a lot happier being inside myself."
The lump in my throat made it impossible to tell Al how
much his offer meant, but that I could not accept it.

That very day Doug Coe sent me a handwritten note. All the brothers would volunteer to serve my sentence, he explained, and then added:

> These past three weeks you have been on my mind constantly. . . . Chuck, a band of like-minded men is being formed by God around the world. The thing you always dreamed of doing for our country and for the people—peace and a better life—can still take place—only now God will get the credit. God only needs men totally committed to Him—and then the mobilization of His resources for the common good of all people can take place. . . .
>
> If I could I would gladly give my life so you could use the wonderful gifts of God that He has entrusted you with, to the glory of God.
>
> I love you, friend—all your companions love you!!
>
> As always,
> Doug.

It was almost more than I imagined possible, this love of one man for another. Christ's love. Al Quie would give up his whole career, Doug Coe would lay down his life, Graham [Purcell] and Harold [Hughes] too. Isn't that what it's really all about? Isn't that the overwhelming gain of knowing Christ Jesus which makes all else as "loss"?[2] And this day I knew Him as never before. I'd felt His presence all right, but now I knew His power and love through the deep caring of four men. All the pain and agony to mind and body was small in comparison.

It was that night in the quiet of my room that I made the total surrender, completing what had begun in Tom Phillips's driveway eighteen long months before. "Lord, if this is what it's all about," I said, "then I thank You. I praise You for leaving me in prison, for letting them take away my license to practice law, yes, even for my son being arrested. I praise You for giving me Your love through these men, for being God, for just letting me walk with Jesus."

With those words came the greatest joy of all, the final release—turning it all over to God as my brother Harold [Hughes] had told me to do. And in the hours that followed, I discovered more strength than I'd ever known before. This was the real mountaintop experience. Above and around me the world was filled with joy and love and beauty. For the first time I felt truly free, even as the fortunes of my life seemed at their lowest ebb.

Forty-eight hours later, at five o'clock on Friday afternoon, Judge Gerhard Gesell telephoned Dave Shapiro. Because of family problems—what had happened to Chris— an order was being prepared to release Charles Colson from prison immediately.

Hours later Jack, the marshal who had been so sympathetic, ran over to us as Patty and I were standing at the front gate at Holabird, bidding good-bye to the small band of inmates.

"The Lord really takes care of His own men," Jack said. "I kind of knew He would set you free today."

"Thank you, brother," I said, "but He did it two nights ago."

* * *

They called it the "Concrete Mama," the nearly one-hundred-year-old patchwork of brick and concrete surrounded by thirty-foot walls set amid the beautiful hill country of Washington state. Mama wasn't beautiful inside, however— not on that October morning in 1979 when I first visited the place.

The state penitentiary at Walla Walla, considered one of the toughest prisons in America, had been cited by an inspection report of the American Corrections Association as overcrowded, filthy, and out of control. The inmates carried knives; homosexuals and drug pushers in silk shirts roamed the cellblocks; an inmate biker gang ran roughshod over underpaid and ill-trained guards as well as the other inmates. Walla Walla was, in the words of a long-time California warden, "simply the worst prison in the U.S."

Four months before our visit a guard had been killed, and Walla Walla had been locked down ever since. That meant the prisoners were confined to their cells for twenty-three out of every twenty-four hours. Fifty-eight guards had gone on strike during the lockdown. Most had subsequently been fired. Morale was miserable.

"When were the men released from lockdown?" I asked the officer at the gate, privately wondering who in my office had managed this kind of scheduling.

"Yesterday," he said, straightening his visored cap and squinting into the sun. "But don't worry, riot police are standing by."

As I was digesting this heartwarming piece of information, the assistant warden, a former Jesuit priest, arrived at the gatehouse.

"Glad you're here, Mr. Colson," he said cheerily. I wasn't sure I was.

"What's it like inside?" I asked.

He shrugged. "Tense, I guess. I don't really know. I don't get into the yard much. Whatever you can do I'm sure will help, though."

Unaccompanied by guards, we toured the concrete prison yard, and the cellblocks confirmed that the ACA had not exaggerated the conditions. The filth and overcrowding were incredible, and the tension in the air was as palpable as the concrete. The two thousand men in Walla Walla were angry.

At the moment their anger was directed at something that had happened during lockdown, Senior Chaplain Jerry Jacobson told me. The one relief from the sterile cement world inside the walls had been a grass playing field in the center of the compound. There the inmates could lounge on the grass and play football. But when the men had been released from lockdown the day before, they discovered that their field had been covered by tons of concrete.

Officials said it had been done for security reasons—the men hid weapons in the grass. Valid or not, the fact was that the prison was now solid concrete. And to make it worse, during the days the men had been locked in, the concrete pad had absorbed the heat of the hot autumn days. In every way Walla Walla was heated to the boiling point.

Chaplain Jacobson accompanied me on my tour, which included a visit to the dungeon-like basement cellblock containing the more than ninety prisoners in protective custody. These were inmates who could not be mixed with the rest of the prison population: informers, psychopaths, and sex offenders. As we completed the tour, a crackling loudspeaker invited all inmates to the auditorium to hear me speak immediately after lunch.

The auditorium was a cavernous room that seated a thousand men. The acoustics were terrible, but the only other meeting place was the chapel, and no one would attend if it was held there, since the chapel was used chiefly as a meeting place for homosexuals.

At two o'clock Jerry introduced me. In front of 850 empty chairs and 150 pairs of unresponsive eyes, I told how Prison Fellowship began, using lines that never failed to produce laughter. There was stony silence.

Two older inmates stared intently from the front row. Both sat erect, arms folded across their chests with an air of authority. I concentrated on them as I concluded my talk.

Later, as I walked across the yard to leave, consoling myself that at least there had been no trouble, I heard a gruff voice call my name. I turned and saw the two inmates from the front row. The first, a man in his forties with graying hair, stuck out his hand.

"I'm Don Dennis. We've been talking, and we believe you," he said without expression.

The other inmate slapped me on the back. "Yeah," he said, grinning, "you're one helluva guy."

"We'll do everything we can to help you guys," I said, grabbing their hands. I didn't realize what that promise would mean.

The following week I asked George Saltau, Prison Fellowship's most experienced instructor, to conduct two Bible study seminars at Walla Walla.

When George arrived at the penitentiary, the chief of security told him that he expected a blood bath any day. So George didn't know what to expect as he went to the private meeting that inmate Don Dennis had requested. With Dennis were six young prisoners who had long sentences, nothing to lose, and were ready, as Don put it, to "blow this place." George's palms were moist as he shook hands with each of the men.

From them George learned what we had not known the week before. After my sermon, inmate leaders had called off a riot they had planned. Six guards had been targeted for murder; there had even been talk of taking me hostage. Instead the inmates had decided they could trust us and sought our help in working out their grievances.

George was face-to-face with the kind of hatred and anger that leads men to kill. People's lives were in his hands. One misstep and the pent-up fury of the four-month lockdown would be unleashed. George conducted a series of intense meetings with convict groups. When he learned that there had been no communication between inmates and prison officials for eighteen months, he approached the warden, who promised he would consider meeting with inmate leaders.

That promise at least bought time. When George returned to Walla Walla a week later, there was a glimmer of hope. The inmate power bases—the lifers, the bikers, the native Americans, the Hispanics and others—who were almost perpetually at war with each other, were talking, at least for the moment. Two men had become Christians in George's seminar, and they, along with Don Dennis, were gradually taking some leadership. Several guards who had been charged with brutality had been dismissed, and the warden was still promising to meet with the prisoners.

Over the next few months George Saltau and Al Elliott, another Prison Fellowship staffer, shuttled in and out of

Walla Walla, meeting with prison officials and convict leaders. Progress was slow, but violence was at a minimum. One night, however, frustrations erupted. To protest conditions, several men slashed their wrists and barricaded themselves in their cells.

Al Elliott was called to the scene. He stood alone outside the barricaded cells and pleaded with the men. Pools of blood gathered on the concrete floor. As Al talked, one man surrendered, then another, and finally the whole group. Medics rushed in with gurneys and plasma.

Later Al was in the mess hall when a chant began at several corner tables. The noise grew louder, echoing off the high ceilings. Al climbed on top of his table and shouted, trying to make himself heard above the clamor. Gradually the voices subsided. "Don't blow this thing," he begged. "The politicians are finally beginning to listen. But you'll lose it all if there's bloodshed. Chuck Colson has been asked to address the state legislature about the situation." At that there was a loud roar of approval.

Two Christian politicians, Bob Utter, chief justice of the Washington State Supreme Court, and Skeeter Ellis, a newly elected Republican representative, had proposed that I speak to the Republican caucus committee about the conditions at the prison. When I laid out the hard facts of what I had seen at Walla Walla and what needed to be done, the legislators seemed interested, even receptive. Later that day I gave the same message to an equally responsive Democratic caucus, and shortly thereafter the House passed a resolution vowing to deal with conditions at Walla Walla. While this had no legal effect, it signaled to the inmates that those in power were listening.

Justice Utter then organized a committee of prominent Christians to work with the legislators who were developing model legislation. My associate, attorney Dan Van Ness, and a Christian attorney in Seattle, Skip Li, proposed several significant amendments which were incorporated in the reform package. After his election Governor John Spellman appointed Amos Reed, a committed Christian, to head the state corrections system. Amos immediately backed the proposed bill. Meanwhile a federal court was nearing a decision on an inmate lawsuit complaining of conditions at Walla Walla. Indications were that the case would go against the state.

These developments electrified the atmosphere at the prison. "Someone has finally heard us," an inmate told Al Elliot while choking back his tears.

During those months I also met with representatives from each of the ruling inmate gangs. Al warned me that they were a tough and unusual bunch of characters. *They can't be any more unusual,* I thought, *than anyone else I've met in Walla Walla.* I was mistaken.

At the first meeting they were waiting for me, shoulder to shoulder in a tight semicircle, at the bikers' club headquarters, a small, bare-walled room with one barred window. One by one I greeted them, some of the toughest inmates I'd ever seen. Their leader, Bobby, had black hair hanging over a leather headstrap adorned with badges; a bushy beard flowed down the front of his leather jacket.

"Bobby," I said as I gripped his tattooed hand, "I'm here to help you." His response was a nod and a grunt.

The next inmate wore elaborate eye makeup and deep red lipstick. He took my hand limply and said in a high-pitched voice, "Thank you, Mr. Colson." My eyes opened wide with shock; this was Bobby's cellmate, a transvestite and leader of the "Queens." Walla Walla had its own rules, its own code for survival. The inmates' hard eyes defied me to pass judgment.

In May, 1980, the U. S. District Court ruled that Walla Walla had violated the constitutional prohibition against "cruel and unusual punishment." Trial testimony had produced a litany of horrors: an inmate sodomized by a guard, another whose leg had to be amputated because gangrene was neglected, a third held naked in isolation for four days. But what proved decisive was the startlingly honest admission under oath of Warden James Spaulding. His prison, he said, ought to be "closed down." It was simply beyond saving.

The inmates were jubilant. Help might finally be coming. George and Al cut back their Walla Walla trips to once a
month.

Even the guards seemed to breathe easier as the court
order transferred inmates to other prisons and relieved the
overcrowding. But the transferred inmates created dangerous
overcrowding at the other prisons, and by the end of the year
bloody riots erupted. One inmate was killed, twenty-five
were injured, and there was $2 million in property damage.
The tension affected the entire prison system, and officials
imposed new restrictions at Walla Walla.

Despite the best efforts of inmate leaders, by early 1981
the prison was again seething. A gang burned a prison office
building. The warden threw the troublemakers, along with
several inmate leaders who had nothing to do with the riot,
into segregation. The arbitrary order infuriated the inmates,
who retaliated with a work strike. Their one demand was the
removal of Warden Spaulding.

Spaulding ordered another lockdown, and I returned to
Walla Walla, where an inmate whispered to me, "Visit the
hole. Don't announce it. Just walk in." I followed his advice.
When the guards grudgingly swung open the heavy steel gate
of B tier of segregation, I immediately stepped back. A foul
mist hung in the air, giving an eerie glow to the dim overhead
lights. Piles of rotting food and human excrement littered the
floor. I had to force myself forward.

At the first cell the inmate rubbed his eyes. "You
Colson?" he asked. "What can you do?" as if my answer
couldn't matter anyway. I thought, *Maybe he's right.* I asked
his name. It sounded familiar.

"No," he shook his head. "You might have heard the
name, but that's my brother. He hung himself in here last
week. Just couldn't take no more after a year."

"A year!" I exclaimed.

"Man, that ain't nothin'. Some dudes been in here like
two or three years."

Once outside I bent over, my hands on my knees, almost
retching as I gulped the cold air of the prison yard. My face

was flushed, hot with anger. How could human beings be allowed to live in such degradation? I made my way to Warden Spaulding's office.

Jim Spaulding was a decent and intelligent man, seemingly unflappable, but like his predecessors he had wrestled with the beast of Walla Walla and had lost. "Jim," I said, "you'll have to clean up segregation. Today. Use fire hoses or whatever it takes, but that swill has got to go."

"Wait a minute," he snapped. "What can I do? They throw everything possible at the officers. I can't order my men to clean it up."

"Have you been in that place?" I asked. He shook his head.

The next day I held a press conference at which I described Walla Walla's segregation unit in detail. Spaulding fired back in the press, saying that the inmates "wouldn't let the staff clean the building." Soon thereafter, after a state investigation, Jim Spaulding was transferred.

In the spring of 1981, almost two years after the Walla Walla lockdown began, the Washington state legislature passed the first in a series of reforms. A new sentencing commission established a policy to put nonviolent offenders into alternative programs. Early-release plans relieved overcrowding, and several million dollars were allocated to clean up and refurbish the state prison.

Easter morning 1985 I returned to Walla Walla. From the road approaching the gatehouse, nothing seemed to have changed. "Concrete Mama" still loomed on the hilltop, as forbidding as it had looked nearly six years earlier.

The new warden, Larry Kinchloe, met us at the gate. "Wait till you see this place," he said enthusiastically.

Our first service was in the protective-custody wing. The floors were scrubbed clean, most of the cells newly painted, and recreation areas had been constructed in every block. It was still a prison, cold and sterile, but it had been miraculously—if that's a fair term to apply to a building—transformed. The prison population was stable, conditions were decent, and alternative programs were beginning. The reform legislation was working, and millions of state tax dollars were being saved.

The service for the maximum-security unit was held in the brand new chapel. As I stood at the door greeting the men while they crowded in, I recognized some I had met years before as angry, hostile convicts; by their open faces and enthusiastic greetings I realized they were now brothers in Christ.

Then came one vibrant, middle-aged inmate surrounded by a cluster of friends. "Remember me?" he grinned and grabbed my hand. I struggled for recognition. "Don't blame you," he laughed, stroking his clean-shaven chin. "I'm Bobby."

It was Bobby, the boss biker who had lived with the transvestite. He was a Christian now and sat through the service with a broad smile on his face, holding a well-worn Bible.

I watched in amazement, realizing that it was not just an institution that had been transformed. The story of Walla Walla was more than legislation and fresh prison paint, important as those changes were. It was the story of transformed lives.

As I flew back home after that glorious Easter week end in Washington state, I was exuberant. But as I started to put words on paper I was stopped by the realization that I couldn't definitively say how the changes had come about at Walla Walla or who was responsible. Certainly George Soltau and Al Elliott had risked their lives going in there in the early days when the situation was red hot. Don Dennis, Bobby the Biker, and others played a vital role in convincing angry cons to talk with bitter guards and exhausted administrators. And then there was the work of Christian lawyers, legislators, and politicians—men like Amos Reed, Bob Utter, Skip Li, Skeeter Ellis, Dan Van Ness.

But the real transforming miracle at Walla Walla had been accomplished, not by the efforts of all these people, but by the unseen work of the hand of God.

I suddenly saw on the page before me the words of Christ—that the signs of the Kingdom of God are like a man planting seed.[3] We do our part, but then God makes the seed—or the prison reform—grow. It is God who produces the signs of His Kingdom on this earth. We are merely the instruments.

We need constantly to be reminded that our efforts, vital as they are, will never bring utopia to this earth. Walla Walla, after all, is still bleak. It is still a prison filled with the angry, desperate, broken lives of those who seem unable to live in society. But it has changed. Because of God's power, not ours, Walla Walla is a "concrete" example of the Kingdom of God transforming places of hopelessness in the kingdom of man. Justice and hope can now be found where there was once only inequity and despair.

Should Christians get involved in political issues and social reform? Can anyone look at the story of Walla Walla and believe otherwise?

NOTES

1. For further information regarding Prison Fellowship write to Box 17500, Washington, DC 20041.
2. Philippians 3:7-8.
3. Mark 4:3ff.

AFTERWORD

by Michael K. MacIntosh, 1944-
Editor's Note

While the editorial work was progressing on this twentieth-century volume, it became evident that a balance in the makeup was needed. To be fair, some representation of fin-de-siécle (end of century) Christian expression was required.

Many are concerned today to see parts of the church sink into a morass of materialism, apathy, compromise, and even immorality. It seemed important that this decline be addressed. In the following sermon excerpt, Michael MacIntosh calls the church to commitment and godly living.

A child of a broken home, Michael Kirk MacIntosh was born and reared in Portland, Oregon. He joined the Jesus movement that emerged out of the drug culture on the west coast in the late sixties and early seventies. After dropping out of high school, he worked in a steel mill, and then drifted around the United States and Mexico until he "made the scene" on the California beaches. There he went through a cycle of drugs, divorce, despair, and eventually psychotherapy. It was a pathetic slide—one from which thousands of other young Americans never recovered.

But Mike found Christ at age twenty-six in a church that had become a mecca for transient and floundering youth, Calvary Chapel in Costa Mesa, California. How he came to himself, how his marriage was healed, and how the Bible came to dominate his life are told in my book For the Love of Mike *published in 1984 by Thomas Nelson. His Horizon Christian Fellowship Church, which began with fourteen young people, is today the largest congregation in San Diego,*

California with worldwide impact. It is still composed mostly of young people, half of them single. His radio ministry extends to many major American cities. Mike is also a chaplain of the San Diego police force.

Michael MacIntosh understands his generation, its cars, its language, its music, and its problems. He brings a desperately needed word for the church at the end of this century. This sermon, titled "God's Great Love," was preached in San Diego to 5,000 people in the summer of 1989 and has been edited for publication. It is reproduced by permission.

*   *   *

Because of the Lord's great love we are not consumed, for his compassions never fail. They are new every morning; great is your faithfulness. I say to myself, "The Lord is my portion; therefore I will wait for him." The Lord is good to those whose hope is in him, to the one who seeks him; it is good to wait quietly for the salvation of the Lord. It is good for a man to bear the yoke while he is young.

                    Lamentations of Jeremiah 3:22-27

Jeremiah was a faithful representative of the Lord; and because he was faithful in little, God gave him more. He became God's spokesman, a prophet who influenced the whole nation of Israel. But the greater his responsibility, the greater the pressure grew on his life. Jeremiah saw that whatever we do for God comes down to an individual level, starting with the person who delivers the message.

Centuries later the Apostle Peter came under the same conviction, as he wrote in his first letter to the Christians of his day. He stated that in the last times judgment must begin at the house of God. Why? Because the house of God, the Christian community, is supposed to be representing God. That means the judgment hits every pastor, every evangelist, every deacon, every elder, every leader before it hits you, who are the body of believers. James, the Lord's brother, also warns in his letter that teachers will be judged the more strictly precisely because they are teachers.

But the New Testament speaks to the whole church. How can the Christian community proclaim to the rest of the people that they are headed straight for judgment, that they need to repent of their sins and stop aborting their babies, robbing, stealing, mugging, raping, and building monuments to themselves while ripping off the rest of us—how can we do all that while we in the church are doing the same things? How can we say we are Christians when we're living with someone we're not married to? That's what Jeremiah and Peter are saying. God is a righteous God, and judgment must begin with us.

When the end comes, Jesus warned us not to pull up the wheat, because the devil would sow tares in the midst of the wheat. Those tares are weeds, and Jesus said we might pull up the good stuff along with the weeds. Instead he told us, "My angels will do the job" (Matthew 13:39). That shows us that we pastors and evangelists and church planters and elders and deacons should not be quick to judge; we don't always have the discernment to see "who's who in the zoo!"

I could look at all of you and say, "What a wonderful Christian crowd!" But you're not all Christians. Some of you tell me, "I haven't been in church for fifteen years and can't believe I'm in church today!" Some of you are here because your girlfriend said, "All right, I'll go out with you, but this is your last chance. I'll keep dating you if you'll go to church with me tomorrow." Some call it friendship evangelism; others call it Christian dating or Christian mating. What's the difference?

But we are the ones Jesus is calling upon to represent Him. That's why judgment first comes to the Christian community. For Him to be a righteous God, a righteous judge, He has to get the hypocrisy and deceitfulness and sin out of His body and glorify Himself through it as the Head of the body. It is not an easy life that Jesus calls us to. If anyone will come after me, He said, let him deny himself, and pick up his cross daily, and follow Me (Luke 9:23).

The prophet Jeremiah was a man with a tender heart. He himself had been broken and humbled, and now he was warning his fellow citizens, for he knew that the heart of the people was sick. A lot of people in our own generation are going to be crushed simply because they didn't humble themselves on the Rock, Jesus Christ, and let Him break them.

Perhaps you are a Christian, a member of the household of faith. And yet you're not really Christlike. People have not seen Jesus Christ in your lifestyle, your attitude, your words, your heart, or your spirit. Or perhaps you're not a Christian because you feel alienated from God. As a little boy or a little girl you may have known Him, but today you feel that God isn't for you. He isn't for hep people or cool people or Bartles-and-James people. You think God is for down-and-outers. Or you may be part of a group that swings the other way and thinks you have to be rich to prove you are a Christian.

No, you just have to be you, and let Him be Him, and be faithful to Him in what He gives you to do.

Now, except for the grace of God, Jeremiah had no more right than anyone else to give out truth to people. But by grace God did call him, and so speaking by grace, Jeremiah tells us, "Because of the Lord's great love we are not consumed, for his compassions never fail." The Lord's great love! Some describe it as an ocean, others as a feeling. I too was always looking for love, but as a popular song expresses it, "looking for love in all the wrong places, and looking for it in all the wrong faces." Then I met the Lord, and it was all different. I found the amazing simplicity of His great love.

Statistics tell us that the average American youth has had three loves by the time he or she gets out of high school. Some of those loves prove devastating. Let's say you broke off one, and then there was another, and another. You told somebody, "I love you. I care for you." A song written for Pogo says, "Well, go ahead and call it love if you want to, if that's what it takes."

How many times have you girls heard guys say, "I can't tell you I love you. You want me to? Is that all it's going to take, and then we can get on with the show?" So he makes up a lie, and you know it's a lie, but you still want to hear, "I love you."

Now, when it comes to you from God, it is not love that fades away. But when it's our love for Him, that's different. Our love is fickle. It's not constant. We are like the people of Israel whose sins had found them out. Our love is based on emotion. If we're feeling good and have had enough coffee, we may work up sufficient energy to love God; but as soon as we get pulled over by a traffic officer, our day starts being "bummed." So when we get to where we are going, there is no parking place. We drive around for twenty minutes, and then somebody dents our fender. By the time we finally pull into a place, we get a ticket for parking next to a hydrant. We go into a building and find the lines are all full. And so it goes on and on!

But God is so different. Oh, thank God for His great love! There are no surprises for Him. Thank God, He does not get upset. His day is never "bummed."

The Apostle Paul wrote, "Behold, if any man be in Christ, he is a new creation; all the old things are passed away and everything has become brand new" (2 Corinthians 5:17). That's what God's great love does for us. He tells us we are not to be living in the past, for we are accountable for today. We are to live for Him today. Forget the past.

So often we are like the little boy who was out playing in the mud and wouldn't come to dinner. Finally his father went out and took him by the ear and said, "You go upstairs and take a bath. We're going to wait dinner till you are cleaned up." So the family waited and waited until finally Dad goes upstairs, and there is his little son standing with the towel wrapped around him, and he is clean, but the bathtub is full of muddy water. And his father says, "Son, what's taking you so long?"

And the boy tells him, "Well, Dad, I've just been standing by the tub, admiring how dirty I used to be." And a lot of people are doing just that, admiring how dirty they used to be instead of going to the dinner table and getting fed.

Many people are saying, "I'm not responsible. I'm a weak person. I have this problem, this gambling thing, but it's something I can't control." Or a husband will say to his wife, "I didn't really commit adultery with her. You can't call it adultery because, you see, I don't love you any more." Or some youngster will tell the judge, "I'm just a kid. I'm not responsible. Not accountable. I mean the gun was in my hand, and I had all this rock cocaine, and ten thousand in cash in my pocket, and he was moving onto my turf. Give me a break!"

That's what we have come to. And that's where Jeremiah says Israel was. The people's sins had been found out, and now they were captives in Babylon. He was writing to exiles and in his Lamentations he pours out his heart: "Because of God's great love we are not consumed." But the question remains in our own generation, how how much longer will God's love put up with us?

And Jeremiah's beautiful answer is, "God never rejects us. His compassions never fail. They are new and fresh every morning."

Many people seem to carry around with them a misconception of God. I know I did. That was before I met Him as a Person. He really is a great God, a wonderful God, and we all need to know Him in our lives, to learn what a unique and marvelous Person he is, and what a great love He has for us, as Jeremiah tells us; for He holds the key to life.

Our love and God's great love remain two different things. The papers tell us that 46 percent of all marriages in America today are remarriages. But God's great love does not separate us; it binds us together, no matter where we are. Fifty percent of all American mothers with infants are either gainfully employed or are presently looking for a job. But the Lord said He would lead His flock like a shepherd and carry the little lambs in His bosom (Isaiah 40:11).

You know how important it is for an infant to be in the arms of its mother rather than some stranger's . . . how important it is for the baby to look up out of its crib and find out who all the members of the family are! Imagine the tenderness of a mother contrasted with the oversight of someone who really doesn't care for the baby.

But the mother is out looking for work. Why?

Perhaps she wants a new television set. But not just a nineteen-inch RCA, but perhaps a twenty-six-inch. Isn't everybody going beyond that? What about the thirty-five-inch, or the forty-eight-inch? Or here is a fifty-one-inch on sale; a truckload has just come in, and no payments are due until six months from now. And while you're there, why not pick up a good deal on a Fisher stereo?

"I will lead my flock like a shepherd . . ."

Fifty percent of all Americans say they watch television during dinner. That leaves no time for discussion with the family; but God tells us in His great compassion He will never let distractions interfere with His love for us. Judith Wallenstein, director of the Center for Families in Transition, has written a book titled, *Second Chance* in which she states that almost 50 percent of all children of divorce in America enter adulthood as worried, under-achieving, self-deprecating, and often angry. Three out of five admit they feel rejected by at least one parent. Half of all these children, she reports, grew up in settings where the parents were warring with each other even after the divorce.

But God's great love says, "I will never leave you nor forsake you" (Deuteronomy 31:6).

Another survey tells us that 34 percent of Americans say they strongly object to working with people who have AIDS. But 38 percent of Americans also strongly object to working with people who don't use deodorants!

Our love is strangely different; but God's great love is never strange. He never rejects us. Never. Not even those of us without deodorant.

. . . There is no instability in the household of God. His disciplines are the same, His justice is the same, His voice is the same, His wisdom is the same. Jesus Christ is the same yesterday, today, and forever. The same Jesus who stood before Pontius Pilate and heard him ask, "What is truth?" is the one who said to Philip, "I am the way, the truth and the life" (John 14:6). He is the same one who told His Jewish followers, "You shall know the truth, and the truth shall make you free." He is the same one who said, "Whosoever will, let him come to me. I will in no wise reject you or turn you away" (John 6:37).

We tend to have our own opinions about God and how things should be done. We're stubborn, we're strong-willed. But it's God's great love that we are not consumed, for His compassions never fail. They are new every morning. In the psalms we read that God loads us daily with benefits. The New Testament tells us that Jesus, seeing the multitudes, had compassion on them.

My compassion happens to be based on the depth of my resources—physical, spiritual, emotional. If I have just taken a long flight on a jet plane, only to board a train and ride for several hours, sitting in an upright position, with cigarette smoke circulating through my nostrils, and someone wants to start talking to me, I find my compassion has dried up. If you come to me when I'm in good health and rested, and you need assistance, but my checkbook doesn't have the right amount in it to be compassionate, you're still in trouble.

There it is: His resources as opposed to our resources. His great love, as opposed to our short supply. And His compassions never fail; they are new every morning. If they were not, they would soon go stale, like left-over manna on the desert floor. But the freshness is there every day. Yesterday you blew it, but His compassions helped you out, didn't they? This morning you blew it again. . . .

One of our Sunday school teachers asked his pupils where the holiest place is. A little boy raised his hand and said, "It's the church parking lot!"

The teacher was interested. "Why do you say the parking lot is the holiest place?"

"Well," said the boy, "when we get up in the morning, Mom's always yelling at the kids to get dressed. Dad's shaving so she's yelling at him, and he's yelling at Mom and at all of us. We sit at the table and throw our food down and are told, 'Don't spill the milk.' Then we argue and fight all the way to church, but as soon as we get to the parking lot, everybody's different. It's 'Hi, how are you!' So I figure the parking lot is the holiest place."

Franklin Roosevelt once said, "Eternal truths are neither true nor eternal unless they have fresh meaning for every new social situation." This is God's great love in action: it's new, it's fresh, it's daily, it's personal, and it's for you. It works in every situation, even with your boss. For example, "A soft answer turns away wrath." Out of His great compassion, God gave us that little key.

* * *

Think of the desperate situations you have been in, where your marriage could have been dissolved, or the probation officer could have thumped you, or something else could have happened, but in each case God gave understanding and compassion because His love is so great!

Jeremiah tells us in this passage, "The Lord is good to those whose hope is in him." I had to think about that. The key, as I understand it, is that He is good to those whose *hope* is in Him, rather than to those who are "hoping" in Him. There is a difference. To many people God is like a lucky charm, a rabbit's foot, a shamrock, a horseshoe, or something that has been blessed or dipped in holy water. Let's say I have a splitting headache. I'll take two Excedrin tablets, and I'll pray. But my *hope* is probably in the Excedrin, not in God; I'm just "hoping" in God. In the same way I'm "hoping" in a lottery ticket, I'm "hoping" in a tax refund, I'm "hoping" in a raise, I'm "hoping" that my checks won't bounce before the thirty-first, and yes I'm "hoping" in God. But God is looking at the person whose overarching *hope* is in Him for everything; whose *hope* rests in the Lord in whom we live and move and have our being. They are the ones He is blessing. They are the ones who are receiving times of refreshing from the presence of the Lord. "Hoping" can be simply wishing, but real *hope* is *trust*.

My *hope*, my life, my whole sustenance is in God. Not in the Bible study group, or the local body of believers, or the organization, or the church universal, or in religion—it is in God who is our life through Jesus Christ, the Person, who shed His blood upon the cross to take away my sins. Were it not for Him, I would exist in a vacuum. So as Jeremiah says, "The Lord is good to those who seek him," and he adds in our text, "The Lord is my portion; therefore I will wait for him. It is good to wait quietly for the salvation of the Lord."

Not long ago I was asked to visit a state penitentiary by a local pastor, and after addressing the inmates, we requested permission to talk to the men on death row. It was granted. To get there, my friend and I had to walk along a narrow hallway and pass three steel doors. Eventually we found five men in cells, awaiting execution. One was a satanist who had shot and killed the parents of a seventeen-year-old boy who happened to be in the cell at the other end of the row.

This boy's parents were wealthy, and the murder had been a brutal one. The satanist wouldn't talk to us; he simply pulled a sheet over his head. After we had visited the others, we came to the end cell where the boy was a prisoner. He had been tried, convicted, and sentenced to die because he had hired the satanist killer, promising him that after he had inherited his parents' millions, he would pay the man a hundred thousand dollars. So they both proceeded to get stoned on drugs before the killer perpetrated his terrible act.

In the boy's cell we found posters of fancy automobiles pasted on the walls: Porsches, Ferraris, Lamberginis, Contouches—every kind of fancy car that a young boy would want. But it was dark in that hole; the boy was in a corner, almost in a fetal position.

"Hey, we'd like to talk to you about the Lord."

"Oh, no, don't talk to me about the Lord!"

"We just want to tell you how much—"

"No, don't tell me. He can't love a guy like me. I killed my Mom and Dad!"

"Please, we don't want to cause you any pain. We just—do you mind if we read with you?"

We started reading some Scripture to him, and eventually that boy prayed. He couldn't believe God's great love. With his hands on the cell bars and tears rolling down his face, he said, "God, if there's any way You can forgive me, forgive me of my sin, and for what I did, I'm so—" And he broke. He told the Lord that he deserved to be put to death, but he wanted to be forgiven. And he accepted the Lord into his heart. My pastor friend arranged for further visits.

On the way out we paused at the first cell where the satanist was being held, and I told him, "Now listen, your friend down there is really sorry for what he did. He has repented. But I hear you worship Satan, and that you called on Satan when you killed his parents. You probably think you have a lot of evil power, and you are a bad, mean, nasty guy, but—well, I want you to know that Jesus will set you free."

He said, "I don't want it, I don't need it, and I don't care."

"But do you realize where you're going?"

"I know where hell is. I know very well what hell is about."

"But don't you want to humble yourself?"

"No."

He turned and crawled under his sheet and hid himself from us. But the great love of God was in that cell block for both of those young men. His compassions were new that morning and available for both of them, but both did not accept them.

As we went out, the warden told us sadly that the boy had a sister three years his senior, who actually received the inheritance. She had run off to Europe with her boyfriend and was spending the money as fast as she could, while tantalizing her brother by sending him postcards and car pictures from Paris and Switzerland.

But God is not mocking that boy on death row as his sister did; He is loving him. Jeremiah wrote that "it is good to wait quietly for the salvation of the Lord." That is what the young man is doing, sitting and waiting.

Jeremiah also wrote that it is good for a man to bear the yoke while he is young. Each week I address a church audience made up mostly of hundreds of young men and women, together with some others who are young in heart because they know Jesus Christ, the Eternal One. I tell them that they are an army assembled by the Lord to battle for the souls of men and women. You have the weapons of your warfare: the helmet of salvation, the breastplate of righteousness, the shield of faith, the sword of the Spirit. It's good that you should bear the yoke of Jesus Christ while you're young and strong. It's good for you to get away from the things that are dissipating your health, to get rid of the videos that are tearing up your soul, and the personal relationships that have you burning with lust, and all those situations in the world which are making you carnal and jaded, so that your heart is becoming as hard as flint. It is good to get away and to bear the yoke of God while you are young.

Jesus said, "Take my yoke and learn of me. My yoke is easy and my burden is light" (Matthew 11:30). So I am saying to young men—stand up and be a man, be a godly man, not some guy hanging out at a sleazy place, drooling over naked women dancing on a bar. Be a MAN! Don't get into a sexual crisis of identity as to whether you are a man or a woman; don't nitpick as to whether this or that is right or wrong. Take up the sword, take up a cause, get some meaning for your life! The reason you're not a godly man today is that you have no purpose in your life, so you're entertaining yourself, you're stroking yourself, you're going around in circles, you're covering yourself with gold and watches and cars and all the trinkets you can find to make you look like a cool person, but you're not a MAN! Take the yoke of God upon you and be a godly man. Hold your head high, your shoulders back, your stomach in, your chest out, and stand up and plead the cause of the poor. Defend the widow, speak out for the fatherless. The letter of James says that pure, undefiled religion is visiting the widows and fatherless in their affliction. It does not consist in heaping up all your money for yourself or spending all your time on yourself.

Be a man who treats women as ladies. Be a gentle man. Women are our equals, yet they are fragile. They need respect. They don't need to be lusted after, to be stripped by your eyes as they walk into a room; rather they need to be treated with honor and respect.

Be a man who can control his own feelings, his own emotions, his own desires. Be a godly husband. Be a godly employer. Be a godly employee. Be a good man, a godly man, and be a man for God. Be a role model for the next generation that is so lost, so sick, so violent, so polluted, often finding so little meaning to life. Many of our generation don't know a single person who has found meaning in life.

We've got to put a stop to this mess before the whole country goes down to destruction. Men will have to stand up and resist the powers of evil and put their foot down. They will have to get involved, become active, vote for the right people, run for the city council. When those young Chinese boys and girls were mowed down by their own troops in Beijing's Tiananmen Square, many of them didn't even know the meaning of freedom and democracy. But you have it all, and don't do anything. Be MEN!

Become leaders of your communities. Don't leave everything to the politicians. Stand up to the drug lords. When you go to a stadium to watch a football or baseball game, summon the policeman and tell him, "Those people are passing marijuana joints back and forth, and I want them out of my row NOW!" I tell you the officers will be glad to do it. They're not afraid. They're men, they're women who will stand up to be counted.

I have seen some policewomen, just five-foot-two inches tall, on duty in the street, standing up to some of the biggest, meanest men in our city. I've heard them say, "Up against the wall!"

"Oh, you've got to be kidding!"

Wham! Boom! "Yes, ma'am, what do you want me to do?"

"Spread those legs!"

"You've got 'em!"

You men need to pick up the sword of the Spirit, the Word of God, and live a life so godly that among high school youngsters the peer pressure will reverse the other way, and the kids themselves will boot the drug dealers and drug users out, because godly men like you are standing with them. Not just big brothers—MEN! Godly men! And men of God! Not sissies and wimps! Men who will stand on solid rock instead of shifting sand and will step out and speak out.

A. W. Tozer, the great preacher and editor of a few years ago, wrote, "In most places today it is scarcely possible to get anyone to attend a meeting where the only attraction is God."

Where are the men at such meetings? The women of our cities don't see very many real men. They see egotists and wimps and flamboyant characters cruising around town, "scoring" wherever they can, whether in safe sex or unsafe. They aren't seeing men who are leading their households as husbands. They're seeing indecisive, wishy-washy men, not able to balance their checkbooks, not making decisions unless it's something for themselves, such as a decision to go surfing, or fishing, or camping, or writing a check to cover the liquor tab.

For such men the world may seem an alluring place, but God is calling you to service today and telling you to bear the yoke now, while you are young and have the health. God wants Jeremiahs for our own day to stand up in education, in politics, in finance, in the building industry, in the environment. You have a moral and ethical obligation as a man to protect your brother and sister, and to do it now.

Ah yes, but then the question always arises, who is my brother? My answer is, show me a man who doesn't know who his brother is, and I'll show you a man who doesn't know God. Each one of us in the human race is a brother and sister. Many of us are brothers and sisters in God's Kingdom. And we men have been called to stand up as men and be what God created us to be: leaders, resisting darkness, resisting the bottle, resisting the pornography, resisting the cocaine, resisting temptations to lie, to flim-flam, and to swindle.

Satan has managed to wipe out so many men of this generation, but not all, thank God! The real men are on their knees praying. Not many people will see them or even be aware of them, but the real men are studying the Scriptures to show themselves approved to God, rightly dividing the word of truth. They are not ashamed even though some observers will question their behavior.

Bear the yoke of the Lord in your youth, as Jeremiah said we are to do. Stand for God, men, or there is a good chance you'll fall for anything.

Finally, let me call your attention to another verse in the third chapter of Lamentations: "Let us examine our ways, and test them, and let us return to the Lord" (Lamentations 3:40). Notice these three simple words: *examine*, *test*, and *return*. Perhaps right now you need to return to the Lord. Take a moment for introspection. Consider if it's possible that God is speaking to you. Examine yourself. Test your motives. Perhaps then you will come back to the Lord and become the person who will represent God to this generation against all odds, as Jeremiah the prophet did in his day.

Remember that what Jeremiah did was not popular. He represented a holy God, a pure God, and he paid a heavy price for doing so. Let the Holy Spirit speak to you now, challenging you to leave mediocrity and to reach for excellence. God is a great God of love. He is full of compassion and offers us newness every day, every morning. His faithfulness is great. Ask Him to fill you with His Holy Spirit's power, as He did Jeremiah, and to make you the man or woman He would have you to be, to represent Him in the name and for the glory of Jesus Christ.